Domain-Driven Refactoring

A hands-on DDD guide to transforming monoliths into modular systems and microservices

Alessandro Colla
Alberto Acerbis

Domain-Driven Refactoring

Portfolio Director: Kunal Chaudhari

Relationship Lead: Srishti Seth

Project Manager: Ashwin Dinesh Kharwa

Content Engineer: Divya Anne Selvaraj

Technical Editor: Kushal Sharma

Copy Editor: Safis Editing

Indexer: Tejal Soni

Proofreader: Divya Anne Selvaraj

Production Designer: Jyoti Kadam

Growth Lead: Mansi Shah

First published: April 2025

Production reference: 1240425

Published by Packt Publishing Ltd.

Grosvenor House

11 St Paul's Square

Birmingham

B3 1RB, UK.

ISBN 978-1-83588-910-7

www.packtpub.com

To my wife, Daniela, my loving partner in this incredible life journey we share. Thank you for your unwavering support, even in the smallest things. You are my refuge and my inspiration.

— Alessandro Colla

To Alessandra, my unwavering partner and constant support, and to Marco and Nicolò, two wonderful sides of the same coin. This book is a testament to the love and strength you bring to my world.

— Alberto Acerbis

Foreword

I first met Alessandro and Alberto at their workshop *Bounded Context is Not Enough* at the Explore DDD conference in snowy Denver in 2024. With live coding, storytelling, and banter infused with Italian humor, they guided us from a tangled legacy code base toward clear, domain-driven architectures. Their subsequent workshop, *Who Fears the Sagas?*, at KanDDDinsky in Berlin only deepened my appreciation for their ability to make complex learning engaging and fun.

That same clarity and playfulness runs through this book. Despite years of practice and consulting work in **Domain-Driven Design (DDD)**, I found myself rethinking long-held ideas and discovering fresh ways to apply them.

"Show me the code!" Alessandro and Alberto lead readers through a journey of legacy modernization, moving from a "big ball of mud" to modular monoliths, event-sourced systems, microservices, and sagas. Each style is presented with practical trade-offs, grounded in domain-driven thinking.

"Teach me the concepts!" The book's opening chapters distill essential DDD concepts, software design principles, and refactoring techniques into an exceptionally compact, insightful, and accessible format. Principles such as the **Single Responsibility Principle (SRP)**, the **Open-Closed Principle (OCP)**, and specification testing come vividly to life through clear visualizations and thoughtfully curated code examples.

These DDD maestros are also outstanding systems thinkers, fluidly connecting the many complex dots in software's problem space with their unique style of making DDD incredibly practical. Their forward-looking perspective on refactoring is particularly compelling – not simply addressing past technical debt, but strategically expanding the software's readiness for future evolution. Domain-driven refactoring, as presented in this book, doesn't just repair yesterday's mistakes; it paves the way for tomorrow's innovations.

This book is essential reading for anyone dedicated to building software that gracefully evolves with the complexities of real-world business domains. Whether you're new to DDD or a seasoned architect, it helps you roll up your sleeves and confidently embark on your DDD or refactoring journey – one small, incremental step at a time.

Xin Yao

Independent DDD consultant & Sociotechnical Architect

March 2025, Copenhagen

Contributors

About the authors

Alessandro Colla is a seasoned e-commerce specialist, C# programmer, and domain-driven design expert with over 30 years of experience in the IT industry. He has built management software and ERP systems from the ground up for diverse industries and has guided teams in improving their skills and practices. Alessandro actively contributes to and maintains open source projects, is the co-author of *Cronache di Domain-Driven Design,* and co-founded DDD Open, an initiative promoting knowledge sharing and collaboration in the software development community.

I would like to thank my wife for her unrelenting support and patience, not only during the process of writing this book but throughout the life we've shared so far.

Alberto Acerbis is a hands-on software architect and trainer with 30+ years of experience in IT. A .NET specialist, C# programmer, and Microsoft MVP, he applies domain-driven design in financial and IIoT projects. He actively contributes to open source, speaks at Microsoft and DDD conferences, and co-authored *Cronache di Domain-Driven Design*. As a co-founder of DDD Open, he promotes knowledge sharing and collaboration in the software development community.

I would like to first and foremost thank my loving and patient wife for her continued support, patience, and encouragement throughout the long process of writing this book.

About the reviewers

Wei Wang (David) is the founder and CEO of Nanyang Version Management Lab Pte. Ltd. and the creator of Gitme.ai, an AI-powered software knowledge platform. With 20 years of experience, including principal consultant roles at Zhipu Technology and Thoughtworks, David drives digital transformation and legacy modernization across industries. A leader in domain-driven design, he co-founded DDDChina and is a frequent speaker at international conferences.

I'd like to thank Alessandro and Alberto for inviting me to review this brilliant book: Domain-Driven Refactoring. It's been an incredible learning experience, and I'm grateful to contribute. The domain-driven design community is inspiring, and its impact will only grow in the AI era. Thank you to everyone advancing this field and making it such an exciting space!

Stephen Wille, with nearly two decades of experience in IT, has progressed from tier-one support to lead software engineer at a Fortune 500 company. His extensive experience provides him with a deep and broad knowledge base, enabling him to elevate engineering standards across diverse projects. A strong advocate for continuous learning, Stephen is passionate about sharing his expertise and empowering teams to achieve higher levels of performance.

My gratitude to those in the field who relentlessly push for excellence.

Erikson Murrugarra Sifuentes, a 15-year tech veteran, delivers robust, secure, domain-driven solutions across LATAM, USA, and Europe, from start-ups to major enterprises, including collaborations with Tech Seals and DigitalPark. Based in the Netherlands, he consults for leading companies and architects domain-driven AI agentics. Passionate about DDD and security by design, he writes, speaks, and mentors in South America, offering free lessons and publications.

My deepest gratitude to my beloved family for their unwavering support. A special thank you to Lori, who has been an integral part of this incredible journey.

Join us on Discord!

Read this book alongside other users, developers, experts, and the author himself.

Ask questions, provide solutions to other readers, chat with the author via Ask Me Anything sessions, and much more. Scan the QR code or visit the link to join the community.

https://packt.link/domain-driven-refactoring

Table of Contents

Part II: Refactoring Legacy Systems

Preface

The software development domain is constantly evolving, driven by the increasing demands of businesses and the growing complexity of technological ecosystems. Applications must now adapt to distributed architectures, support rapid changes, and remain resilient under immense pressure—all while aligning closely with business goals. These challenges are both exciting and daunting, requiring developers and architects to think beyond code and embrace methodologies that bridge the gap between technical precision and business alignment.

Modern software development operates at a crossroads where business innovation and technical challenges intersect. As organizations grow and adapt, the demands on software systems build up. Legacy architectures, once sufficient for simpler times, often struggle to keep pace with the agility and scalability required today. Distributed systems have become the norm, promising flexibility but introducing their own challenges, such as eventual consistency, fault tolerance, and coordination across services. In such an environment, it is easy to lose sight of the domain—the heart of the problem the software aims to solve.

This is where **Domain-Driven Design (DDD)** steps in. Since its introduction by Eric Evans in 2003, DDD has served as a transformative approach for designing software systems that reflect the intricacies of real-world domains. The approach offers strategies for modeling complexity, structuring applications, and enabling effective collaboration between technical and business teams. This book is our contribution to the rich ecosystem of DDD knowledge, aiming to guide you through the principles, patterns, and practices that make DDD not just a philosophy but a practical toolset for modern software development.

Who this book is for

Whether you are a software developer, architect, or team lead, this book is crafted to enhance your ability to build systems that are robust, scalable, and aligned with the business they support. Specifically, this book is for the following people:

- **Developers** who want to move beyond coding and understand how to design systems that solve real-world problems effectively
- **Architects** tasked with creating modular, maintainable, and scalable solutions in increasingly complex environments
- **Technical leaders** who seek to foster collaboration between cross-functional teams and ensure that technical decisions support business goals

No matter your role, if you're passionate about creating software that not only works but thrives under complexity, this book is for you.

What this book covers

Chapter 1, Evolution of Domain-Driven Design, introduces the origins of DDD, tracing its development from early software engineering practices to its current role in addressing complexity. This chapter explores the fundamental challenges that DDD aims to solve and provides an overview of its key principles, including ubiquitous language and bounded contexts.

Chapter 2, Understanding Complexity: Problem and Solution Space, dives into the nature of complexity in software systems and teaches you how to distinguish between essential and accidental complexity. This chapter introduces tools such as the Cynefin framework and EventStorming, equipping you to navigate problem and solution spaces effectively.

Chapter 3, Strategic Patterns, covers the strategic aspects of DDD, focusing on dividing domains into bounded contexts and defining clear relationships between them. This chapter teaches you how to apply techniques such as context mapping and how to create a ubiquitous language that fosters collaboration and reduces ambiguity.

Chapter 4, Tactical Patterns, provides an overview of the tactical building blocks of DDD, such as entities, value objects, aggregates, repositories, and domain services, with practical examples of implementing these patterns in code while maintaining alignment with business rules.

Chapter 5, Introducing Refactoring Principles, teaches you how to identify and address technical debt in legacy systems using DDD principles. This chapter introduces key refactoring strategies, emphasizing the importance of modularity and incremental change to improve the maintainability and scalability supported by various kinds of tests.

Chapter 6, Transitioning from Chaos, focuses on transforming monolithic systems into modular architectures. This chapter explores practical steps for decoupling tightly coupled services, identifying bounded contexts, and implementing clear interfaces to simplify interactions.

Chapter 7, Integrating Events with CQRS, shows you how to implement Command Query Responsibility Segregation with EventSourcing (CQRS+ES). This chapter explains how to use events to decouple systems, ensure scalability, and maintain consistency while managing eventual consistency challenges.

Chapter 8, Refactoring the Database, provides strategies for aligning database schemas with bounded contexts and refactoring shared tables, as well as introducing patterns such as Expand/Contract. This chapter also covers techniques for handling data consistency in distributed systems.

Chapter 9, DDD Patterns for Continuous Integration and Continuous Refactoring, explores how to integrate DDD with continuous integration and delivery practices. This chapter focuses on automation, iterative design, and maintaining alignment between domain models and technical implementation.

Chapter 10, When and Why You Should Transition to a Microservices Architecture, provides guidance on transitioning from a modular monolith to a microservices architecture. This chapter highlights the trade-offs and complexities of distributed systems and explains how DDD principles can help with this evolution.

Chapter 11, Dealing with Events and Their Evolution, explains how to manage event versioning in event-sourced systems to ensure compatibility and adaptability over time. This chapter introduces strategies such as upcasting, schema evolution, and content negotiation.

Chapter 12, Orchestrating Complexity: Advanced Approaches to Business Processes, explores advanced DDD techniques for managing distributed systems and business processes. Topics covered in this chapter include sagas, choreography versus orchestration, and ensuring system consistency in the face of failures.

To get the most out of this book

This book is designed to be a practical guide for mastering DDD and applying its principles in real-world scenarios. Whether you're new to DDD or have some prior experience, this book provides a structured approach to help you navigate the complexities of modern software development. At the time of writing this book, all the code was tested with .NET 8 running under Docker Desktop for Windows version 4.36.

Software/hardware covered in the book	Operating system requirements
Docker	Windows, macOS, or Linux
C#	Windows, macOS, or Linux
RabbitMQ	Windows, macOS, or Linux
Kurrent (formerly EventStoreDB)	Windows, macOS, or Linux

Download the example code files

The code bundle for the book is hosted on GitHub at https://github.com/PacktPublishing/Domain-driven-Refactoring/branches. We also have other code bundles from our rich catalog of books and videos available at https://github.com/PacktPublishing. Check them out!

Download the color images

We also provide a PDF file that has color images of the screenshots/diagrams used in this book. You can download it here: https://packt.link/gbp/9781835885949.

Conventions used

There are a number of text conventions used throughout this book.

CodeInText: Indicates code words in text, database table names, folder names, filenames, file extensions, pathnames, dummy URLs, user input, and Twitter handles. For example: "A possible implementation, again using SalesOrderCreated with the added IsReseller property, could be as follows."

A block of code is set as follows:

```
public class DiscountService {
    public decimal CalculateDiscount(SalesOrder order) {
        if (order.Discount == null) {
            return 0;
        }
```

```
        var result = //... do some calculations...
        return result
    }
}
```

When we wish to draw your attention to a particular part of a code block, the relevant lines or items are set in bold:

```
namespace BrewUp.Sales.Acl;

public sealed class
AvailabilityUpdatedForNotificationEventHandler(ILoggerFactory
loggerFactory, IServiceBus serviceBus) : IntegrationEventHandlerAsync
<AvailabilityUpdatedForNotification>(loggerFactory)
```

Bold: Indicates a new term, an important word, or words that you see on the screen. For instance, words in menus or dialog boxes appear in the text like this. For example: "One of the first tools we would like to introduce to you is the **Cynefin framework**."

Warnings or important notes appear like this.

Tips and tricks appear like this.

Get in touch

Feedback from our readers is always welcome.

General feedback: Email feedback@packtpub.com and mention the book's title in the subject of your message. If you have questions about any aspect of this book, please email us at questions@packtpub.com.

Errata: Although we have taken every care to ensure the accuracy of our content, mistakes do happen. If you have found a mistake in this book, we would be grateful if you reported this to us. Please visit http://www.packtpub.com/submit-errata, click **Submit Errata**, and fill in the form.

Piracy: If you come across any illegal copies of our works in any form on the internet, we would be grateful if you would provide us with the location address or website name. Please contact us at copyright@packtpub.com with a link to the material.

If you are interested in becoming an author: If there is a topic that you have expertise in and you are interested in either writing or contributing to a book, please visit http://authors.packtpub.com/.

Free benefits with your book

This book comes with free benefits to support your learning. Activate them now for instant access (see the "*How to Unlock*" section for instructions).

Here's a quick overview of what you can instantly unlock with your purchase:

DRM-Free PDF Version

Download DRM-free PDF and ePub copies of this book.

7-Day Packt Library Access

Get 7-day unlimited access to 8,000+ books and videos. No credit card required.

Available for first-time Packt+ trial users only.

Next-Gen Reader Access

Read this book on Packt Reader with progress sync, dark mode and note-taking.

How to unlock

Scan the QR code (or go to `packtpub.com/unlock`). Search for this book by name, confirm the edition, and then follow the steps on the page.

UNLOCK NOW

Note: Keep your invoice handy. Purchases made directly from Packt don't require one

Share your thoughts

Once you've read *Domain-Driven Refactoring*, we'd love to hear your thoughts! Scan the QR code below to go straight to the Amazon review page for this book and share your feedback.

`https://packt.link/r/1835889115`

Your review is important to us and the tech community and will help us make sure we're delivering excellent quality content.

Part 1

Why Use Domain-Driven Design to Tackle Complexity?

In this first part of the book, you'll develop a solid understanding of **Domain-Driven Design (DDD)** and its fundamental concepts. We'll explore how DDD has evolved, tackle the challenges of understanding complexity, and introduce you to the core strategic and tactical patterns. By the end of this part of the book, you'll have the knowledge needed to start modeling and managing complex software systems with confidence.

This part of the book includes the following chapters:

- *Chapter 1, Evolution of Domain-Driven Design*
- *Chapter 2, Understanding Complexity: Problem and Solution Space*
- *Chapter 3, Strategic Patterns*
- *Chapter 4, Tactical Patterns*

1

Evolution of Domain-Driven Design

Since the birth of software development in the 1960s, developers strived to create better applications to deal with the complexity of the world. During the following 20 years, many reports emerged pointing out the inefficiency of software systems and their design processes. We also went through the infamous software crisis that led to many incidents, such as the Therac-25 (`https://en.wikipedia.org/wiki/Therac-25`).

One of the main problems during that time was that software development followed a "code-and-fix" approach. That is, developing software without a clear view of the project and the problem to solve. This led to incomplete software that quite always went over budget and missing deadlines seemed to be normal.

The turning point arrived in 1968 during the NATO conference where the issue was acknowledged, and people started laying the groundwork for software engineering as a formal discipline (`https://docslib.org/doc/9230794/crisis-what-crisis-reconsidering-the-software-crisis-of-the-1960s-and-the-origins-of-software-engineering`).

In this chapter, we will delve into the following main topics:

- Progression of the software development approaches
- The story so far
- What is **domain-driven design (DDD)**?
- How it changes the approach to the problem

Progression of the software development approaches

Between the 1980s and 1990s, the awareness of the software crisis led to the rise of various "silver-bullet" approaches that did not, however, provide a definitive solution. The famous article, *No Silver Bullets*, written by Fred Brooks, took the problem head-on and brought to the attention of the reader that there are mainly two different kinds of complexity; essential and accidental (you will read in depth about them in *Chapter 2*).

In Steve McConnell's book, *Software Estimation: Demystifying the Black Art*, there is a really interesting concept called "cone of uncertainty," which exposes part of the problem with a simple diagram (*Figure 1.1*). This diagram points out that estimates created early in the project are subject to a high degree of error. As you can see, these estimates can be off by a factor of four both in high and lower ends. The application of this concept was in the estimate process, but it maps very well to the problem that DDD tries to solve. A deep understanding of the domain leads to stronger models, greater project resilience, and more accurate estimates. This could be only obtained by investing time in understanding the problem. As also stated in the book itself,*The reason the estimate contains variability is that the software project itself contains variability."*

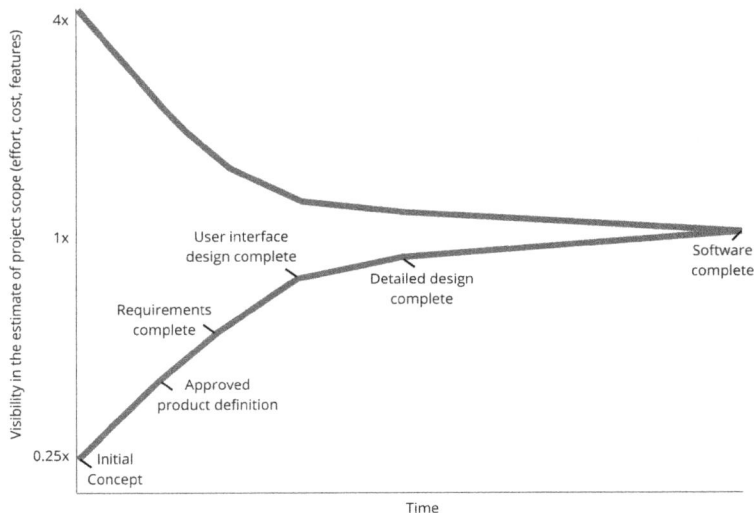

Figure 1.1 – Cone of uncertainty

As a result of this awareness, as predicted by F. Brooks, and the evolution of development methods, such as object-oriented programming, we assisted in the rise of new development tools called RAD (e.g., Delphi, Visual Basic, Paradox, Visual FoxPro), which provided solutions to the accidental complexity of the problem, while still leaving room for improvement to essential complexity.

The summary of these inefficiencies put the roots for the birth of DDD.

The story so far

Back in 2003, Eric Evans, through his popular book, *Domain-Driven Design: Tackling Complexity in the Heart of Software* (often referred to as "the blue book" because of its distinctive blue hard cover), introduced an innovative approach to software design and development. Since then, an ever-growing slice of the software community has begun to shift their approach to software design by applying what he suggested.

This new way of developing software was driven by the need to find a new and more efficient way to tackle the intricacies of an already complex world. What Evans tried to put down in his seminal book is a completely novel approach to what is defined as E-programs of Lehman's law (https://en.wikipedia.org/wiki/Lehman%27s_laws_of_software_evolution).

What he realized was that the traditional approach in software design was focused on translating the complexity of the business flows with just technical solutions (DB first, anyone?).

His proposal was to first do a deep exploration and modeling of the problem space (we will delve into it in *Chapter 2*) and only then try to find an acceptable solution. This approach could only be achieved by involving a continuous collaboration between developers and domain experts.

As paradoxical as it seems, DDD has reached widespread acceptance and use with the advent of microservices. As with every tremendous change, it takes time for the community to understand and refine these concepts. In fact, the early adopters started to slowly implement it circa 2004-2006. The landscape has shifted significantly since that time. During this period, the first use cases started to appear in various developers' communities and mostly in complex systems, such as telecommunication and healthcare.

In 2006, Jimmy Nilsson authored the book titled *Applying Domain-Driven Design and Patterns with Examples in C# and .NET*. The book's approach was very practical and the first one with a fully-fledged application so that the readers could see a method for implementing the main concepts of DDD. This book contributed heavily to further popularizing the approach.

Soon after, Floyd Marinescu and Abel Avram published *Domain-Driven Design Quickly*, where they tried to *"concisely summarize the essence of DDD."* Their work was based mainly on Evans' and Nilsson's books but also used other communities' forums to try to organize and simplify the fundamental concepts of DDD.

After a period of relative calm, in 2009, Greg Young came up with the term **Command Query Responsibility Segregation (CQRS)** (You can learn more at https://cqrs.wordpress.com/wp-content/uploads/2010/11/cqrs_documents.pdf), which is built upon Bertrand Mayer's CQS (as described in his book *Object-Oriented Software Construction*) and further powered by **event sourcing (ES)** to handle complex domain logic (the famous CQRS + ES). This is a pattern that strongly complements DDD by separating read and write operations. But another big push to DDD arrived around 2012 when its patterns influenced in a way the emerging microservices architecture (https://en.wikipedia.org/wiki/Microservices) with bounded contexts offering a natural way to define service boundaries, leading to a resurgence in DDD interest.

Just a year later, two big things happened simultaneously. Vaughn Vernon published *Implementing Domain-Driven Design* (the so-called "red book"), a book which, like Evans', we have studied at least three times during the years. This publication provides great guidance on applying DDD concepts and patterns in real-world projects, bridging the gap between theory and practical implementation. This book introduced a concrete example of the use of events in a complex domain (we will see how they can help our refactoring process in *Chapter 11*). The second massive thing that will heavily influence the community in the coming years was Alberto Brandolini's first post on **EventStorming** (http://ziobrando.blogspot.com/2013/11/introducing-event-storming.html). This workshop format has been widely adopted for collaborative domain modeling since it helps create better communication and understanding between domain experts and developers. As we will see in *Chapter 2*, staying in the problem space as long as possible is a good thing.

As if the preceding year were not full of things to study and reflect upon, the following year, another interesting book saw the light, *Patterns, Principles, and Practices of Domain-Driven Design* by Scott Millett and Nick Tune. This book offers an in-depth exploration of DDD patterns and practices, enriched with case studies, and has become a key resource for experienced developers and architects.

Then, in 2016, the first big conference on DDD was born. The first edition of DDD Europe was held in Bruxelles with an already impressive number of participants as a testimony of the unstoppable interest that DDD has created. Since then, the conference moved to Amsterdam and every year, more than 700 participants attend, with tons of talks and workshops.

In the following years, lots of other communities and conferences were born and we are sure today you can find at least one local meetup near your town with other passionate developers willing to share their struggles and successes with DDD.

In 2019, Alexey Zimarev published *Hands-On Domain Driven Design with .NET: Tackling complexity in the heart of software by putting the DDD principles to practice*, a well-structured book with a plethora of examples in C# with .NET Core.

Finally, in 2021 another terrific book was published, *Learning Domain-Driven Design: Aligning Software Architecture and Business Strategy* by Vlad Khononov. This incredible book focuses on providing a modern perspective of DDD by giving the reader practical implementation practices for modern complex software development.

Last but not least, in 2024, we were lucky enough to be part of the celebration of the 20th anniversary of the Explore DDD Conference held in Denver, CO.

These milestones highlight the growth and adaptation of DDD principles in response to evolving software development challenges, proving the enduring relevance and impact of DDD in the field. We surely forgot some other important events that contributed to the definition of what is today DDD, but they are the ones that we lived through personally and shaped us as developers still trying to find the light in a fast-paced world continuously growing in complexity.

What is domain-driven design (DDD)?

First, we can say what DDD is not. It is not a framework, or a library, to be installed on our computers to guide us in the development of software systems.

At the heart of DDD are two interconnected principles: ubiquitous language and bounded context.

Ubiquitous language is a shared vocabulary consistently used by all stakeholders, including domain experts, developers, and business teams. It eliminates ambiguities in communication, ensuring that everyone involved speaks the same language when discussing the domain. This shared understanding directly influences the accuracy and clarity of the software model, aligning it closely with the business domain.

Bounded context defines the boundaries within which a specific domain model and its associated ubiquitous language apply. These boundaries prevent overlaps or inconsistencies between different parts of a system, enabling teams to work independently within their assigned contexts. This modular approach simplifies the management of complex systems and ensures that changes within one context do not unintentionally affect others.

As an example, you can think of the game that many Agile coaches use, the broken telephone. The game points out how with each hand-off of information from one person to another, the information is always altered due to the interpretation of each individual.

In human conversations, context is naturally developed as people engage in dialog. When someone enters the discussion midway, they often ask, "Who or what are you talking about?" rather than directly inquiring, "What is the context?"

Without context, meaning can be ambiguous, distorted, or even completely lost. A lack of context when joining a conversation can lead to misunderstandings, as the newcomer may make incorrect assumptions about the subject at hand. Similarly, an abstraction can only be as accurate as the shared understanding of the context among all participants in the communication.

As stated before, one of the main goals of DDD is to reduce as much as possible this phenomenon by establishing a common language to make explicit the implicit.

| How the Customer explained it | What the Project Manager understood | How the Analyst designed it | What the Programmer wrote | What the Customer really needed |

Figure 1.2 – The broken telephone applied to a project

Communication is key to understanding the problem we need to solve. DDD wants to be an alternative to an anemic list of requirements and delivery of the software. This can be achieved by starting by trying to understand the problem instead of defining a list of requirements. We should not start with one, or more, ready-made solutions, because requirements are in fact a solution to the problem and are given to us at the beginning of the project exactly when we do not know anything about the domain. This means that we are unable to clearly understand whether they really are the solution or not. Requirements capture a stakeholder's perspective of the system at a particular point in time and are subject to change.

DDD aims to help create software more aligned with the business goals, more adaptable to change, and easier to maintain over time. To ease the conversation, DDD focuses on the business **domain**, so it is necessary to clarify its meaning right from the start.

Throughout this book, you will evolve an **Enterprise Resource Planning (ERP)** system that handles production, shipping, and orders of a brewery (yes, we love beer). You will start from a legacy system and by applying all the patterns that DDD gives us we will refactor and improve it.

What you will do, exactly, is better understand the business domain, which is the main area of activity of our brewery, and refactor your way toward a more resilient and scalable application using baby steps instead of a "big bang change" (or nuclear option, as we call it).

Now that we know what "domain" is, why "**driven**"? By the book, the term implies that the design of the software is guided by someone or something. In our case, it is based on a deep understanding of the domain, and only after understanding a domain, we'll introduce technical considerations or implementation details.

Finally, "**design**" simply refers to the process of creating a solution.

Refactoring is a crucial part of the DDD approach. It involves restructuring existing code without changing its external behavior to improve nonfunctional attributes. In the context of DDD, refactoring is not just about code; it's about refining the model to better reflect the domain as your understanding deepens.

This continuous alignment of the software model with the evolving understanding of the business domain is one of the key principles of DDD. Regularly revisiting and refining the model ensures it accurately represents the current state of the domain. This iterative process of refining and improving the model is where refactoring comes into play.

In practice, refactoring with DDD involves several steps:

1. **Understanding the Domain**: Before any refactoring, you need a deep understanding of the business domain. Engage with domain experts to gather insights and ensure the model accurately reflects the domain knowledge.

2. **Identifying Areas for Improvement**: Look for parts of the code where the domain model is not well represented or where technical debt has accumulated. These are prime candidates for refactoring.

3. **Applying DDD Patterns**: Use DDD patterns, such as aggregates, entities, value objects, and services, to restructure the code. Ensure that these patterns are applied in a way that enhances the clarity and integrity of the domain model.

4. **Maintaining Functionality**: Refactor in small steps to ensure that the system remains functional throughout the process. Use automated tests to verify that existing functionality is preserved.

5. **Continuous Integration**: Integrate changes frequently to catch issues early and ensure that the refactored code works well with the rest of the system.

6. **Feedback Loop**: Regularly review the changes with domain experts to ensure that the refactoring aligns with their understanding of the domain. Use their feedback to further refine the model.

This iterative process ensures that the software remains adaptable to changes in business requirements and it is easier to maintain and extend over time.

How DDD changes the approach to the problem

DDD fundamentally transforms the approach to software development by placing the business domain at the heart of the development process. Traditional software development methodologies often start with technical considerations, such as data modeling, database design, or user interface wireframes.

While these aspects are essential, DDD shifts the focus from technical priorities to aligning software design with fundamental business concepts, resulting in more relevant, flexible, and maintainable systems.

DDD emphasized the importance of explicitly defining context to ensure the precise interpretation of an abstraction. It advocates for a mindset shift where the primary focus is the alignment between all the members of the team and avoiding misunderstanding. This is one of the primary ways DDD is used to change the approach to problem-solving. This common language is something shared between the stakeholders, domain experts, developers, and end users and is as strict as a programming language. The good thing is that it is a vocabulary that is understood by each party and its consistent use allows every team member to easily refactor parts of the code that do not align with business requirements. It also strongly reduces misunderstandings and ensures that the code base evolves in harmony with the business.

DDD encourages developers to immerse themselves in domain knowledge and collaborate closely with domain experts (e.g., business analysts, end users, etc.). This deep exploration of the domain allows developers to gain a comprehensive understanding of the concepts, rules, processes, and behaviors that govern the real-world problem space. Obviously, this is not something that is achieved easily, but requires exploration and experimentation with several iterations with a lot of the time spent, as we will see in the next chapter, in what is called the problem space.

Just as in human conversations, fully grasping a model requires establishing the appropriate context and clear boundaries. A model, as we have noted, is a structured system of abstractions. Beware that a model remains an oversimplification of reality as defined by Rebecca Wirfs-Brock (`https://weave-it.org/blog/overcoming-additive-bias-software-design`):

> *A model is a simplified representation of a thing or phenomenon that intentionally emphasizes certain aspects while ignoring others. Abstraction with a specific use in mind.*

These contexts help manage the complexity of large software systems by allowing different parts of the system to evolve independently. Each bounded context contains its own domain model, which is consistent and isolated from other contexts. This modularization is crucial for refactoring as it allows changes to be made within one context without impacting others, thus reducing the risk of introducing errors and improving the system's overall maintainability.

In addition to bounded contexts, DDD leverages tactical patterns such as entities, value objects, aggregates, repositories, and services. These patterns provide a structured approach to encapsulating domain logic, ensuring that changes can be implemented cleanly and systematically. For example, entities represent objects that have a distinct identity and life cycle, while value objects encapsulate attributes and behaviors without identity. Aggregates are clusters of related entities and value objects that are treated as a single unit for data changes, ensuring consistency and integrity within the model.

Repositories abstract the data access layer, providing a clean interface for storing and retrieving aggregates. As described in Martin Fowler's book, *Patterns of Enterprise Application Architecture*, (`https://martinfowler.com/eaaCatalog/repository.html`) a repository mediates between the domain and data mapping layers, acting like an in-memory domain object collection.

Domain services encapsulate domain logic that does not naturally fit within an aggregate, promoting a clear separation of concerns. Its main use is to coordinate one or more aggregates removing as much as possible the coupling between them.

These patterns not only facilitate cleaner and more maintainable code but also make it easier to refactor and extend the system in response to the ever-changing business requirements.

Furthermore, DDD encourages iterative development and continuous refactoring. This iterative process allows teams to incrementally improve the system, making small, manageable changes that collectively lead to significant enhancements in the code base's quality and functionality. These concepts do not apply to a green field project but are also true for the refactoring of a legacy system.

To close, by placing the domain at the center of the design process, DDD helps bridge the gap between the technical and business perspectives. As already stated, it significantly changes the approach to problem-solving in software development by prioritizing a deep understanding of the business domain, fostering clear communication through a ubiquitous language, and structuring the system using bounded contexts and well-defined design patterns. This methodology not only makes the refactoring process more efficient and effective but also ensures that the software evolves in alignment with the business's needs, resulting in more robust and maintainable systems.

Summary

Since Evans' 2003 book, *Domain-Driven Design: Tackling Complexity in the Heart of Software*, the software community has increasingly adopted the DDD approach. Evans' emphasis on understanding and modeling the problem space before implementing technical solutions marked a significant shift from traditional methodologies, especially in refactoring.

This chapter highlights the evolution of DDD and its influence on refactoring practices. Key contributions include Nilsson's practical applications, Greg Young's CQRS pattern for complex domain logic, and the resurgence of DDD with microservices architecture. Vaughn Vernon's work gave practical examples, while Alberto Brandolini's EventStorming improved communication between domain experts and developers.

In conclusion, DDD transforms refactoring by prioritizing domain understanding and communication, leading to more intuitive, business-aligned, and resilient software solutions.

In the next chapter, you will refresh, or learn if you are new to these concepts, the principal strategic patterns that you need to know foreffective refactoring the DDD way.

2

Understanding Complexity: Problem and Solution Space

In the previous chapter, we went through the history of DDD and what it tries to solve. We also started to talk about the need to explore the domain, improve our knowledge of it, and find solutions in an iterative way. In this chapter, we will delve into problem and solution spaces, and by the end of it, you will have a clear understanding of their importance not only when approaching a greenfield project but also when refactoring one that already exists. Such a project may already be drifting away with useless features or complexity that do not represent the business anymore. You have probably seen many such types of projects that try to solve problems they themselves create, rather than adding value for the user.

We will explore the intricate nature of modern complex systems and how to navigate their inherent complexity. Understanding these concepts is a fundamental skill for DDD as it allows us to deconstruct and manage the various components that define your system.

Specifically, we'll cover the following main topics in this chapter:

- Dealing with complexity
- Problem and solution space
- Decision-making and biases

Dealing with complexity

One of the best things about the nineties was that you could deploy new versions of systems with ease. When you were ready, you simply took down the application, upgraded it, and then put it back online. The same was true for our awesome SQL scripts that updated the DB in one fell swoop and, until the end of the nineties, most systems were deployed this way.

These days, you can no longer afford to do this anymore because you do not have the luxury of being able to take down all the components of a system and upgrade them all at once. You must take into account that different teams are working on different components at different speeds, and there could be a lot of DBs that need to be kept somewhat aligned. What we are trying to say here is that the main reason this is not an acceptable way of doing things anymore is because at the root of everything lies complexity. Modern systems are so big and complicated that complexity itself is an inherent characteristic. No matter what you are dealing with, complexity arises from various sources—such as the sheer number of components, their interdependencies, and the dynamic nature of their interactions.

Understanding complexity involves recognizing its multifaceted nature and can be classified into two main types: essential complexity and accidental complexity. Essential complexity is intrinsic to the problem domain and cannot be removed. It is the complexity that arises from the nature of the problem itself. For example, the complexity of a financial trading system is inherent due to the numerous rules, regulations, and market conditions it must adhere to.

Accidental complexity, on the other hand, stems from the solution domain. It is the unnecessary complexity introduced by poor design decisions, inefficient processes, or inadequate tools. Reducing accidental complexity is mandatory for managing and simplifying systems.

Figure 2.1 is a summary of the key points to classify complexity.

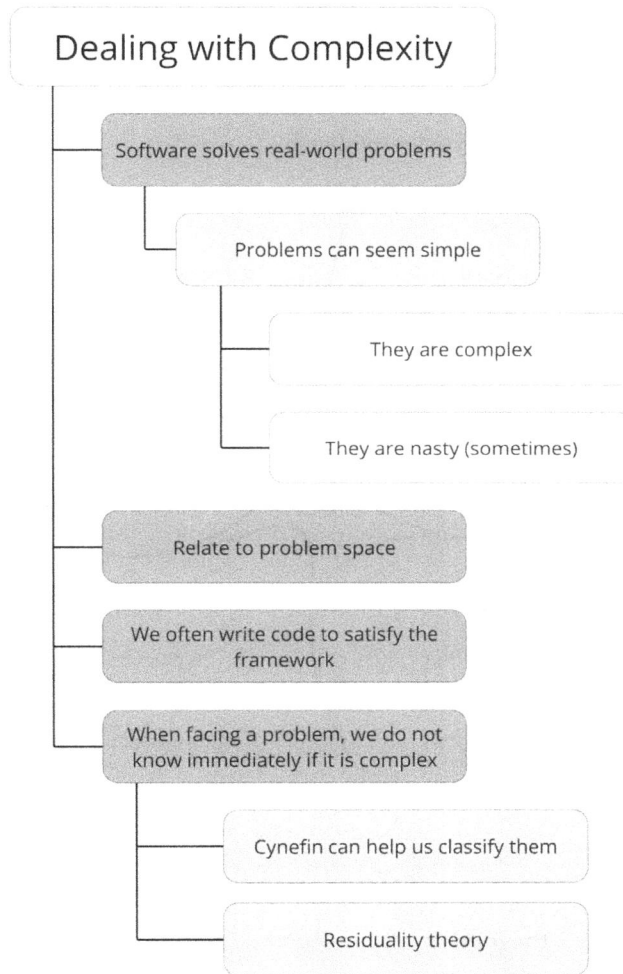

Dealing with Complexity

- Software solves real-world problems
  - Problems can seem simple
    - They are complex
    - They are nasty (sometimes)
- Relate to problem space
- We often write code to satisfy the framework
- When facing a problem, we do not know immediately if it is complex
  - Cynefin can help us classify them
  - Residuality theory

Figure 2.1 – Key points when dealing with complexity

As we can see in *Figure 2.1*, there is a lot to take into consideration when dealing with complexity, but do not worry; we have tools created by very smart people that can help us tackle it.

One of the first tools we would like to introduce to you is the **Cynefin framework** (`https://en.wikipedia.org/wiki/Cynefin_framework`).

Cynefin framework

The Cynefin framework was developed by Dave Snowden in 1999, and its name, pronounced /kəˈnɛvɪn/ kuh-NEV-in, is a Welsh word that means "habitat." We can sum it up by saying that it is a sense-making device that helps individuals and organizations understand and navigate complexity. *Figure 2.2* shows the Cynefin template.

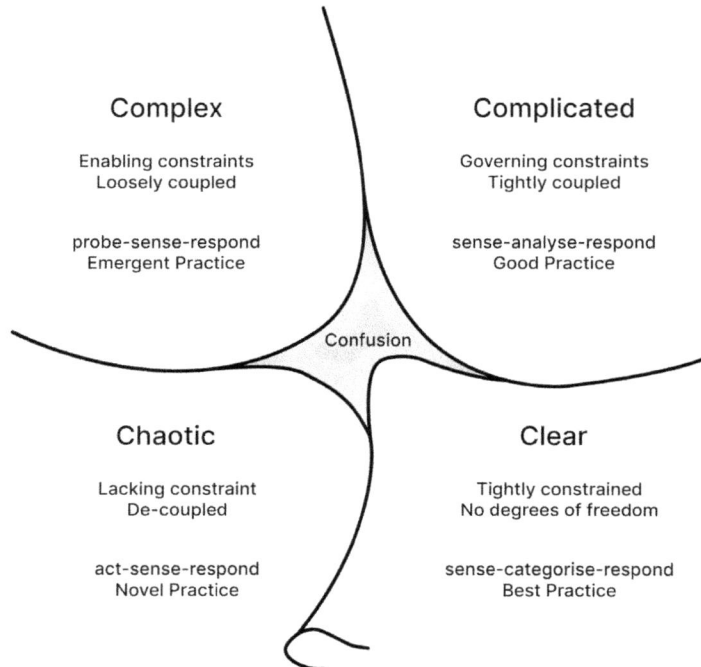

Complex

Enabling constraints
Loosely coupled

probe-sense-respond
Emergent Practice

Complicated

Governing constraints
Tightly coupled

sense-analyse-respond
Good Practice

Confusion

Chaotic

Lacking constraint
De-coupled

act-sense-respond
Novel Practice

Clear

Tightly constrained
No degrees of freedom

sense-categorise-respond
Best Practice

Figure 2.2 – Cynefin framework, taken from Wikipedia

As we can see in *Figure 2.2*, the framework categorizes situations into five distinct contexts.

Clear context

Clear context represents the "known knowns." This means that the relationship between cause and effect requires analysis or expertise but is still predictable. Best practices or well-defined rules are already in place. In this situation, the advice is to "sense–categorize–respond": first, establish the facts ("sense"), then categorize them, and finally, respond by following the rules or applying the best practices. Here, the DDD strategic patterns are useless because we already have a clear vision of the domain and so we can move directly to implementing tactical patterns.

Complicated context

Complicated context represents the "known unknowns"—situations where the relationship between cause and effect requires analysis or expertise but it is still predictable. Good practice and expert advice are applicable. As we can see in *Figure 2.2*, the framework suggests "sense–analyze–respond": assess the facts, analyze, and apply the appropriate good operating practice. In this specific domain, strategic and tactical patterns are essential to increase its understanding and start moving to a clear context.

Complex context

Complex context represents the "unknown unknowns." As it were, it is when cause and effect are deducible only in retrospect, there are no right answers, and patterns emerge through interaction. Emergent practices are needed here. "Probe–sense–respond" takes place: small-scale experiments ("probe") to explore the space and generate data, sense the results, and respond with actions. Strategic patterns with explorative tools come to the rescue to help us root a better vision and comprehension of this context. Tactical patterns are useless here.

Chaotic context

In a **chaotic context** situation, cause and effect are unclear because there is no clear relationship, and immediate action is required to stabilize the situation. We must "act–sense–respond": act to establish order, sense where stability lies, and respond to try to turn a chaotic context into a complex context. Novel practices emerge. In this specific context, the pattern of DDD does not help, but we should use other exploration tools to give us a starting point on which we could start to apply strategic patterns.

Confusion context

The **confusion context** is in the center of *Figure 2.2* and represents situations where there is no clarity about which of the other contexts apply. As written by Snowden and Boone in their article *A Leader's Framework for Decision Making* (https://strategicleadership.com.au/wp-content/uploads/2017/06/A-Leader%E2%80%99s-Framework-for-Decision-Making-HBR-Nov-2007.pdf): "*Here, multiple perspectives jostle for prominence, factional leaders argue with one another, and cacophony rules.*"

Table 2.1 summarizes when we should use strategic, tactical, and explorative patterns.

	Strategic patterns	**Tactical patterns**	**Explorative patterns**
Clear	No	Yes	No
Complicated	Yes	Yes	No
Complex	Yes	No	Yes
Chaotic	No	No	Yes
Confusion	No	No	Yes

Table 2.1 – A recap of when we should use strategic, tactical, and explorative patterns

To conclude with a practical example, let us look at the one given by the author himself in 2007. It refers to an incident that happened in 1993 at the Brown's Chicken and Pasta restaurant in Palatine, Illinois. A shooter murdered seven employees, and as a result, Deputy Police Chief Walt Gasior had to deal with a situation in which the local police faced all the domains. He had to act immediately to manage the initial panic (chaotic), keep the department running by following standard procedures (simple), ask for expert help (complicated), and keep the community calm in the following weeks (complex).

Residuality theory

Another powerful tool we have in our toolbox is **residuality theory** (https://www.sciencedirect.com/science/article/pii/S1877050921007420). Formulated by Barry O'Reilly, it states that the future of a system is determined by its residues, which are the remnants left behind after the system has been affected by a stressor.

Residuality theory is a pivotal concept in the realm of DDD, offering a structured approach to understanding and improving complex systems. At its core, residuality theory examines how a system retains its structure and behavior after being subjected to changes or disruptions, referred to as stressors.

Imagine a legacy e-commerce platform that struggles to handle peak shopping seasons, such as Christmas or Black Friday. Each peak period acts as a stressor, revealing underlying issues such as slow performance or system crashes. By applying the residuality theory, we analyze these stress responses to identify persistent problems and areas resistant to change.

This method allows us to target refactoring efforts more effectively, ensuring that improvements address the root causes of system fragility. By refactoring this aspect, we enhance the system's robustness, making it more resilient to future stressors. With this approach, we can better pinpoint which area of our system needs refactoring and design a system that gracefully adapts to evolving demands and challenges.

O'Reilly's residuality theory presents a nuanced understanding of how systems evolve and sustain themselves through the continuous accumulation of past states and interactions. This theory wants to shift our perspective on change, suggesting that systems (what he calls naïve architectures) do not simply go through isolated, linear steps but are profoundly shaped by the "residue" that remains when facing changes. These residues are active, influential components that affect how systems adapt, resist, and evolve over time.

To truly understand a system, one must consider these residuals, which manifest in various forms, such as legacy code in software, ingrained processes in organizations, or established cultural norms within communities. Each of these residues carries with it the weight of past decisions, interactions, and contexts, creating a complex web that influences current and future states. For example, in the realm of software development, understanding the intricacies of legacy code is essential for making informed decisions about future development and integrations.

Residuality theory advocates for a holistic approach to change management and system design. It encourages us to look beyond immediate actions and outcomes and to consider the deeper, more persistent influences that shape a system's behavior. By doing so, we can better predict potential challenges, identify areas of resistance, and develop strategies that are more aligned with the underlying reality of the system. This approach contrasts sharply with traditional models of change that often overlook the importance of historical context and residual effects, leading to strategies that may be effective in the short term but fail to sustain over time.

In practical terms, applying residuality theory means engaging in a continuous process of reflection and analysis, where past experiences are not just acknowledged but are critically examined to understand their ongoing impact. This involves not only identifying the residues but also interpreting their significance and leveraging this understanding to inform future actions. For instance, in a business context, leaders might analyze past project failures and successes to identify persistent patterns that could influence current initiatives. In software development, teams might conduct thorough code reviews to understand how past coding practices and design decisions affect current performance and scalability.

Stressors and refactoring

A **stressor**, in the context of refactoring, is any external factor or event that places pressure on the system and tests its stability, performance, and resilience. As per the example before, this pressure can be caused by a spike in the number of users, unexpected behaviors, and network or hardware failures. These are practical tests that reveal the system's weaknesses and bottlenecks. Do not equate this with Netflix's Chaos Monkey though. You identify stressors with brainstorming sessions, analysis of the production system in its ecosystem, or by using random simulation.

Observing and analyzing how your system behaves under these stress scenarios allows you to gain critical insights into system weaknesses and bottlenecks. This understanding is crucial for effective refactoring, enhancing the system's ability to handle future stressors, and improving overall robustness and reliability.

If you want to learn more on the topic, we suggest watching the speech O'Reilly gave at NDC Oslo in 2023 on YouTube (`https://www.youtube.com/watch?v=0wcUG2EV-7E`).

EventStorming

Last but not least, we want to bring your attention to **EventStorming** (`https://www.eventstorming.com/`), a tool created by Alberto Brandolini. This tool is especially useful for the exploration of your domain and is different from other similar tools (i.e., domain storytelling). The idea behind it is quite simple; since your goal is to understand the complexity of the domain, bring all the interested parties, from domain experts to stakeholders, to the table and build a domain model together that is understandable to everyone. There is no single format for EventStorming; it is more of a family of workshops aimed at graphically representing the complexity of key information flows within organizations using events as an exploration tool. There are three main kinds of formats we can choose from, and every single one is specifically designed for different moments of exploration. Let's go through them in the next sub-sections.

Big picture

When you must deal with the refactoring of a code base, you need to understand what this solution solves, and you need to talk to all the stakeholders of the project, all the businesspeople, and all the developers. The goal is to build a model that represents the flow of all data in your domain. Everything starts by hanging a sheet of paper on the wall, typically 10-15 meters in length (but it usually grows a lot more), and applying fundamental ingredients on it—orange sticky notes. These notes represent events that occur in the domain, and, usually, after a couple of hours of discussions and writing of orange stickies, you will see that processes start to emerge on the wall as a flow represented by all the orange sticky notes. From here, you will be able to start exploring with the stakeholders the different ways in which they perceive the same problem.

In this phase, it is important to understand whether these ways are simply different in solving the problem or whether each stakeholder has a different point of view on it. You will end up with a defined common language between developers, business experts, and stakeholders. *Figure 2.3* shows an example of events in an EventStorming session with added notes about topics that must be covered during the detailed analysis of the flow. The scope of the big picture is to highlight the main events and potential pain points throughout the business flow.

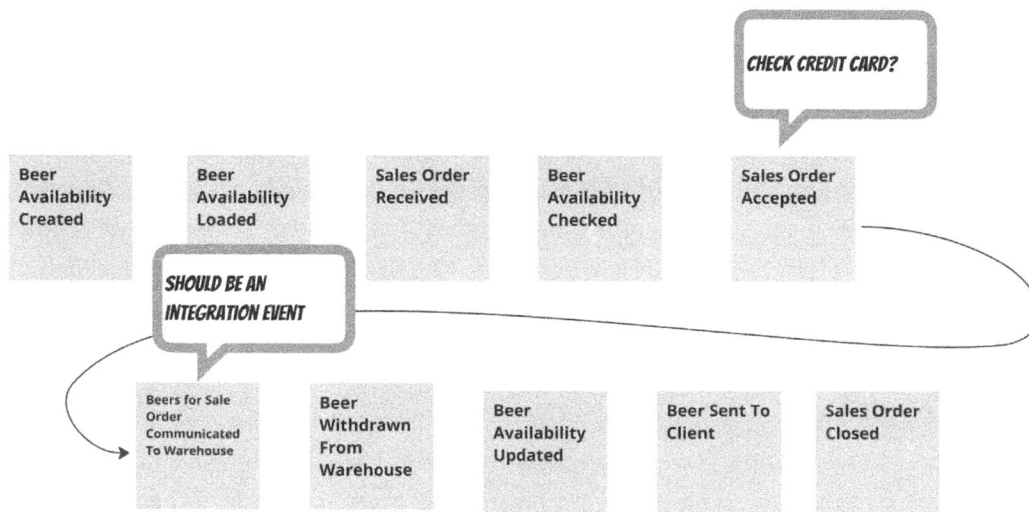

Figure 2.3 – EventStorming big picture result

Process modeling

In this case, the scope of the exploration is more limited, and so is the team dimension. You need to create a space in which each stakeholder can contribute to creating the model, and for this reason, you cannot use tools such as UML, otherwise, only developers could participate, or Business Process Modeling Notation, because only businesspeople could participate. You need to enable conversations between all the members of the domain so that you can create a model to share between them.

In *Figure 2.4*, you can see all the types of sticky notes that you can use during an EventStorming session. Having a common model avoids misinterpretation, and with that, you don't lose any details on the business flow.

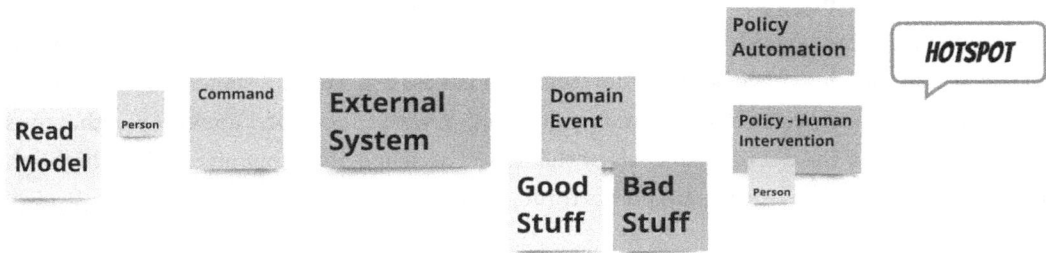

Figure 2.4 – The grammar of EventStorming process modeling

To achieve this goal, you have to add more types of sticky notes to EventStorming's grammar. You do not need a design of the processes as a result of your exploration, but to encourage the conversation, so that you can use a tool as simple as possible to be understood by everyone. For example, during refactoring, it is very important to identify the right boundaries to split our monolith with. That separation represents the way in which you will extrapolate the microservices architecture.

Software design

With the previous workshop, you end up with a clear definition of the domain boundaries. Now, with this third format, you are going to explore in detail every single one of them, so that the grammar will be richer.

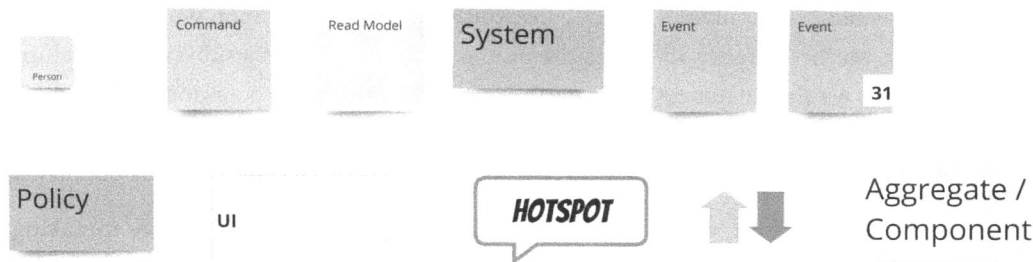

Figure 2.5 – All of the elements used during EventStorming

With this workshop, you will identify the *aggregate* of your *bounded context*, as well as the *domain events*, *commands*, *services* (internal and external), *policy*, and all the objects you need to design your solution. The aim of this workshop is to provide a detailed structure of the software for the team using the language that you discovered during the previous EventStorming sessions, and the details of all objects discovered in this one.

Now that you have understood the importance of knowledge, you can discover how deep you can go into the problem and try to solve it.

Problem and solution space

Among the many phrases apocryphally attributed (`https://quoteinvestigator.com/2014/05/22/solve/`) to Albert Einstein, there is one that goes as follows:

> *"If I had an hour to save the world, I would spend 55 minutes defining the problem and only 5 minutes finding the solutions."*

We could summarize this statement by saying that the problem space is the set of all the problems that your application should solve, while the solution space is the set of all solutions that address each given problem.

Allen Newell and Herbert Simon in their book *Human Problem Solving* argue that we, as human beings, tend to be problem solvers. We see this daily in our team while developing software. We tend to seek and try to find a solution as quickly as possible and leave the problem space as quickly too. We are uncomfortable staying in this area, but it is where our client needs to reside; it is the zone that allows us to acquire more information about the problems our client asks us to solve through the software we will develop for them because writing software means solving business problems! Essentially, this space constitutes the foundation upon which the solution space will rest. Mathematically speaking, the problem space is always a subset of the solution space. Therefore, we should not rush to leave the former to move, with poor domain knowledge, to the latter. As developers, to demonstrate our capabilities, we tend to provide a solution as soon as possible, as if to show that we are good at our job by providing solutions fast to our clients.

By acting this way, however, we do not delve deeply enough into the problem; we are taking a shortcut to exit an uncomfortable zone. If we are then given requirements, our biases suggest the solution to propose! Unfortunately, such a solution will always be incomplete, at best, and wrong, at worst, because it is at this stage that projects begin to fail. We will realize it later when it is already too late, but the root of the failure lies in not having thoroughly investigated the problem space.

Staying in the problem space means resisting the urge to prematurely jump into solutions. It requires a disciplined approach to fully understand and articulate the problem before considering any solution. This involves engaging with stakeholders to capture their perspectives, conducting thorough research, and employing techniques such as domain modeling and scenario analysis to explore all facets of the problem.

By deeply investigating the problem space, we uncover the underlying causes, constraints, and nuances that might not be immediately obvious. This process often reveals critical insights that significantly influence the design and implementation of the solution. It ensures that the problem is framed correctly, which is essential for creating effective and sustainable solutions.

Furthermore, staying in the problem space helps to mitigate biases and assumptions that can cloud judgment. It promotes a culture of curiosity and continuous learning within the team, where questions are encouraged, and diverse viewpoints are valued. This collaborative exploration fosters a shared understanding of the problem, aligning all stakeholders around a common goal.

Neglecting this phase leads to superficial solutions that fail to address the core issues. Projects that skip through problem investigation often suffer from scope creep, missed requirements, and ultimately, failure to deliver value. In contrast, a robust exploration of the problem space lays a solid foundation for successful projects, ensuring that solutions are not only technically sound but also relevant and impactful.

Figure 2.6 summarizes the differences between them.

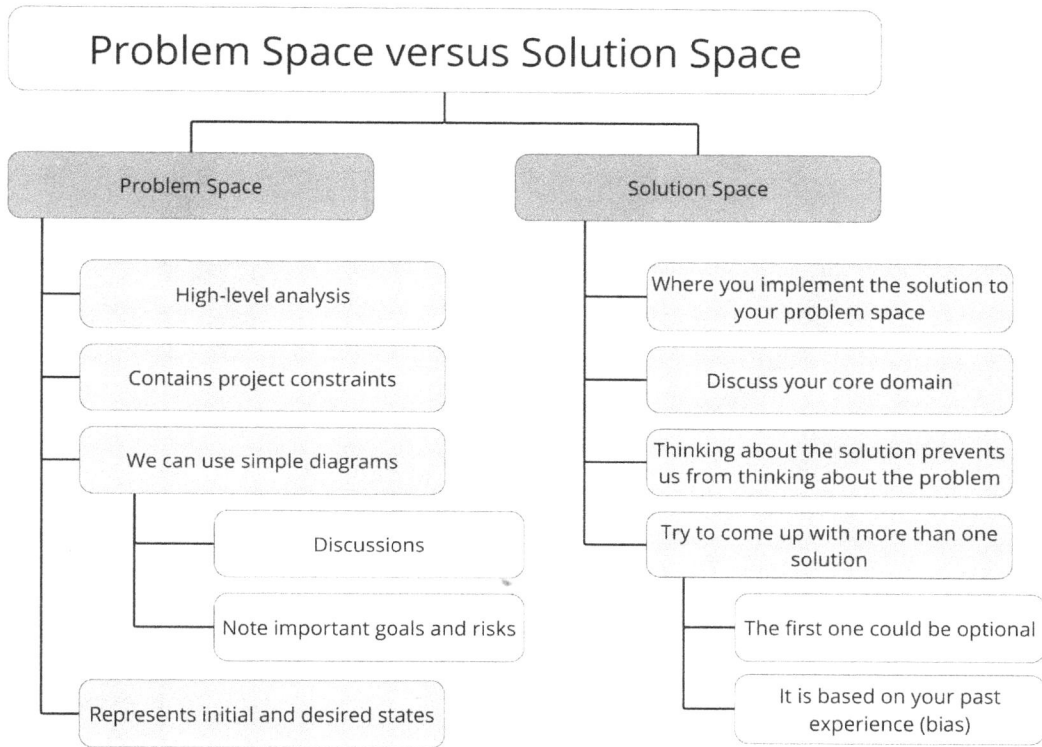

Problem Space versus Solution Space

Problem Space
- High-level analysis
- Contains project constraints
- We can use simple diagrams
  - Discussions
  - Note important goals and risks
- Represents initial and desired states

Solution Space
- Where you implement the solution to your problem space
- Discuss your core domain
- Thinking about the solution prevents us from thinking about the problem
- Try to come up with more than one solution
  - The first one could be optional
  - It is based on your past experience (bias)

Figure 2.6 – Problem space versus solution space

The urge to provide an adequate solution soon from the start means starting off on the wrong foot. We all know that our applications start small but are destined to grow over time, some very quickly: as customer demands grow, a small deviation at the beginning of the journey will lead us to a destination different from what was imagined, making it increasingly difficult to align our solution with the actual problem solution.

How can we avoid all of this? By staying in the problem space as long as possible, just like in Einstein's quote. Even Evans proposes an exploratory model, consisting of continuous iterations of analysis, proposal, and feedback, as shown in *Figure 2.7*.

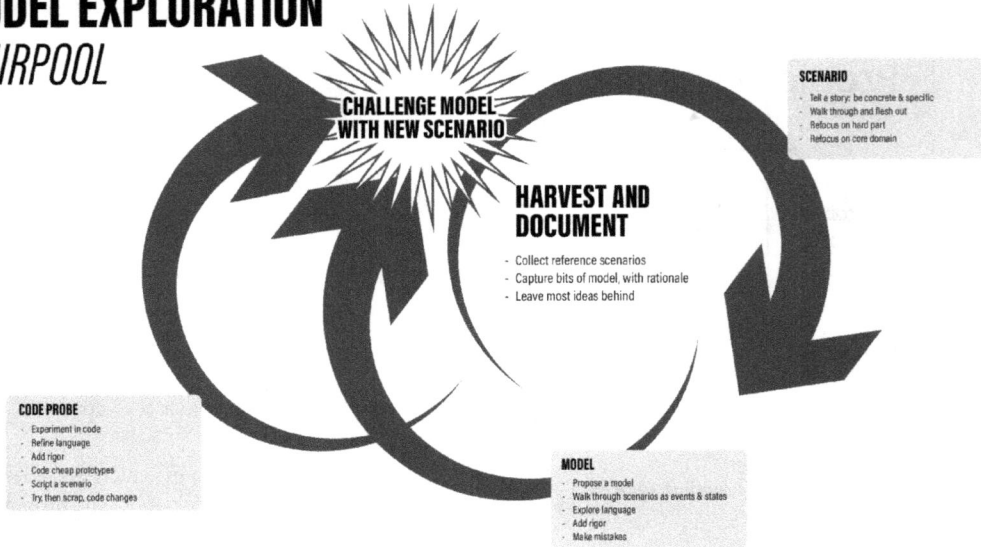

MODEL EXPLORATION
WHIRPOOL

CHALLENGE MODEL WITH NEW SCENARIO

SCENARIO
- Tell a story: be concrete & specific
- Walk through and flesh out
- Refocus on hard part
- Refocus on core domain

HARVEST AND DOCUMENT
- Collect reference scenarios
- Capture bits of model, with rationale
- Leave most ideas behind

CODE PROBE
- Experiment in code
- Refine language
- Add rigor
- Code cheap prototypes
- Script a scenario
- Try then scrap, code changes

MODEL
- Propose a model
- Walk through scenarios as events & states
- Explore language
- Add rigor
- Make mistakes

Figure 2.7 – Model exploration whirlpool

Evans defines the action of finding a solution from the beginning to the entire problem as what we colloquially call big front design: a block "locking in our ignorance." The problem with this type of approach is that we are forced to make a lot of important decisions about our solution when we have less knowledge of the problem itself.

To counter this, Dan North suggests extreme caution in moving toward a definitive solution. In his article *Introducing Deliberate Discovery* (https://dannorth.net/introducing-deliberate-discovery/), he advocates for a proactive exploration of the domain knowledge, emphasizing the importance of identifying and understanding what we do not yet know about the domain. Let's spend some time going through the important parts of the article.

Deliberate discovery

The main terms covered in North's article are as follows:

- **Deliberate discovery**: Emphasizes the importance of actively seeking knowledge to reduce ignorance in projects.

- **Learning versus ignorance**: Identifies ignorance as a primary constraint to project success and highlights the need for proactive learning

- **Accidental versus deliberate learning**: Contrasts passive, accidental learning with intentional, deliberate discovery to accelerate knowledge acquisition

- **Non-linear discovery**: Discusses how learning happens in irregular, often unexpected ways
- **Assumption of problems**: Advocates planning with the expectation that unpredictable problems will arise, thus preparing better responses

The key recommendations made by North are as follows:

- Focus planning on knowledge acquisition rather than merely estimating the task
- Recognize and address various forms of ignorance (technical, domain-specific, organizational)
- Make deliberate efforts in discovery to significantly improve project outcomes by reducing unknowns early
- Acknowledge that learning happens in spurts, often influenced by unforeseen challenges
- Prepare for bad events proactively to mitigate their impact on projects

Now let us look at another perspective that delves into the risks of big front design stemming from lack of awareness. Interestingly, "lack of awareness" is termed as the "2nd order of ignorance" in Phillip G. Armour's article titled *The Five Orders of Ignorance* (`https://cacm.acm.org/opinion/the-five-orders-of-ignorance/`)

.Five orders of ignorance

The main argument in Armour's article is that the true product of software development is the knowledge embedded in the software; creating functional software requires understanding what "works."

If knowledge is the key, then the following is also true:

- Building effective software is primarily about acquiring the necessary knowledge
- Software development should be viewed as a knowledge-acquisition process rather than a product-production activity

Starting with these considerations, we end up with **five orders of ignorance**:

- **0th order ignorance (0OI)**: Lack of ignorance – you know something and can demonstrate it
- **1st order ignorance (1OI)**: Lack of knowledge – you don't know something, but you know what you don't know
- **2nd order ignorance (2OI)**: Lack of awareness – you don't know you don't know

- **3rd order ignorance (3OI)**: Lack of process – you don't know a suitable process to find out what you don't know
- **4th order ignorance (4OI)**: Meta ignorance – you don't know about the five orders of ignorance

If ignorance is the opposite of knowledge, how can we remain in the problem space to bridge 1OI and increase awareness of 2OI? How do we control our tendency to propose solutions too quickly?

Bridging gaps in ignorance

To address the challenge of navigating between known and unknown gaps in knowledge, we recommend the following useful tips:

- **Maintain control of the discussion**: You don't have to talk continuously, but you have to avoid the discussion converging too quickly to a conclusion. Often, a signal to a colleague is enough to change the focus of the conversation with the client. The main reason for maintaining control of the discussion is that clients—or their representatives—often assume certain information is understood and leave it unsaid, so it's up to us to surface and clarify those assumptions.
- **Listen to different solutions**: In initial meetings with a client, participants are often hesitant to speak or propose ideas. Then, after the ice is broken thanks to our capable agile coach, solutions start to emerge and sometimes conflict with each other. It is important to maintain a healthy and positive environment by including everyone's suggestions in the solution space.
- **Keep the main solution hidden**: As the moderator of the problem exploration, your task is to keep the solutions that globally prove to be valid hidden for as long as possible. For example, if you use EventStorming as an exploration tool, let participants continue to attach sticky notes to the wall, and perhaps guide them in a direction so that the main solution emerges autonomously. Highlight solutions that seem similar and focus attention on them to understand whether they are different expressions of the same solution or totally different ones.

Staying in the problem space is certainly uncomfortable for both parties: the client and the supplier. The former feels a bit under pressure due to the countless questions they keep receiving, and the latter, often us, can't wait to propose a solution. Completely addressing the client's problem takes time, and it's not always convenient to insist on deeper investigation or prolonged questioning during the first meeting. The important thing is to identify the boundaries of the problem and start proposing a solution that can be revisited for feedback and continued after potentially adjusting the course.

Our domain will always be in constant evolution, if only for everything that belongs to the level of unknown unknowns – the things we still don't know we don't know but will discover as we become greater experts in the domain we are working on. At this point, we need to understand how to approach such a solution, from an architectural point of view. And for this, we need to explore the domain before creating a model.

Deleuzian walk

We have already seen how the abstractions of reality can be dangerous to solve a problem. Creating a good model is the primary goal, either during the first design of your solution or while you are working to refactor it. But how do we do this? EventStorming, like storytelling and other tools, is good for exploring the domain together with all team members before creating a model. However, an alternative way to run an exploration is to simply experience the domain itself, just as we explore the territory around us when we walk.

This form of exploration is known as the Deleuzian walk and describes an alternative way of learning. The term comes from the ideas of Gilles Deleuze, as described in his 1968 book *Difference and Repetition*, which can be summarized as follows:

- **Philosophy of difference**: Deleuze challenges traditional philosophy's focus on identity and sameness, advocating for a deeper exploration of differences

- **Repetition and novelty**: He explores how repetition can generate new meanings or variations, challenging the idea that repetition simply reinforces what already exists or remains the same.

- **Ontology**: Deleuze presents being as inherently different, emphasizing uniqueness over uniformity

- **Time and memory**: The roles of time and memory are scrutinized for their impact on cultivating differences

- **Conceptual tools**: Deleuze navigates through his arguments employing complex philosophical constructs such as the virtual, the actual, and intensity

When you walk along a new path for the first time, you are totally involved in looking at the map to be sure to get back home safely. After a few times, you start to discover new things on your journey because now you know the path, and you can pay attention to the environment around you, the mountains around the valley, or the river at the bottom. You will see new landscapes or discover new alternative ways of traveling in the same space. When you bring your friends with you, they will see different things, because their interests are different from yours. Instead of understanding the world around you, you are contemplating it, and you become very rich. You are changing your way of thinking, from learning from the map (linear), in which the map provides an objective, well-defined, description of the walk, to observing the world around you with your eyes and discovering new things (laterally).

This metaphor is quite fitting for domain exploration. As the environment changes during the different seasons, your domain also changes due to new business requirements, or simply because the world changes constantly and so does the business flow. This means that our structure is constantly changing, and implementing certain structures too early could be very dangerous and unproductive.

During domain exploration, knowledge is much preferable in contrast to the developer's need for an immediate concrete implementation. So, Deleuze's ideas map perfectly with the model exploration whirlpool shown in *Figure 2.7*. Basically, it is important to discover your domain iteratively and increase your knowledge of the domain step by step. Remember that you are a developer and do not necessarily know from the start the domain you will work on.

Decision-making and biases

By now, it should be clear why it is important to spend most of our time understanding the problem instead of finding a solution, and now we can delve into the last aspect of handling complexity. This includes cognitive aspects of decision-making and how biases can impact the process, especially in the context of refactoring complex systems using DDD patterns and principles. Understanding these cognitive processes will help you make more informed and rational decisions during your refactoring journey.

Understanding System 1 and System 2

Daniel Kahneman, a renowned psychologist and Nobel laureate, introduced the concept of two systems of thinking in his book *Thinking, Fast and Slow*. These systems are fundamental to understanding human decision-making processes and are called **System 1** and **System 2**.

System 1 is efficient for routine tasks and familiar situations but can be prone to biases and errors when dealing with complex or unfamiliar problems. System 2, on the other hand, is slower and more deliberate and allows us to make more rational and informed decisions, especially when dealing with unfamiliar or complex situations. Their key traits are as follows:

- **System 1 – fast and intuitive**: System 1 operates automatically and quickly, with little or no effort and no sense of voluntary control. It is our intuitive system, which we use for quick judgments and decisions. Examples of System 1 thinking include the following:

    - Recognizing a familiar face in a crowd
    - Answering simple arithmetic questions (e.g., 2 + 2 = 4)
    - Driving a car on an empty road

- **System 2 – slow and deliberate**: System 2 allocates attention to the effortful mental activities that demand it, including complex computations. It is our analytical system, which we use for critical thinking and complex problem-solving. Examples of System 2 thinking include the following:

    - Solving a complex mathematical problem
    - Making a strategic decision in a business context
    - Refactoring a complex software system

The importance of Systems 1 and 2 in refactoring

Refactoring, particularly in complex systems, requires a balance between intuitive and deliberate thinking. Here's how understanding and applying System 1 and System 2 can enhance your refactoring efforts.

To leverage both systems, you must understand when and how to use them during the refactoring process. Starting with System 1, an experienced developer can quickly recognize patterns, code smells, and where to start a refactoring process through past experiences. Also, for minor tasks, such as extracting small methods, System 1 can be effective. System 2 kicks in when you deal with large-scale refactoring, such as restructuring an entire module or re-architecting a system. Here, deliberate thinking is crucial. It also helps in creating a refactoring plan and identifying potential risks ahead. As a last important thing, System 2 can help mitigate biases that could emerge with System 1.

Common cognitive biases in refactoring

Refactoring is as much a mental process as a technical one, and our cognitive biases can significantly impact the outcomes. Recognizing these biases and taking steps to counteract them can help you avoid potential pitfalls. Let's look at the main ones and what you can consider doing to mitigate them.

Anchoring bias

Anchoring bias occurs when we rely too heavily on the first piece of information encountered (the "anchor") when making decisions. As stated, this might mean sticking to the first solution or design without considering other alternatives. You should encourage team discussions and explore multiple solutions before settling on a decision.

Here's how to counteract it:

- **Encourage exploration**: Actively brainstorm multiple solutions before committing to one. Use tools such as design spikes or proof-of-concept development to evaluate alternatives.
- **Adopt decision frameworks**: Use structured techniques such as decision matrices to evaluate options objectively.
- **Set a "cooling-off period"**: Give the team time to reflect on initial ideas before making a final decision.

Confirmation bias

Confirmation bias is the tendency to search for and remember information that confirms one's preconceptions. This can lead to ignoring critical feedback or alternative approaches during refactoring. To mitigate this bias, you can seek different opinions and rely on thorough code reviews to challenge your decisions.

Here's how to counteract it:

- **Foster a culture of challenge**: Encourage team members to play devil's advocate during discussions. Assign someone to question the prevailing assumptions in every meeting.
- **Emphasize diverse perspectives**: Actively involve people from different roles or with varying expertise to review designs and refactoring plans.
- **Automate feedback**: Use tools such as static code analyzers and automated tests to surface objective insights, reducing reliance on subjective interpretations.

Availability heuristic

The **availability heuristic** involves prioritizing events based on vividness or recency instead of their frequency, such as a plane crash versus a car crash. The latter is more frequent, but we tend to think of the former more often. This can result in overestimating the importance of recent events that are not the norm and potentially lead us to suboptimal refactoring decisions. We should force ourselves to base our decisions on objective data rather than recent experiences alone.

Here's how to counteract it:

- **Rely on historical data**: Analyze metrics such as defect rates, code churn, or feature usage to guide refactoring priorities
- **Maintain a refactoring log**: Document past refactoring efforts, lessons learned, and their outcomes to ground future decisions in accumulated knowledge
- **Encourage structured retrospectives**: Reflect regularly on past decisions to identify patterns that can inform better judgment

Practical example – refactoring a legacy system

Let's consider a practical example to illustrate the application of System 1 and System 2 thinking in refactoring a complex system. Imagine you are tasked with refactoring a monolithic application into a more modular and maintainable structure using DDD principles. This scenario provides an excellent opportunity to demonstrate how both types of thinking can be leveraged throughout the refactoring process.

Your approach would likely begin with an initial assessment, combining both System 1 and System 2 thinking. You'd use your intuitive System 1 to quickly identify obvious code smells and areas that need improvement. Simultaneously, you'd engage your analytical System 2 thinking to perform a detailed analysis of the system's architecture, dependencies, and business domains. This deeper, more deliberate analysis provides a comprehensive understanding of the system's complexity.

With a clear picture of the system, you move on to strategic planning, which primarily involves System 2 thinking. You develop a strategic plan for the refactoring process, carefully breaking down the monolith into bounded contexts. This step requires thoughtful consideration of the system's structure and business logic. As part of this planning, you identify key aggregate roots, entities, and value objects within each bounded context (we will do a recap on these terms in *Chapters 3* and *4*), laying the groundwork for a more modular and domain-aligned architecture.

The actual refactoring process is where both System 1 and System 2 thinking truly shine in tandem. You apply System 1 thinking for straightforward refactoring tasks within each bounded context. These might include simple code cleanup, renaming for clarity, or extracting obvious methods. For more complex tasks, you switch to System 2 thinking. This includes defining new interfaces, decoupling dependencies, and ensuring data consistency across the newly defined boundaries. The interplay between quick, intuitive decisions and deeper, more analytical thinking allows for efficient progress while maintaining the integrity of the refactoring effort.

Throughout the refactoring process, continuous review and adaptation are crucial. You regularly review the refactoring progress with your team, using System 1 thinking to identify quick wins and immediate improvements. At the same time, you employ System 2 thinking to address any emerging challenges or changes in requirements. This balanced approach ensures that you can make rapid progress while also adapting to the evolving needs of the project and catching any potential issues before they become significant problems.

By understanding the dual systems of thinking and recognizing common cognitive biases, you can improve your decision-making process during refactoring. Leveraging System 1 for routine tasks and System 2 for complex problem-solving allows for a balanced and effective approach. Always remain vigilant of biases, seek diverse perspectives, and apply deliberate thinking to tackle the complexity inherent in refactoring.

Summary

In this chapter, you discovered tools to help understand and pragmatically approach complexity. You gained a comprehensive understanding of handling modern systems' complexity by effectively separating and navigating the problem and solution spaces while mitigating biases in decision-making. You learned how to approach the complexity of modern systems, the importance of remaining in the problem space as long as possible, and how thinking about the solution changes from thinking about the problem. Additionally, you explored the differences between System 1 and System 2.

In the next chapter, we will delve into context mapping and strategic patterns. You will learn how to identify and map the various contexts within your domain, understand the relationships between them, and apply strategic patterns to manage these contexts effectively. This will enable you to align your system's design with its business goals, ensuring a more cohesive and adaptable architecture.

3

Strategic Patterns

As you learned in previous chapters, the biggest challenge at the start of any project—whether it's a greenfield project or a refactoring effort—is the language. By now, the importance of understanding the domain and defining a shared language to build knowledge should be evident. However, creating a ubiquitous language comes with hidden challenges, often stemming from human behavior.

Now that you know how to avoid these mistakes, you are ready to discover the patterns that domain-driven design gives us and learn how to use them during the refactoring of your system.

To do so, we'll cover the following main topics in this chapter:

- Defining terms clearly
- Dividing the domain
- Dealing with communication between bounded contexts

By the end of the chapter, you will know how to strategically divide a domain into subdomains, understand their roles in your domain, and determine the optimal communication patterns. This refactoring operation will result in a modular solution that is also scalable and maintainable.

Defining terms clearly will solve half of the problem

In his book, Evans makes clear the importance of using the ubiquitous language in conversation with domain experts, and with all team members. To ensure that the comprehension of the problem is clear and without ambiguity due to an incorrect translation from the domain language to the technical language, it is important that the language used in our code base is as close as possible to the domain model. That is because the product that we deploy in production uses the technical language, not the business language.

To achieve that, during the conversation between teammates, no one needs to translate terms from one language to another. Since the software does not cope with ambiguity, we should base the conversation on the domain model. We will explain the domain model concept better later in the *What is a bounded context?* section of this chapter.

Evans is uncompromising about this:

"By using the model-based language pervasively and not being satisfied until it flows, we approach a model that is complete and comprehensible, made up of simple elements that combine to express complex ideas...

"...Domain experts should object to terms or structures that are awkward or inadequate to convey domain understanding; developers should watch for ambiguity or inconsistency that will trip up design"

The ubiquitous language is not just a vocabulary; it is a rigorous language between all teammates who aim to remove all ambiguity and create a base to identify the boundaries around the business problem they have to solve.

During refactoring, it's important to understand the model underlying the software we are working on before starting to modify the code. Having a common model of the business that every teammate can understand is the key to obtaining a clear architecture for the solution. It helps us to clearly identify the boundaries around the business problem, and having a common language is the first step. Try to think about a customer model; it seems easy to create a model of our customer, just including all properties such as invoice data, personal data, delivery addresses, headquarters addresses, and so on. We would then have a complete model of our customer. Most of the software that you are working on probably has a model similar to this one, and this is the primary pain point when you have to modify the behavior of the program or implement a new feature.

If you have to implement a new feature, for example, in the logistics area of your application, you probably have to modify the customer model. So far, you have usually been forced to change the model even in the sales area and purchases area, at minimum. As you already know, changing code in many areas is one of the main fears for a developer since it's impossible to know what will happen in the system when you modify many components in your code base. By now, you should have started to understand the importance of having a model aligned with your business problem. A model that is too large forces you to change it every time you need to modify your code. A model that is too small is not enough to describe the problem itself. How can you design the right model? When you were younger, you probably played the telephone game. It was hilarious to discover that the sentence at the end of the line was totally different from the one at the beginning of it. At each step, when a child whispered the sentence to the ear of the next one in the line, the sentence invariably changed, leading to hilarious results.

Figure 3.1 shows the telephone game pattern in a real business situation. A domain expert explains their problem to an analyst, who explains the same (are you sure?) problem to an architect, and so on until it reaches the development team. They create a solution that will be deployed. Can you see the problem? Any person involved in this pattern has their own interpretation of the problem, which is different from that of the previous person in the line.

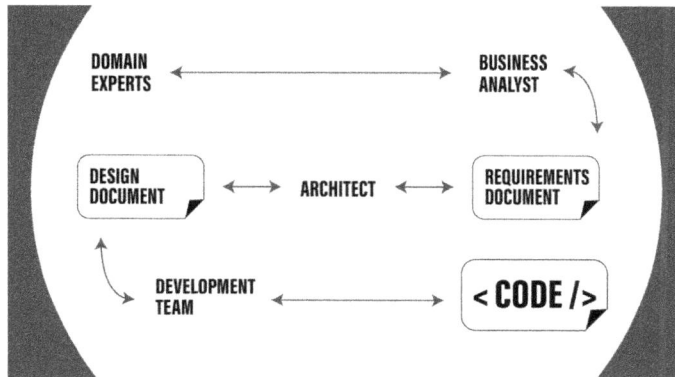

Figure 3.1 – The telephone game in a business situation

While the outcome is hilarious while playing the game, it is not so funny in the business world. Each time businesspeople try to explain a problem to technical people, they use their own language. To businesspeople, their own language is unambiguous. Since they know the problem, and they talk about it every day with colleagues or customers, they assume that the same mutual understanding exists with others.

This led to the creation of a solid language to communicate needs and solutions between the two groups. The technical people also have their own language, which is totally different from the one of the business. So, when these people have to create a model to solve the business problem described by the businesspeople, they have to translate a language into another one. Every time you translate something, you could lose important information or, worse, you might need to use your own words to describe what you understood.

This process is repeated at every step, from the customer to the analyst to the developer. Remember what we said about complexity, bias, and so on in the previous chapter?

How can you avoid this mistake? The first and simplest solution could be to remove the line between business experts and developers and get these people to communicate directly. Unfortunately, they use different languages, and this type of communication is impossible.

Figure 3.2 explains this solution. Domain experts and the development team talk among themselves directly, without any mediator. In this case, the problem isn't the loss of information, but the language. Each of them uses a different language and cannot understand what the other says.

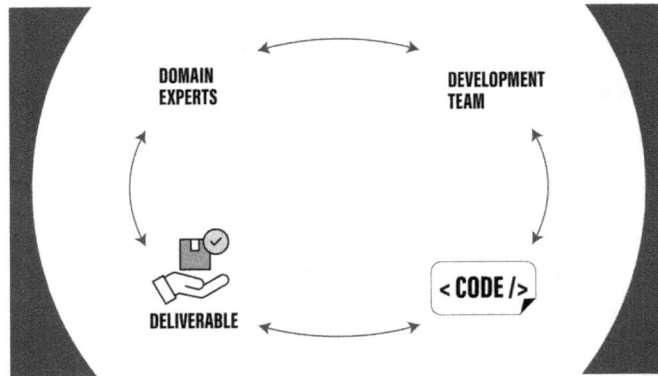

Figure 3.2 – Letting business- and technical people talk directly

Hopefully, you are now seeing the importance of a ubiquitous language within the team. It guarantees the absence of ambiguity inside the communication, and it is the first step to building a domain model that is really helpful for everyone.

Finally, you can see the solution to the problem in *Figure 3.3*. Using a ubiquitous language, each member of the team understands the other, and together they can build a domain model that's helpful for everyone.

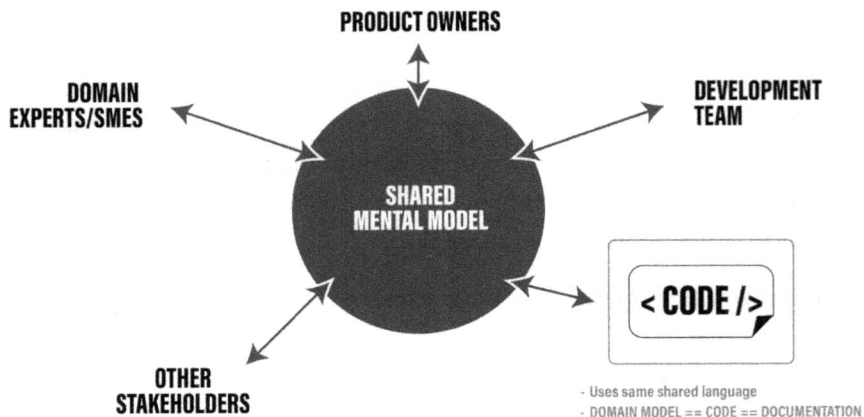

Figure 3.3 – Common domain model

Having a model aligned with the business simplifies the refactor because now you and your business experts can understand each other without the need for translations or interpreters, and every new request that arrives will be perfectly aligned with your model. In addition, if the new request involves changing the model, you can rest easy knowing that changing the model will not affect the other functionalities of the system.

However, why do you need to create many models, and not just one, for your whole business? If the goal is creating software that can evolve, you need to create many small models, each of which is isolated from the other one. This is what bounded contexts are responsible for.

What is a bounded context?

A bounded context is a fundamental pattern of domain-driven design. It is the focus of strategic patterns and a central concept when you deal with large models because it allows you to split a big problem into smaller problems or a large model into smaller models.

Having small models helps us solve business problems and maintain our code in the future. To identify the boundaries around this fine-grained model, you have to use the ubiquitous language discovered previously to identify the pivotal events that move the discussion around the business problem from one context to another.

In our journey to discover the patterns inside domain-driven design and its implementation, we will use an ERP to manage a brewery. In this example, as you will see, we will start with an Event-Storming workshop. You will meet the **domain event**, a pattern that we will discuss in *Chapter 4, Tactical Patterns*, of this book. For the moment, you need to know that there are special events, the pivotal events, that help us to identify these boundaries because they have some specific properties.

One of these events is SalesOrderCreated. It is an event that changes the flow of the process. For instance, after a sales order is created, you have to verify the plafond availability of your customer, the beer availability in the warehouse, and the shipping conditions in the logistic area. The rules of the game have changed! After this event, you probably need new policies to handle all those cases. These policies could be in a different model that could also be in different bounded contexts.

You have to keep in mind that the core of domain-driven design is about designing software based on a model, one that all the teammates can understand. When this model will not map the business flow anymore due to the increased complexity and the components involved in it, you are definitely moving outside of the model boundary. When you deal with the refactoring of an old project, it is important to identify these boundaries, because the first thing you have to do after discovering them is to remove the coupling between objects that belong to different bounded contexts. Removing these coupling enables you to modify part of the system without the fear of breaking others, and that is a fundamental step!

Another element that you can use to draw boundaries between contexts is human behaviors. Back to the example of the sales order created, the behavior of the people involved in the payment system will be different from the people involved in the logistics department because they will have different tasks to perform. You have to capture these differences and use them to identify the boundaries of your contexts.

Once you have split the whole domain into many different bounded contexts, you need to find how these contexts communicate with one another. Like in the real world, each part of the system contributes to the final success, and the only way to achieve this is *collaboration*.

Dividing the domain into meaningful boundaries

The most obvious advantage of having a ubiquitous language is the ability to easily identify the boundaries around a business problem and split the domain into many subdomains. A business domain is the main area of activity of a company. In the example we will use in this book, the business domain is *brewery management*. The service that our hypothetical company provides is the production and selling of the best beer in the world! Easy.

It is important to understand that the business domain is not a software application. The software provides the solution you create to help your customer manage their business. A business domain is generally big and complex. So, as you have already discovered, having just one model to describe the whole business is impossible, and it is probably the situation that you will find yourself in when approaching refactoring. You can see the problem of having a "one-size-fits-all" model. It is a constraint for every new request and creates a fear of changing anything in your code due to the strong coupling between the components of your legacy application.

As in the real world, a company achieves its business domain goals by splitting the business itself into multiple areas. Domain-driven design does the same by splitting the domain into multiple subdomains. A subdomain is a small part of the whole domain and focuses on a particular aspect of the business. It is an important strategic pattern within domain-driven design. Therefore, a single subdomain is not enough to guarantee the success of a company. It is a cog in a more complex system: the domain.

In a complex system, each gear is assembled so that the whole system can fulfill its task; not every gear is important in the same way. In the context of a wheel, if you break a spoke, you can continue pedaling and finish your ride. However, if you puncture the tire, you must stop your ride, repair the tire, and then finish your ride. Both the tire and spoke are part of the wheel, but the tire is more important than the spoke. Likewise, if the goal of your company is to produce the best beer, having a good warehouse system will be important to stock the beers before selling them, but less important than having a perfect production department. None of these departments on their own will make your brewery profitable; all of these, and probably others, are necessary to achieve the goal, but it is imperative to identify the responsibilities of each one.

To identify the boundaries around these subdomains, you have to use the ubiquitous language discovered in the exploration phase with the domain experts and stakeholders. Any inconsistency in the ubiquitous language is a warning that something should be investigated more. That is because we could be talking about the same things but with different names, or we could be looking at a totally different thing that might belong to a different bounded context. You need to learn how to force your business experts to stay inside the problem space because you know how important this is. You need to identify whether you are talking about the customer for a sale order, or the customer for a delivery. You are certainly talking about a customer in either case, but in two different ways. That means having two different models, and, in this case, two different subdomains. You already know that a subdomain is a smaller area of knowledge or activity within a larger domain. Now you have also discovered that, as in the case of a cog or wheel, some subdomains are more important than others and there are different types of them. Splitting the whole domain into many subdomains means that you can create a smaller model and talk with specific domain experts to go deeply into the modeling. During the first part of the refactor, distilling a domain is extremely important to start with a good strategic design. The refactoring process is intended to improve the design, structure, and implementation of the software, as well as its *non-functional* attributes, without changing the functionalities.

Your goal is to reduce accidental complexity and improve code readability without side effects. Remember that you cannot transform a *big ball of mud* into a microservices solution in one step. Always keep *Gall's law* in mind:

"A complex system that works is invariably found to have evolved from a simple system that worked. The inverse proposition also appears to be true: a complex system designed from scratch never works and cannot be made to work. You have to start over, beginning with a working simple system."

Generally, refactoring involves implementing a set of standardized small-scale modifications where each change is a minor adjustment to the source code of a computer program. These adjustments typically maintain the software's existing functionality or, at the very least, do not alter its adherence to functional specifications. The author of *Refactoring To Patterns*, *Joshua Kerievsky*, wrote the following:

"By continuously improving the design of code, we make it easier and easier to work with. This is in sharp contrast to what typically happens: little refactoring and a great deal of attention paid to expediently add new features. If you get into the hygienic habit of refactoring continuously, you'll find that it is easier to extend and maintain code."

Splitting the whole domain into many subdomains is the first step of this process and is called **context mapping**.

It's important to clarify that dividing a domain into multiple subdomains doesn't necessarily require creating multiple autonomous services. The implementation could take the form of a modular monolith or a microservices-based solution. What truly matters is ensuring that a bounded context remains self-contained and does not span across multiple services or modules.

Context mapping

Context mapping is a technique used to visualize and understand the relationships and interactions between bounded contexts within a system. It involves creating a map that highlights how contexts relate to each other, identifies integration points, and exposes potential issues. This map becomes a critical tool in managing the complexity of large systems.

Drawing this map is not an easy task, however, and you should follow a series of steps to execute in a loop until you and your team reach a consensus on the outcome.

As a first step, identify the bounded contexts within your system. Each context should have a clear boundary and a specific domain model. Once you have your boundaries, you can move on to the next step, which could seem daunting at first. It involves defining how these contexts interact with each other. Are they dependent on each other? Do they share data or services?

Once you overcome this task with a reasonable, understandable web of connections, you should try to highlight the points where contexts integrate or need to communicate.

Lastly, you should be able to draw a visual representation of the contexts and their relationships. At the end of this chapter, you will end up with a complete diagram that illustrates the flow of information and its dependencies, as shown in *Figure 3.12*. However, before going straight to it, let's break it up into smaller steps so as to fully understand context mapping.

Firstly, *Figure 3.4* shows how we could draw the context map of our ERP using the bounded contexts of customer, sales, warehouse, and shipping.

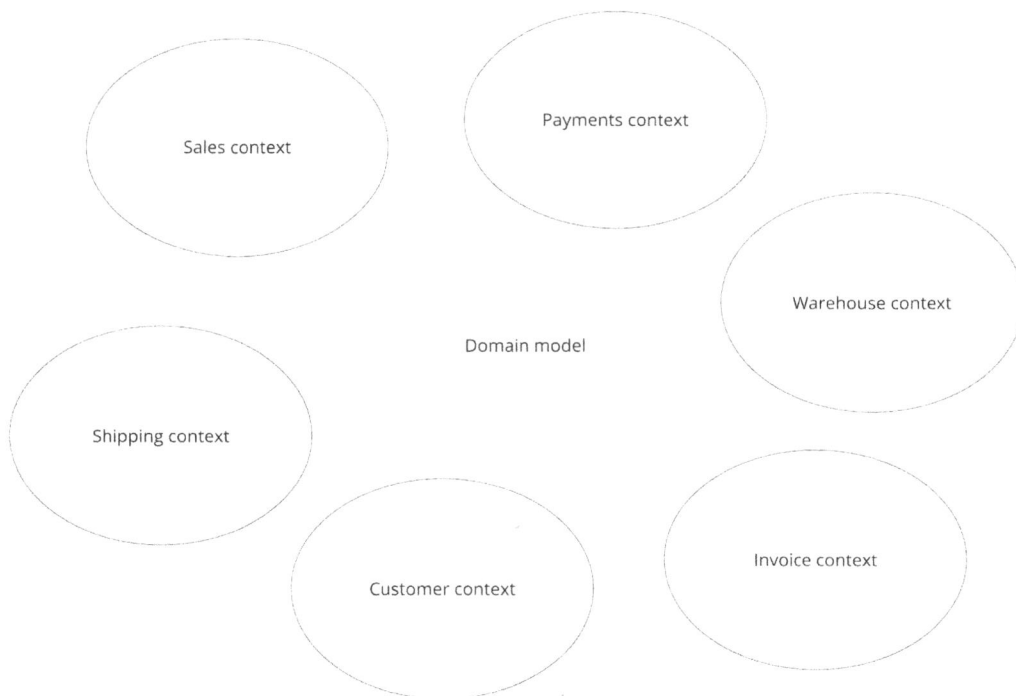

Figure 3.4 – A portion of our brewery's context map

Types of subdomains

In our list of tasks to achieve a good mapping, the first step is to define specific domain models. However, what does that mean?

It means that every bounded context fills a specific role in your architecture, and you have to determine the importance of each one. This involves identifying which bounded contexts represent your core business logic, which ones support that core, and which ones are more generic in nature. By doing this, you can prioritize your efforts and resources effectively.

To achieve this, you need to analyze each bounded context and categorize it into one of the various subdomain types. This categorization helps you understand the strategic significance of each part of your system. Subdomains represent specific areas within a domain. They correspond to individual bounded contexts with their own set of rules and logic.

In context mapping, there are several types of subdomains you can choose from based on their role in your system. These are as follows:

- Core subdomain
- Supporting subdomain
- Generic subdomain

By identifying which type each of your bounded contexts falls into, you can make informed decisions about how to approach their development, integration, and maintenance. For instance, you would likely invest more resources and innovation into your core domain, while perhaps looking for off-the-shelf solutions for generic domains.

This process of identification and categorization is crucial as it forms the foundation of your context map, guiding your overall architectural strategy and helping to align your technical efforts with your business priorities. Also, it deeply impacts how you structure your teams and the members within each one. For example, the team working on the core domain will probably be composed of the more experienced developers at first and maybe, at a later point, you will move some of them to other teams to share knowledge.

Now that you understand context maps, let us see what exactly they are and what purposes they serve.

Core subdomain

The core subdomain is the heart of your business. It is where your company's unique value proposition lies and where you have a competitive advantage. This is the most critical and complex part of your system, requiring the most attention and resources. For our ERP, the sales system is the core domain, as it is central to the business' operations and success.

Supporting subdomain

Supporting subdomains, while important, are not the primary focus of the business. They complement and enable the core subdomain but don't provide the main competitive advantage. These subdomains are necessary for the business to function smoothly but aren't where the company differentiates itself. In our ERP example, a customer service module would be a supporting subdomain – it's crucial for customer satisfaction but not the main business driver.

Generic subdomain

Generic subdomains are common across many businesses and aren't specific to your particular enterprise. These are often areas where reinventing the wheel isn't necessary, and you can leverage existing solutions or outsource them. The invoice system is a good example of a generic subdomain – it is essential for monitoring revenue, but it's not where a brewery would focus its innovative efforts.

Figure 3.5 shows a context map with the definition of every subdomain.

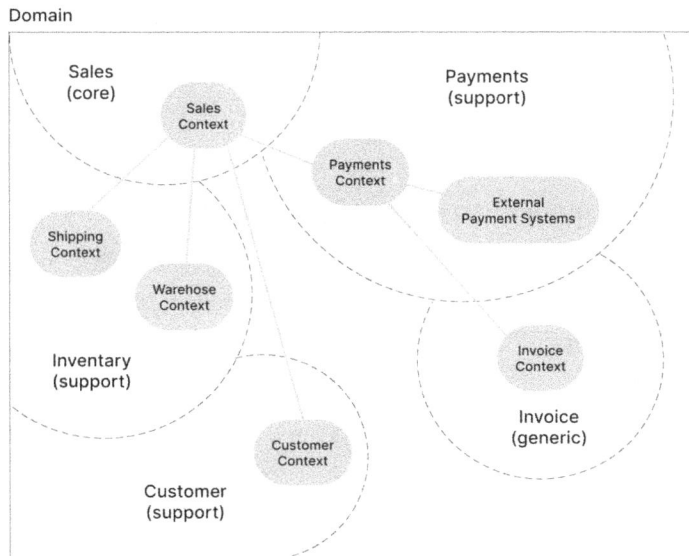

Figure 3.5 – Types of subdomains

Understanding these different types of domains is crucial for effective context mapping and overall system design. It helps in prioritizing development efforts, allocating resources efficiently, and making strategic decisions about system integration and evolution. By recognizing which parts of your system fall into which subdomain categories, you can focus your innovative efforts where they matter most while finding efficient solutions for less critical areas.

Subdomains change over time

What we designed in this chapter is the first context map based on the knowledge acquired during the conversations with the brewery's business experts. It tries to satisfy the business' actual needs. Over time, the knowledge of the domain will improve, and the business flows will change with or without requests from the business experts. So, our bounded contexts or their importance in the domain could change accordingly. Last but not least, if you worked with your teams' rotations, every member should be capable of taking on almost any subdomains.

Dealing with communication between bounded contexts

Now that you have a solid understanding of the importance of well-defined boundaries, we can move on to the last aspect of bounded contexts: communication. To build a cohesive system, these bounded contexts must interact effectively. That is why proper communication between bounded contexts is crucial. Strategic design offers some patterns to help you identify the best solutions based on our context of operation. Your goal here is to have a clear picture of how different parts of the system interact and relate with each other.

Importance of correct communication

Effective communication between bounded contexts ensures that the system functions as a unified whole. When bounded contexts fail to communicate correctly, inconsistencies and integration issues arise, leading to a fragmented system. Proper communication mechanisms help in the following ways:

- **Maintaining consistency**: Ensuring that data and behavior are consistent across the system
- **Enhancing flexibility**: Allowing bounded contexts to evolve independently without breaking the system

- **Reducing coupling**: Minimizing dependencies between different parts of the system, making it easier to manage and refactor
- **Improving clarity**: Providing clear interaction patterns, helping in understanding and maintaining the system

Communication patterns

These strategic patterns are high-level design strategies used to address and manage the relationships between bounded contexts. They provide a blueprint for handling integration, collaboration, and governance across contexts. Some of the most relevant include the following:

- **Shared kernel**
- **Customer-supplier**
- **Conformist**
- **Anticorruption Layer (ACL)**
- **Open Host Service (OHS)**
- **Published language**
- **Separate ways**

Shared kernel

In the shared kernel pattern, two or more bounded contexts share a portion of the same domain model. This shared part is managed collaboratively by the teams responsible for each context. This pattern is useful when contexts have strong interdependency and require a common understanding of specific aspects of the model.

Using our ERP as an example, consider the warehouse and sales contexts that share common details about the beer and stock levels. This shared kernel ensures that both contexts have a consistent understanding of product data, reducing the risk of discrepancies. The warehouse context manages stock levels, beer details, and warehouse locations, while the sales context handles customer orders, order processing, and fulfillment.

The shared kernel in this scenario includes details about the beer such as SKU, description, and price, which are critical for both contexts to function correctly.

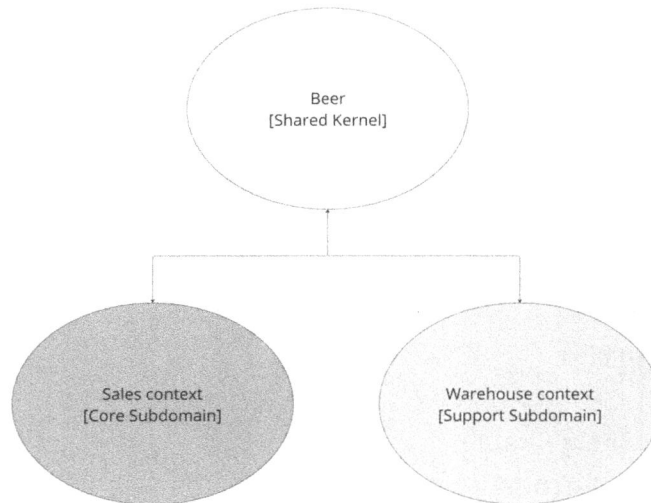

Figure 3.6 – Shared kernel example

Customer-supplier

The customer-supplier pattern establishes a clear upstream-downstream relationship between contexts. The upstream context provides services or data, while the downstream context depends on those services. The supplier (upstream) must ensure that the customer (downstream) can rely on its services, fostering a collaborative relationship.

For instance, the customer context (supplier) provides customer information to the sales context (customer). The sales context depends on accurate customer data to manage orders effectively. The sales context manages orders and payment processing, while the customer context handles plafonds and special categorization. The customer context must ensure that customer information is accurate and available in a timely manner for the sales context to function correctly.

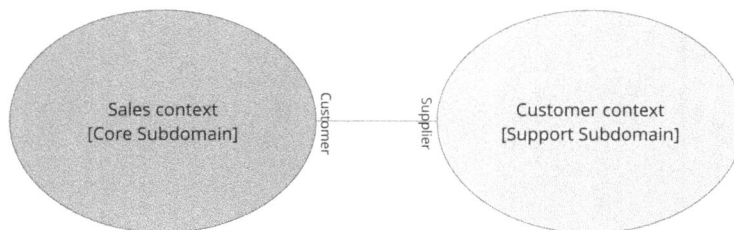

Figure 3.7 – Customer-supplier example

Conformist

In the conformist pattern, the downstream context (conformist) adopts the model and communication protocols of the upstream context without influencing it. This pattern is used when the downstream context has little control over the upstream context and must conform to its way of working.

For example, a third-party payment processing service dictates the data format and interaction protocols, and the internal payments context must conform to these requirements. The payment processing service (external) provides payment gateways, transaction processing, and fraud detection, while the internal payment context manages internal payment flows, user payment data, and transaction records. The internal payment context must adapt to the protocols and data formats specified by the external payment processing service to ensure seamless integration.

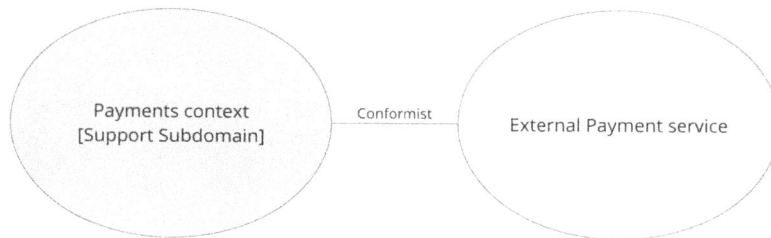

Figure 3.8 – Conformist example

ACL

The ACL pattern introduces a layer that translates and adapts between the models of two bounded contexts. This layer prevents the downstream context from being corrupted by the upstream context's model, allowing each context to maintain its integrity.

In our ERP platform, the sales context might use an ACL to translate data from the legacy CRM system into its own model. This ensures that the sales context is not polluted by the outdated CRM model. The legacy CRM system manages customer relationships, historical data, and sales interactions, while the sales context handles current sales processes, customer interactions, and order management. The ACL translates CRM data into the format and structure required by the sales context, ensuring data integrity and consistency.

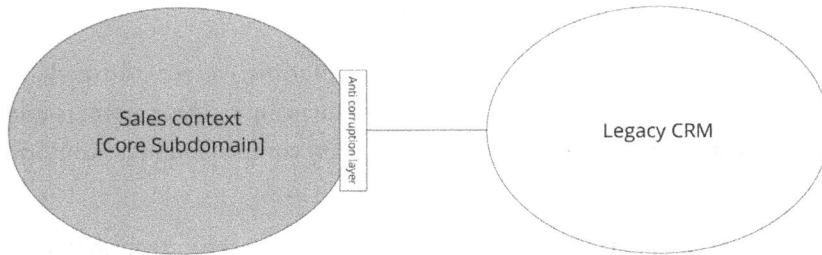

Figure 3.9 – ACL example

OHS

The OHS pattern involves exposing a bounded context's capabilities through a well-defined service interface, making it an open host for other contexts to interact with. This pattern promotes loose coupling and clear contracts between contexts.

For instance, the shipping context might provide an OHS that allows other contexts, such as sales and warehouse, to request shipping services through a standard API. The shipping context manages shipping rates, carriers, and tracking information. The sales context requests shipping services for order fulfillment, and the warehouse context requests shipping information for stock transfers and replenishments. The shipping context exposes its services via an API, enabling other contexts to interact with it without tight coupling.

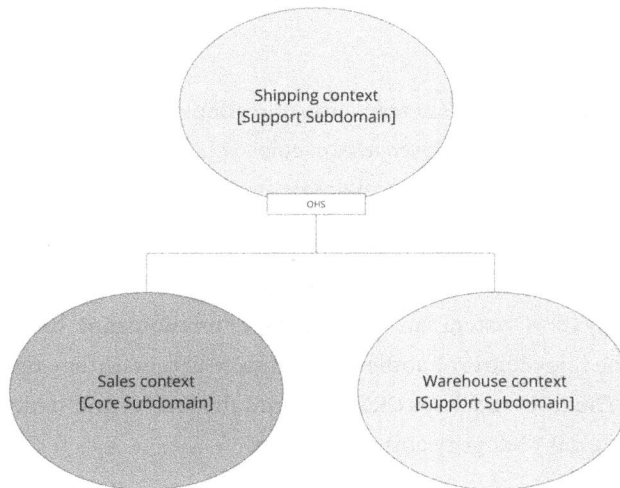

Figure 3.10 – OHS example

Published language

The published language pattern entails defining a shared language (a set of common terms and data structures) that multiple bounded contexts use for communication. This shared language reduces misunderstandings and integration complexity.

In a microservices architecture, a common event schema might be used for inter-service communication. This ensures that all services understand the event data consistently. For example, the sales context publishes order events when new orders are placed. The warehouse context consumes order events to update stock levels, and the invoice context consumes order events to generate invoices. The published language defines a common schema for order events, ensuring that all services can interpret the data correctly.

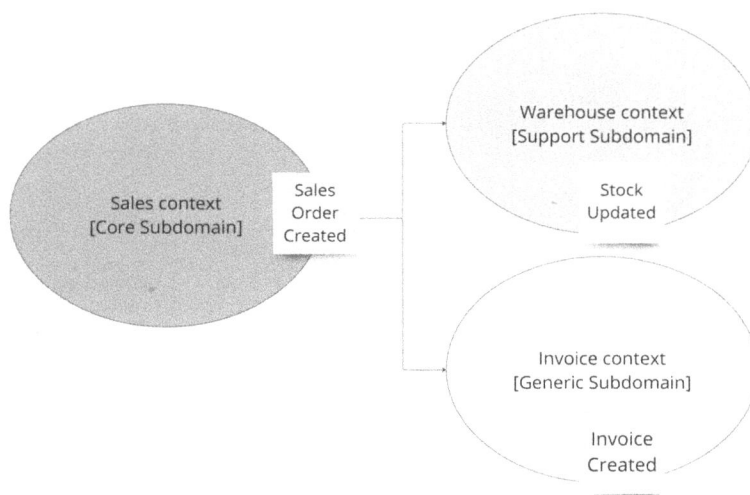

Figure 3.11 – Published language example

Separate ways

The separate ways pattern addresses the complexity that arises when two distinct parts of a system need to evolve independently. This pattern involves identifying bounded contexts within the domain that have minimal interaction and can be developed and maintained separately. By explicitly separating these contexts, teams can focus on the specific needs and rules of each domain area without being hindered by the intricacies of the others. This separation reduces coupling and allows for more agile and responsive development cycles, enabling each context to evolve at its own pace and in its own direction.

Final context map

In *Figure 3.12*, you can see the complete context map of our ERP, describing the communication patterns between each bounded context. You can start with a pattern, such as *conformist*, and then change to *OHS* because you need to maintain a high level of separation between bounded contexts. When you need to communicate with external systems, you can choose to be *conformist* with them or to use an *ACL* to maintain your language inside your domain model. You are not forced to use just one of them; you have to use the right tool in the right place.

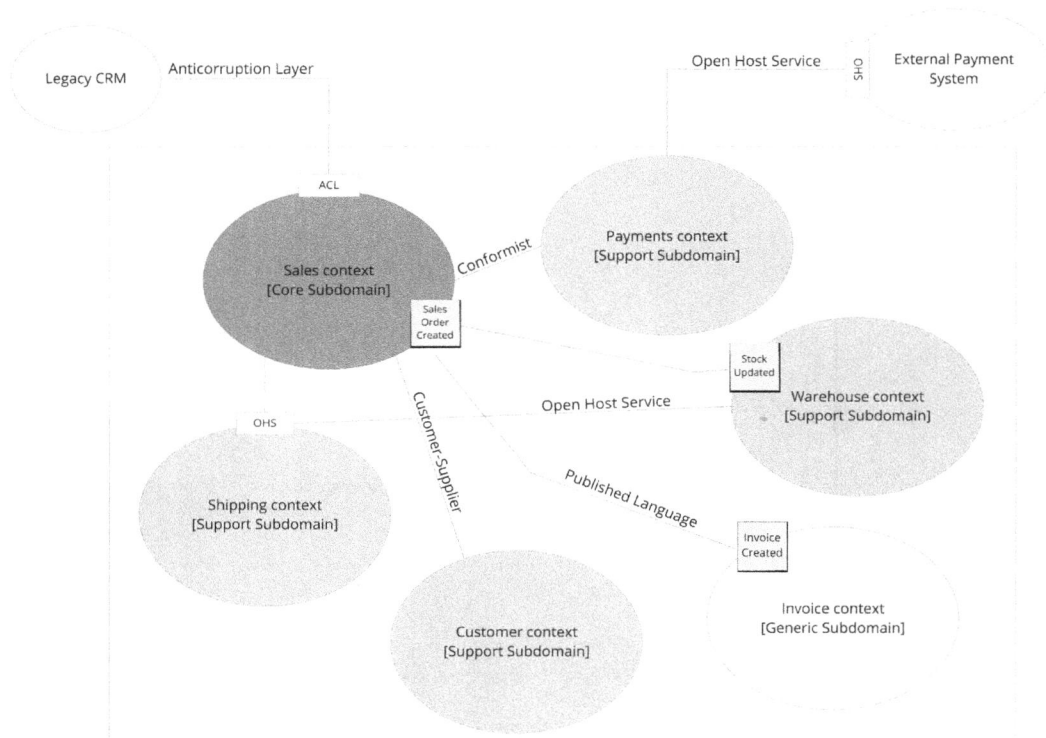

Figure 3.12 – Complete context map

Refactoring complex systems with domain-driven design principles requires careful consideration of how bounded contexts communicate. Proper communication ensures consistency, flexibility, and clarity, enabling the system to function cohesively. By leveraging strategic patterns such as shared kernel, customer-supplier, conformist, ACL, OHS, and published language, teams can manage the relationships and interactions between bounded contexts effectively.

Summary

In this chapter, you delved deep into the strategic patterns of domain-driven design, discovering how vital it is to establish a ubiquitous language to eliminate ambiguity and ensure clear communication among all team members.

You learned that aligning the language used in your code with the domain models helps create a clear and comprehensible architecture, simplifying modifications and reducing errors. You learned how splitting large models into smaller, manageable bounded contexts is crucial for maintaining a system that can evolve without fear of unintended consequences. This approach allows you to isolate different business areas, making it easier to modify parts of your system without disrupting others. Finally, you were also introduced to several strategic patterns that help manage the relationships and interactions between these contexts. These include the shared kernel, customer-supplier, conformist, ACL, PHS, and published language patterns.

Each of these patterns offers a blueprint for maintaining consistency, flexibility, and clarity across the system, ensuring it functions as a cohesive whole. Understanding these patterns equips you to identify the boundaries within your domain and effectively manage the complexity of large systems.

In the next chapter, you will delve into tactical patterns, which will provide you with practical tools and techniques to implement the concepts you've learned so far.

Get this book's PDF version and more

Scan the QR code (or go to `packtpub.com/unlock`). Search for this book by name, confirm the edition, and then follow the steps on the page.

UNLOCK NOW

Note: Keep your invoice handy. Purchases made directly from Packt don't require an invoice.

4

Tactical Patterns

Having explored the key strategic patterns in the previous chapter, we now shift our focus to the tactical patterns of DDD. The patterns we will cover include entities, value objects, aggregates, repositories, services, and modules.

We will conclude the chapter with an in-depth analysis of events, in which we will discuss their significance. We will clarify the distinctions between domain events and integration events, ensuring you grasp their importance and correct application in DDD.

By the end of this chapter, you will have a comprehensive understanding of these tactical patterns and their critical role in effective DDD.

In this chapter, we will cover the following topics:

- Understanding tactical patterns in DDD
- Services and modules
- Domain and integration events

Technical requirements

Starting in this chapter, we will begin incorporating code examples to illustrate the tactical patterns of DDD in a practical context. The code will be written in C#, and while an in-depth knowledge of the language is not mandatory, having a basic understanding will greatly enhance your ability to follow along and comprehend the examples more swiftly.

For those unfamiliar with C#, even a basic grasp of its syntax and core concepts will be beneficial. However, if you are proficient in other programming languages, you should still be able to follow along and understand the examples with ease.

Throughout the book, we will refer to an example application to demonstrate the practical implementation of the concepts discussed. You can access the complete code for this example application on GitHub at the following URL: `https://github.com/PacktPublishing/Domain-driven-Refactoring/branches`. This repository will serve as a valuable resource throughout the rest of the book, allowing you to explore the code in detail and experiment with the patterns we cover.

By the end of this chapter, and as you progress through the book, you will not only gain theoretical knowledge but also practical skills in applying DDD principles using C#. This hands-on approach will solidify your understanding and prepare you to tackle real-world challenges in your software development refactoring.

Understanding tactical patterns in DDD

If the purpose of the strategic pattern is to identify the boundaries to split our domain into many subdomains, the purpose of the tactical pattern is to identify the components inside each bounded context.

In this section, we will cover the tactical aspects of DDD, where different patterns play distinct roles depending on the complexity and strategic importance of the subdomain. We must remember that not all subdomains are created in the same way. Different subdomains have different levels of complexity and different strategic importance. If you are writing code for a generic subdomain, you most likely do not need any special patterns. Sometimes, **create, read, update, and delete (CRUD)** is more than enough! A model that represents the table in your database is enough, and the use of an **object-relational mapper (ORM)** is sometimes helpful.

But what happens if you have to write code for your core subdomain? In this case, you need to have a model that represents your business problem—not just a collection of properties. A model composed of only properties is called an **anemic domain**, and this should not be your goal. A **domain model** has to be a full business model, with properties and behaviors. It has to be consistent from the moment it is instantiated and has to remain consistent in all its states. This consistency is upheld by enforcing business rules, invariants, and transactions, all of which must be guaranteed and protected for the entire lifespan of your domain model.

Take, as an example, our ERP for managing a brewery, and particularly our core subdomain, `Sales`. The flow to create a new sales order has to satisfy the following constraints, and many others:

- The customer should be able to create a new order. They should have enough credit to do that.

- The beers must be available in our warehouse or, at least, we should be able to restock them reasonably quickly.
- The delivery address should be valid and within the delivery area.

The domain model we create must implement behaviors to verify each of the preceding conditions. As you can see, a sales order has many objects and is a useful way to introduce some tactical patterns, which we are going to cover in the following sections.

Entities

An **entity** is an object that is primarily defined by a unique identifier, often referred to as its *identity*. This identity distinguishes one entity from another, even if their other attributes are identical. For example, in a business domain, a customer might be uniquely identified by a customer ID or a government-issued identifier such as a social security number.

What makes entities special is their life cycle: they are created, modified, and eventually deleted, but their identity remains constant throughout. Even if their details (such as a customer's address or phone number) change, the entity itself remains the same as long as its identity is preserved.

Unlike a value object, which we will analyze shortly, the attributes of an entity can change over time. For example, a customer's address or contact information may change but the customer remains the same entity.

Entities are persisted in storage systems such as databases. This persistence ensures that the state of the entity can be retrieved and maintained across the different sessions or uses of the application.

In our sales order, the object that contains the data of the order, such as customer data, order and delivery date, and the payment attribute, represents an entity. We will see that the sales order entity also contains the methods to implement the behavior of our business because we shouldn't create an anemic domain.

The following code shows an example of an entity in our ERP. We use the library named Muflone (https://github.com/CQRS-Muflone/Muflone), which we wrote to support us, and we will get into it in the following chapters. For the moment, assume that Entity is just a base class with basic properties, such as Id:

```
public class SalesOrderRow : Entity
{
    internal BeerId _beerId;
    internal BeerName _beerName;
```

```
    internal Quantity _quantity;
    internal Price _beerPrice;

    protected SalesOrderRow()
    {
    }
}
```

The first thing you will notice is that the SalesOrderRow class implements the base class, Entity.

Secondly, you can see that the property types are not primitive types (e.g., int or decimal) but custom types that come from the ubiquitous language. We cannot stress enough that it is very important to share decisions about the behavior of this object with everyone who is working on it.

Finally, all the properties are declared internal because only the methods inside this namespace are allowed to change their values.

This encapsulation enforces a clear separation between the internal state of the entity and external access. An entity is defined not just by its properties but, more importantly, by the behaviors that operate on those properties.

If you're wondering how application services can access these properties, the answer is: they can't. Instead, a component within the domain (such as a mapper) is responsible for transforming entities into **data transfer objects (DTOs)**. These DTOs are then used by the external layers of the application, preserving the integrity of the domain. Direct exposure of domain objects to external layers would break the principle of encapsulation and could lead to unwanted dependencies.

An entity in DDD is a core concept that emphasizes the importance of a unique identity. This identity remains constant even as the entity's attributes change, making entities suitable for representing objects that need to be tracked individually throughout their life cycle. Understanding entities helps with designing systems that accurately reflect the uniqueness and persistence of real-world objects, ensuring that the business logic can manage these objects' states and identities consistently.

Value objects

A **value object** is defined by its attributes rather than a unique identity. Two value objects are considered equal if all their attributes match, regardless of their location or instance within the system. This lack of identity makes them ideal for representing descriptive concepts in the domain, such as an address or a monetary amount.

A key characteristic of value objects is immutability: once they have been created, their state cannot be changed. If you need to modify a value object, you create a new instance with the updated attributes. This immutability ensures consistency and thread safety, as the state of a value object cannot be altered unexpectedly.

Value objects are typically short-lived and easily replaceable as they describe properties rather than tracking specific instances. For example, an address in a sales order is a value object because the system doesn't need to uniquely identify that address; it only cares about its descriptive attributes.

In DDD, distinguishing between a value object and an entity depends on context. Use a value object when the identity is irrelevant and the focus is on attributes:

- An **address** in an order is a value object because its attributes (e.g., street and city) define its value and it doesn't need a unique identity
- A **customer**, on the other hand, is an entity because it has a unique identifier (e.g., customer ID) that persists over time, even if its properties, such as the address, change

This distinction has practical implications. If a customer's address changes, the old value object can be discarded and a new one created. Since value objects lack unique identities, there's no need to maintain or track the old instance.

When designing a system, it is crucial to decide whether a concept should be modeled as a value object or an entity. This decision affects how you manage persistence, how you handle equality checks, and how you design the overall data model.

The following code is an example of a value object. Just as entities inherit from a common `Entity` base class, value objects inherit from a `ValueObject` base class. This allows you to avoid rewriting shared logic for each value object in your code base:

```
public class Price(decimal value, string currency) : ValueObject
{
    public readonly decimal Value = value;
    public readonly string Currency = currency ?? throw new
NotImplementedException(nameof(currency));

    protected override IEnumerable<object> GetEqualityComponents()
    {
        yield return Value;
        yield return Currency;
    }
}
```

We want to reiterate that the big difference between an entity and a value object is that the former needs to have an ID, while the latter has no ID because it is defined by its attributes.

Notice also that each attribute is readonly. That is because a value object is an immutable object, which means if you need to modify it, you have to replace it with a new one.

Value objects are crucial in DDD for representing concepts that can be defined entirely by their attributes, without needing a unique identity. They are immutable, defined only by their attributes, and are often used to describe aspects or characteristics of entities. Understanding the difference between value objects and entities aids in building a clear and consistent domain model, ensuring that the system accurately represents the real-world processes it supports.

Aggregates

An **aggregate** is a group or cluster of domain objects, which can include entities and value objects. These domain objects are logically related and are treated as a single unit for the purpose of data changes. This means that changes to the state of any part of the aggregate are considered changes to the whole aggregate.

The aggregate has a special entity known as the **aggregate root**. This aggregate root serves as the entry point for accepting and interacting with the objects within the aggregate. It controls all access to the internal objects, ensuring that the integrity and invariants of the aggregate are maintained. The aggregate root is the only object that can be directly referenced from outside the aggregate.

Enforcing that all interactions go through the aggregate root, which encapsulates the internal structure and logic of the aggregate, helps maintain consistency, as the aggregate root can enforce business rules and constraints.

Aggregates define a consistency boundary. Within this boundary, all changes are made together in a single transaction. This means that the aggregate as a whole is always in a consistent state, even if some parts of it change.

Defining appropriate aggregate boundaries is crucial in DDD. Aggregates should not be too large, which can lead to performance and complexity issues, nor too small, which can lead to consistency problems. The goal is to encapsulate related changes and maintain consistency within the aggregate.

Since all changes within an aggregate are made in a single transaction, it's important to design aggregates that can efficiently maintain this consistency without compromising performance. This often involves trade-offs between strong consistency and the scalability of the system.

Figure 4.1 shows the relationships between aggregates. You can see that the entities of an aggregate may only link to the aggregate root of other aggregates. Relationships between entities in different aggregates that are not defined as aggregate roots are not permitted!

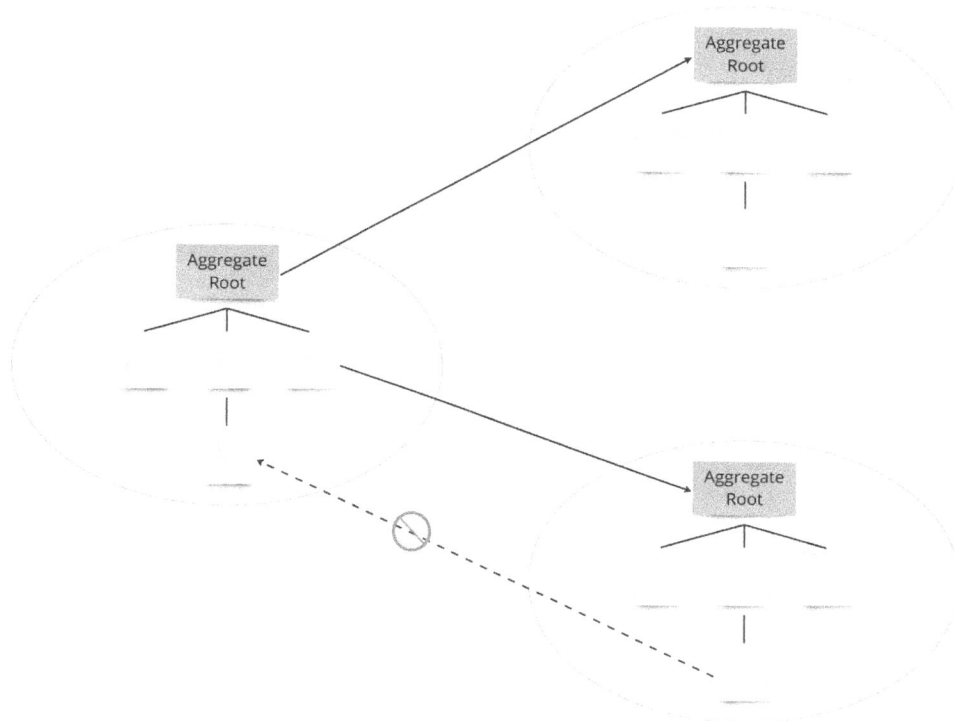

Figure 4.1 – Aggregates

Now, let's move our attention to the SalesOrder aggregate of our ERP by looking at the following piece of code:

```
public class SalesOrder : AggregateRoot
{
    internal SalesOrderNumber _salesOrderNumber;
    internal OrderDate _orderDate;

    internal CustomerId _customerId;
    internal CustomerName _customerName;

    internal IEnumerable<SalesOrderRow> _rows;
```

```
    protected SalesOrder()
    {
    }


    internal static SalesOrder CreateSalesOrder(SalesOrderId salesOrderId,
  Guid correlationId, SalesOrderNumber salesOrderNumber,
        OrderDate orderDate, CustomerId customerId, CustomerName
  customerName, IEnumerable<SalesOrderRowJson> rows)
    {
        return new SalesOrder(salesOrderId, correlationId,
  salesOrderNumber, orderDate, customerId, customerName,
            rows);
    }


    private SalesOrder(SalesOrderId salesOrderId, Guid correlationId,
  SalesOrderNumber salesOrderNumber, OrderDate orderDate,
        CustomerId customerId, CustomerName customerName,
  IEnumerable<SalesOrderRowJson> rows)
    {
        // Check SalesOrder invariants
    }
}
```

The SalesOrder class derives from the AggregateRoot base abstract class so that everyone knows this is the entry point for the SalesOrder aggregate. The goal of this object is to maintain the integrity of SalesOrder as a whole, starting from its creation.

Also, all subsequent changes of status are the responsibility of this object, which exposes the method to implement the business behaviors. These methods can be reached through domain services or command handlers, depending on the pattern you used to implement the aggregate, but you can see all these cases shortly in this chapter.

An aggregate in DDD is a key concept that organizes related domain objects into a cohesive unit. The aggregate root is the only part of the aggregate accessible from outside, ensuring encapsulation and consistency. Aggregates define transaction boundaries, which are crucial for maintaining the integrity of the system's state. By managing how domain objects are accessed and modified, aggregates help enforce business rules and invariants, providing a robust structure for complex business logic.

Repositories

The **repository pattern** acts as an intermediary between the domain model and the data mapping layers. It provides a way to manage access to the data source and ensures that the domain model remains independent of the underlying data access implementation.

It provides an abstraction layer over the data access mechanism and hides the details of data storage, retrieval, and mapping, thus allowing the domain model to focus solely on the business logic. This also decouples the domain layer from the data access, promoting a clean separation of concerns.

The purpose of the repository is to provide an interface for accessing aggregates from a data store. It handles CRUD operations and hides the implementation details of the data source.

In this pattern, a repository interface is defined that includes methods for retrieving and storing objects. For example, a repository interface for the SalesOrder aggregate might look like this:

```
public interface ISalesOrderRepository
{
    SalesOrder GetById(Guid id);
    IEnumerable<SalesOrder> GetAll();
    void Add(SalesOrder salesOrder);
    void Update(SalesOrder salesOrder);
    void Remove(SalesOrder salesOrder);
}
```

This interface provides a contract for data access operations without exposing details about the underlying implementation.

The implementation of the repository interface will vary depending on the data source.

There are many benefits of using the repository pattern, starting with decoupling. The repository pattern decouples the domain logic from data access, allowing the domain object to focus solely on business logic. Using repository interfaces makes it straightforward to replace the data access layer with a mock or stub, facilitating the writing of unit tests. Thinking of the main goal of our exploration (refactoring), the repository centralizes data access logic, making it easier to maintain and modify your code after introducing it. That is possible because the repository ensures consistent handling of data access operations across the application, promoting a single source of truth for data access.

To conclude, repositories are used to manage aggregates rather than individual entities, as aggregates represent the consistency within a domain model. The design of the repository and the domain model should reflect the domain's needs, not the underlying data storage mechanisms. Often, the unit of work pattern is used alongside repositories to manage transactions and ensure the atomicity of operations.

> **Unit of work**
>
> A **unit of work** manages a list of objects impacted by a business transaction and coordinates saving changes and resolving concurrency issues.

Factories

The **factory pattern** is a creational design pattern used in DDD to encapsulate the creation logic of aggregates. The primary purpose of the factory pattern is to provide a way to create objects without exposing the instantiation logic to the client and to ensure that the created objects are in a valid state. By centralizing creation logic in a factory, you maintain consistency, reduce duplication, and encapsulate the construction process.

Creating an aggregate involves complex validation or setting up a graph of objects. A factory can encapsulate this complexity and ensure that the created aggregates always satisfy the business rules and constraints defined in the domain model. By using a factory, you ensure that the objects are always created in a consistent and valid state, preventing inconsistencies that might arise from ad hoc object creation.

Why do you have to use this pattern? Because, like the repository pattern, the factory pattern has many benefits. First, the factory provides a single point to enforce business rules during the creation of objects, ensuring that all created objects are valid. When aggregate creation logic changes, it only needs to be updated in one place, the factory, rather than throughout the application. This is possible because aggregate construction processes, especially those involving the setup of dependencies or state, are abstracted away from the client. To conclude, the factory can be mocked or stubbed in unit tests, allowing more controlled and isolated testing scenarios.

Factories should only be responsible for creating aggregates, not for complex domain logic. They should not perform tasks beyond object creation, such as coordinating activities or managing transactions. The methods in a factory should use terms from the ubiquitous language, making it clear what the factory creates and what parameters are required.

The primary goal of a factory is to ensure that the created aggregates are always in a valid state, adhering to the business rules and constraints of the domain. A good practice is to keep the constructor of entities private or protected and use factory methods for object creation. This ensures that the factory controls the instantiation process, working directly with the aggregate root to maintain the integrity and invariants of the entire aggregate.

While factories ensure that aggregates are created in a consistent and valid state, they do not handle complex domain operations or cross-cutting concerns. This is where services come into play, providing a structured way to encapsulate domain logic that does not naturally belong to an entity or a value object.

Services and modules

In DDD, **services** and **modules** play a pivotal role in maintaining the clarity and separation of concerns within your application. Understanding the distinction between domain services and application services is crucial for architecting a robust and maintainable system.

Let's start with services and see what the two types of service are, the differences between them, and when to use them. As usual, this exploration will be illustrated by examples in the domain of our brewery ERP.

Domain services

Domain services are an integral part of the domain model, encapsulating business logic that doesn't naturally fit within an aggregate. They are used when a particular operation or process spans multiple entities or when the behavior does not belong to any specific entity. Domain services are pure, meaning they do not have side effects and typically do not rely on external systems such as databases or messaging systems.

Consider the brewery ERP system. Imagine you need to calculate the total price of a sales order, including various discounts and taxes. This calculation involves multiple entities and value objects, such as SalesOrder, Customer, Product, and Discount. Placing this logic inside any single entity would violate the **Single Responsibility Principle (SRP)** and make the entity unnecessarily complex. Instead, you would create a domain service, PricingService, to handle this calculation:

```
public class PricingService {
    private readonly TaxCalculator _taxCalculator;
    private readonly DiscountService _discountService;
```

```
    public PricingService(TaxCalculator taxCalculator, DiscountService
discountService) {
        _taxCalculator = taxCalculator;
        _discountService = discountService;
    }


    public decimal CalculateTotalPrice(SalesOrder order) {
        decimal totalPrice = 0;

        // Sum the price for each row in the order
        foreach (var row in order.Rows) {
            totalPrice += row.Quantity * row. Price;
        }

        // Apply discount if applicable
        totalPrice -= _discountService.CalculateDiscount(order);

        // Calculate and add tax
        totalPrice += _taxCalculator.CalculateTax(totalPrice);

        return totalPrice;
    }
}
```

In PricingService, the CalculateTotalPrice method handles the logic of summing the prices of all rows in the sales order, applying any discounts, and then calculating and adding the tax. The tax calculation is delegated to a separate TaxCalculator service, and the discount calculation is delegated to DiscountService, each encapsulating specific parts of the pricing logic.

The TaxCalculator service is responsible for tax calculations. By isolating tax logic in its own service, we adhere to the SRP and ensure that each service has a clear and focused purpose:

```
public class TaxCalculator {
    private readonly decimal _taxRate;

    public TaxCalculator(decimal taxRate) {
        _taxRate = taxRate;
```

```
    }

    public decimal CalculateTax(decimal amount) {
        return amount * _taxRate;
    }
}
```

TaxCalculator takes a tax rate as a dependency and uses it to calculate the tax on a given amount. This service can be easily modified or extended to accommodate different tax rates or complex tax rules without affecting PricingService.

DiscountService is responsible for applying discounts to the sales order. This service ensures that discount logic is encapsulated separately, making it easier to manage and modify. Here is the sample code for a simplified discount service:

```
public class DiscountService {
    public decimal CalculateDiscount(SalesOrder order) {
        if (order.Discount == null) {
            return 0;
        }
        var result = //... do some calculations...
        return result
    }
}
```

DiscountService applies the appropriate discount to the order if one is available. This separation of discount logic allows PricingService to remain focused on its core responsibility of calculating the total price.

Application services

Application services sit above the domain layer, orchestrating the domain objects to fulfill a particular use case. They act as a bridge between the presentation layer (such as a web API or the user interface) and the domain layer, handling tasks such as transaction management, authentication, and authorization. Unlike domain services, application services can have side effects and interact with external systems.

Returning to our brewery ERP, imagine the process of creating a new sales order. This involves several steps: validating the order details, checking product availability, calculating the total price, and finally, saving the order to the database. These steps encompass various domain operations orchestrated by an application service, as shown in the following code:

```
public class SalesOrderService {
    private readonly ISalesOrderRepository _salesOrderRepository;
    private readonly PricingService _pricingService;
    private readonly WarehouseService _warehouseService;

    public SalesOrderService(ISalesOrderRepository salesOrderRepository,
PricingService pricingService, WarehouseService warehouseService) {
        _salesOrderRepository = salesOrderRepository;
        _pricingService = pricingService;
        _warehouseService = warehouseService;
    }

    public SalesOrder CreateSalesOrder(SalesOrderDto orderDto) {
        // Validate order details
        SalesOrder order = new SalesOrder(orderDto);

        // Check product availability
        _warehouseService.CheckAvailability(order);

        // Calculate total price
        decimal totalPrice = _pricingService.CalculateTotalPrice(order);
        order.SetTotalPrice(totalPrice);

        // Save order to the database
        _salesOrderRepository.Save(order);

        return order;
    }
}
```

In the preceding example, SalesOrderService orchestrates the entire process of creating a sales order, utilizing domain services such as PricingService and WarehouseService, and managing persistence through SalesOrderRepository.

`SalesOrderService` starts by validating the order details and converting the DTO into a `SalesOrder` domain entity. It then checks the availability of the products in the order using `WarehouseService`. Next, it calculates the total price of the order, including discounts and taxes, by calling `PricingService`. Finally, it saves the completed order to the database using `SalesOrderRepository`.

Key differences between domain and application services

The primary difference between domain services and application services lies in their focus and scope. Domain services encapsulate domain-specific logic that spans multiple entities, while application services coordinate the use of domain objects to accomplish higher-level tasks.

When you need to encapsulate business logic that pertains to the domain but doesn't naturally belong to a single entity, you should use domain services. This is especially useful for complex business rules or processes that involve multiple entities. On the other hand, application services should be used to manage use cases and workflows that involve multiple domain operations. They handle coordination tasks, transaction management, and interactions with external systems.

To summarize, the proper use of domain and application services ensures a clean separation of concerns, making your code base more maintainable and scalable. In our brewery ERP system, domain services such as `PricingService`, `TaxCalculator`, and `DiscountService`, along with application services such as `SalesOrderService`, work together to handle the complexities of sales order processing, each fulfilling their specific roles within the architecture. By leveraging these concepts, you can build systems that are both robust and adaptable to changing business requirements.

Modules

A module is essentially a way to group related concepts and functionalities within a software system, encapsulating them to reduce interdependencies and promote a clear structure. By organizing code into well-defined modules, you can better maintain, understand, and evolve your application. A module plays a pivotal role in managing the complexity of large systems.

Modules serve as the building blocks for a robust and scalable system architecture in DDD. Their primary purpose is to help you manage the inherent complexity of a large application by dividing it into smaller, more manageable pieces. This modular approach allows each module to focus on a specific aspect of the domain, promoting a high degree of cohesion within the module while minimizing coupling between different modules.

A module encapsulates a cluster of related domain concepts, which might include entities, value objects, aggregates, and services. This encapsulation helps you maintain a clear separation of concerns. Each module handles a specific aspect of the domain, making it easier to understand and manage. Moreover, well-defined interfaces and boundaries between modules simplify the communication between different parts of the system, reducing the risk of unintended side effects and making it easier to understand how different parts of the system interact.

Implementing a modular approach in your projects can offer numerous benefits. Improved maintainability is a significant advantage. By breaking down the system into smaller, self-contained modules, you can make changes to one module without affecting the others. This reduces the risk of introducing bugs and makes it easier to test and maintain the code. Enhanced scalability is another benefit, as modules can be developed, deployed, and scaled independently, allowing you to address performance and scalability concerns more effectively. With clearly defined modules, different teams can work on separate parts of the system concurrently without stepping on each other's toes, facilitating collaboration. Furthermore, modules can be designed to mirror the structure of the business domain, ensuring that the software system evolves in tandem with the business requirements, which leads to better alignment with business goals.

Let's consider our brewery ERP system that handles sales orders to illustrate the concept of modules in DDD. In this system, you might have several modules, each focusing on a different aspect of the brewery's operations. For example, the `Sales` module is responsible for managing sales orders, customer interactions, and invoicing. It might include entities such as `Order`, `Customer`, and `Invoice`, along with services for processing orders and generating invoices. The `Warehouse` module manages the brewery's inventory, tracking the availability of ingredients, finished products, and supplies. This module includes entities such as `Ingredient`, `Product`, and `Stock`, as well as services for updating inventory levels and generating stock reports. The `Production` module oversees the brewing process, including scheduling production runs, monitoring fermentation, and ensuring quality control. It might involve entities such as `Batch`, `Recipe`, and `ProductionSchedule`, with services for managing production workflows and tracking batch quality.

By organizing the brewery ERP system into these modules, you can ensure that each aspect of the brewery's operations is handled independently, with clear boundaries between different areas of functionality.

Modules in refactoring complex systems

Modules are particularly useful during the refactoring process of a complex system. As systems grow and evolve, they often become tangled and difficult to manage. By refactoring the system into well-defined modules, you can achieve several key benefits. One such benefit is the isolation of changes. When you need to modify a specific part of the system, you can do so within the confines of a single module, reducing the risk of unintended side effects. This also improves understanding, as clear module boundaries make it easier to understand the system's structure and behavior, facilitating more effective debugging and problem-solving. Additionally, the modular design promotes incremental improvements. You can refactor and improve one module at a time, gradually enhancing the overall system without requiring a complete rewrite.

For instance, if the brewery ERP system needs to accommodate new sales channels, you can modify the `Sales` module without disrupting the `Inventory` or `Production` modules. This modular approach ensures that changes are contained and the overall system remains stable and maintainable.

While modules help structure and isolate different parts of a complex system, they often need to communicate with each other to reflect meaningful changes. This is where events come into play, enabling decoupled interactions between modules and ensuring that important state changes are properly propagated throughout the system.

Domain and integration events

In the context of software development, **events** are notifications that signify that something significant has occurred within the system. An event represents a change of state or the occurrence of a meaningful action. For instance, in our ERP application, events could include a sales order being placed, a payment being processed, or a beer order being shipped. Events are crucial in decoupling various parts of an application, enabling them to communicate and react to changes without being tightly coupled to one another.

They represent something that has happened in the domain that is of significance to the business. Events are used to communicate changes in the state of the domain. They are immutable facts that capture the state change and are often used to decouple different parts of the system, allowing them to react to changes independently. The fact that they represent something that has happened explains why they are written in past tense.

A practical example is the `SalesOrderCreated` event, which could look something like this:

```
public sealed class SalesOrderCreated(SalesOrderId aggregateId,
Guid commitId, SalesOrderNumber salesOrderNumber, OrderDate
orderDate, CustomerId customerId, CustomerName customerName,
IEnumerable<SalesOrderRow> rows) : DomainEvent(aggregateId, commitId)
{
    public readonly SalesOrderId SalesOrderId = aggregateId;
    public readonly SalesOrderNumber SalesOrderNumber = salesOrderNumber;
    public readonly OrderDate OrderDate = orderDate;

    public readonly CustomerId CustomerId = customerId;
    public readonly CustomerName CustomerName = customerName;

    public readonly IEnumerable<SalesOrderRow> Rows = rows;
}
```

The `SalesOrderCreated` event is a domain event that captures the creation of a sales order. It extends `DomainEvent` and contains essential information such as the order ID, customer details, order date, and the list of order items. By making this event immutable, we ensure that once it is published, its data remains unchanged, accurately representing a past occurrence in the business domain.

Later in this section, we will review the two kinds of events that exist in a DDD-oriented application:

- Domain events
- Integration events

But first, let's review why they are a key concept in a modern application.

Importance of events in modern applications

Modern applications are becoming increasingly complex, often involving multiple services and components that must work together seamlessly. Events provide a way to manage this complexity by promoting a reactive and decoupled architecture. They enable horizontal scaling by allowing different services to process events independently. This scalability is essential for handling large volumes of data and user interactions. Furthermore, events contribute to the resilience of systems, allowing them to continue functioning even if some components are temporarily unavailable. Events can be stored and processed later, ensuring that no data or critical operation is lost. Additionally, events offer flexibility by facilitating the integration of new features and services. New components can subscribe to existing events without necessitating changes to the existing system, promoting a more adaptable architecture. Ultimately, events enable decoupling by separating the sender and receiver, resulting in more maintainable and modular systems.

Domain events

Let's start with the first kind: **domain events**. These events, as you already know, are specific to the business domain and signify something that has happened within that domain. They are a critical concept in DDD, representing things that domain experts care about. For example, in our ERP application, events such as SalesOrderCreated, PaymentConfirmed, and BeerAvailabilityUpdated are domain events. These events reflect significant occurrences from a business perspective, capturing the essence of business operations and processes.

Domain events are characterized by their business relevance and . They represent occurrences that are significant from a business perspective and are of interest to domain experts. Domain events are immutable; once an event is created, it should not change. It captures a past occurrence and should remain a historical record. Additionally, domain events are self-descriptive. They should provide enough information for any interested party to understand what happened without requiring additional context or data.

An example is the BeerAvailabilityUpdated event, as shown in the following snippet:

```
public class BeerAvailabilityUpdated(BeerId aggregateId, Guid commitId,
BeerName beerName, Quantity quantity) : DomainEvent(aggregateId, commitId)
{
    public readonly BeerId BeerId = aggregateId;
    public readonly BeerName BeerName = beerName;
    public readonly Quantity Quantity = quantity;
}
```

The preceding code includes all the information on the availability of a specific beer as a reaction to the payment confirmation for a specific sale order.

Integration events

The second kind of event, and no less important, is **integration events**. They are used to communicate between different bounded contexts or external systems. While domain events are concerned with the business logic within a particular bounded context, integration events ensure that different parts of a distributed system stay in sync. They facilitate communication and coordination between different services or systems that need to work together to achieve a common goal.

Integration events are characterized by their role in cross-boundary communication. They are used to notify other systems or bounded contexts about changes, ensuring that the entire system remains consistent and up to date. Integration events help achieve loose coupling between services, making the system more modular and easier to maintain. This decoupling allows services to evolve independently without disrupting other parts of the system. Additionally, integration events often lead to eventual consistency, where different parts of the system eventually reach a consistent state after processing the events.

Soon enough, during your refactoring journey or development of a new feature, you will reach a point where a domain event in a certain bounded context appears to be identical to the integration event that you wish to send outside to let others synchronize with it. The temptation to use the domain one is high; we know that laziness can sometimes prevail over discipline, but try to refrain from doing it. That's because sooner or later the ubiquitous language of your bounded context will inevitably change, and while there is a chance that you will probably change that domain event, it is not guaranteed that the integration event needs to change accordingly. In such a case, the two events would diverge; if you used the same event for both tasks, you can already imagine the impact on your entire application, not only on a single component.

Use cases in our brewery application

As mentioned in the previous chapters, our brewery application is composed of the following bounded contexts: `Sales`, `Warehouse`, `Payment`, and `Shipping`. Let's explore how domain and integration events can be used within this system to facilitate communication and ensure seamless operations:

- **Sales context**: In the `Sales` context, a significant domain event would be `SalesOrderCreated`. This event is triggered when a customer places an order. It is crucial for the `Sales` context to track new orders and initiate the subsequent processes required to fulfill the order.

- **Warehouse context**: In the `Warehouse` context, a critical domain event would be `BeerAvailabilityUpdated`. This event is triggered when stock is reserved for an order. It is essential for managing inventory within the `Warehouse` context, ensuring that the necessary items are available and reserved for the customer order.

- **Payment context**: In the `Payment` context, a key domain event would be `PaymentProcessed`. This event is triggered when a payment is successfully processed. It is important for the `Payment` context to track the payment status and ensure that the order can proceed to the next stage.

- **Shipping context**: In the Shipping context, a significant domain event would be ShipmentCreated. This event is triggered when a shipment is created for an order. It is crucial for the Shipping context to manage deliveries and ensure that the order is dispatched to the customer.

- **Integration events across contexts**: Integration events play a vital role in ensuring that different bounded contexts within the brewery application stay in sync and communicate effectively. When a SalesOrderCreated domain event is triggered in the Sales context, it will also trigger an integration event (that could have the same name) that is published to other bounded contexts. The Warehouse, Payment, and Shipping contexts subscribe to this event to initiate their respective processes. For example, the Warehouse context allocates stock, triggering the BeerAvailabilityUpdated domain event, which then triggers an integration event to notify the Sales context about stock reservation.

These domain and integration events form a chain of reactions across the system, ensuring that each bounded context remains informed and can act accordingly. To better understand how these events propagate and influence different parts of the application, let's examine the overall event flow and how information moves throughout the system.

Event flow and information flow

To illustrate a complete flow of events and information within our application, consider the diagram in *Figure 4.2*:

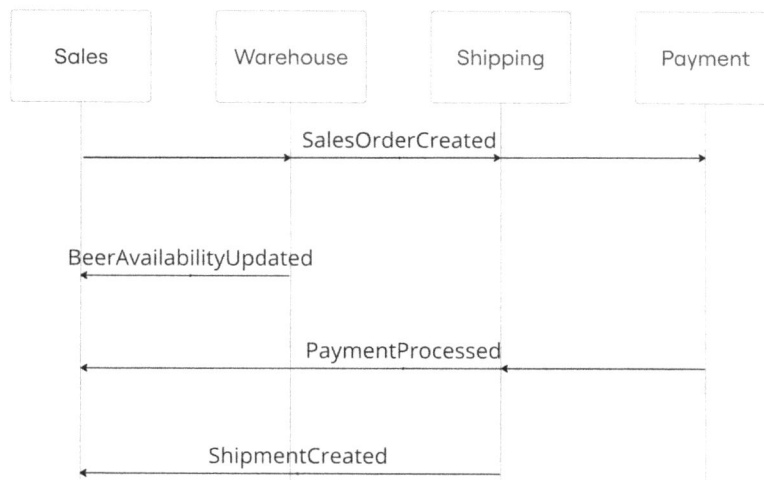

Figure 4.2 – Diagram of a business flow with events

When a customer places an order in the Sales context, the system triggers the SalesOrderCreated domain event. This event is significant within the Sales context as it marks the initiation of the order fulfillment process. Concurrently, an integration event with the same name is published to the Warehouse, Payment, and Shipping contexts.

Upon receiving the SalesOrderCreated integration event, the Warehouse context allocates the necessary stock for the order. This allocation triggers the BeerAvailabilityUpdated domain event, which is crucial for managing inventory within the Warehouse context. The BeerAvailabilityUpdated event then becomes an integration event, notifying the Sales context about the successful reservation of stock for the order.

Meanwhile, the Payment context, upon receiving the SalesOrderCreated event, processes the customer's payment. This action triggers the PaymentProcessed domain event, which is essential for tracking payment status within the Payment context. The PaymentProcessed event becomes an integration event, notifying the Sales and Shipping contexts about the successful payment, allowing them to proceed with their respective processes.

The Shipping context, after receiving both the SalesOrderCreated and PaymentProcessed events, creates a shipment for the order. This action triggers the ShipmentCreated domain event, which is significant for managing deliveries within the Shipping context. The ShipmentCreated event becomes an integration event, notifying the Sales context to update the customer about the shipment status and complete the order fulfillment process.

Sagas

As you will see in *Chapter 12, Orchestrating Complexity: Advanced Approaches to Business Processes*, the flow we have just described is also called a **choreography saga**. In *Chapter 12*, you will delve into the two main sagas that could be used to handle complex business flows.

Events, both domain and integration, play a pivotal role in modern complex applications by promoting decoupling, scalability, and maintainability. In our brewery application, domain events help manage business logic within bounded contexts, while integration events ensure seamless communication and synchronization across contexts. By understanding and leveraging these concepts, developers can build robust, scalable, and maintainable systems.

Summary

In this chapter, we delved deeply into the main tactical patterns of DDD. We started with entities, which are objects defined not by their attributes but by a thread of continuity and identity. These entities possess a distinct identity that runs through different states and transformations over time, making them critical in modeling real-world scenarios where identity persistence is crucial.

We moved on to value objects, which are defined entirely by their attributes. Value objects lack a distinct identity and are inherently immutable, offering a way to model concepts that can be described by their attributes alone, such as a quantity or a price. This immutability simplifies their use and ensures consistency across the system.

Aggregates were introduced as a key concept for maintaining consistency within the system. An aggregate is a cluster of entities and value objects that are treated as a single unit for data changes. The root entity of an aggregate guarantees the consistency of changes within the aggregate boundary, ensuring that all invariants are respected. This structure is vital for managing the complexity of business rules and data integrity.

Repositories were covered next. We explained their role in encapsulating the logic required to access data sources. By using repositories, you can abstract the infrastructure or technology-specific code, providing a clean separation between the domain model and data access layers. This separation enhances the maintainability and testability of the code.

We also explored the concept of services, distinguishing between domain services and application services. Domain services encapsulate domain logic that doesn't naturally fit within entities or value objects, offering a way to express operations and processes within the domain model. In contrast, application services are responsible for orchestrating the application's use cases, serving as a bridge between the user interface and the domain layer.

Modules were presented as a means to organize the domain model into cohesive units, enhancing the clarity and maintainability of the system. By grouping related concepts together, modules help manage complexity and facilitate a clearer understanding of the domain structure.

In the last section of the chapter, we delved into integration and domain events, underscoring their importance in modern application architectures. Integration events are pivotal for communication between bounded contexts or external systems, ensuring that changes in one part of the system are propagated and handled appropriately elsewhere. Domain events capture significant occurrences within the domain, making the system more responsive and robust by explicitly modeling the domain's state changes and reactions.

Events are a key concept in modern complex applications because they enable a decoupled and reactive system design. By embracing an event-driven approach, you can achieve greater scalability and flexibility, handling real-time data and operations more effectively. Events allow different parts of the system to remain loosely coupled while still collaborating seamlessly, facilitating a more resilient and adaptive architecture.

This chapter marks the end of *Part 1*, which reviewed the key concepts of DDD. In the next chapter, we will start to go deep into refactoring. You will learn about the principles of refactoring and how DDD can help in the process.

Part 2

Refactoring Legacy Systems

This second part of the book is all about helping you take control of legacy systems. You'll learn practical refactoring principles, discover how to bring order to chaotic architectures, and explore techniques such as CQRS and event-driven design. You'll also cover refactoring databases and how to use DDD patterns to enable **continuous integration and continuous deployment (CI/CD)**. By the time you finish, you'll be ready to transform even the most stubborn systems into something maintainable and future-proof.

This part of the book includes the following chapters:

- *Chapter 5, Introducing Refactoring Principles*
- *Chapter 6, Transitioning from Chaos*
- *Chapter 7, Integrating Events with CQRS*
- *Chapter 8, Refactoring the Database*
- *Chapter 9, DDD Patterns for Continuous Integration and Continuous Refactoring*

5

Introducing Refactoring Principles

In the previous chapter, we reviewed the tactical patterns of DDD and equipped you with a robust toolkit to model complex systems effectively. As you now understand, tactical patterns are crucial for aligning your software architecture with the core business domain. However, as systems evolve, even well-designed code bases can accumulate technical debt and become harder to maintain. This is where refactoring comes into play.

Starting with this chapter, you will embark on the journey of mastering refactoring principles, a critical skill set for any software developer working within the DDD paradigm. Refactoring is not merely about making your code cleaner—it's about making it more aligned with the underlying business needs, more maintainable, and more resilient to future changes.

The chapter is structured around three core themes:

- Understanding before acting
- The pillars of safe change
- Toward cleaner and more maintainable code

You will first learn the importance of thoroughly analyzing and comprehending the existing code base. This includes gaining insights into the current design, recognizing potential pitfalls, and identifying the right tools to facilitate the refactoring process. You will develop the skills to evaluate code with a critical eye, ensuring that every change is purposeful and aligned with the domain model.

Refactoring can be risky if not performed carefully. You will learn how to establish a safety net through the use of testing patterns, ensuring that every step of your refactoring journey is validated by reliable tests. This section will teach you how to create, maintain, and use these tests to detect unintended consequences early, minimizing risks and preserving the integrity of your application.

Finally, you will explore the application of design principles that guide effective incremental refactoring. By applying these principles, you will learn how to evolve your code base incrementally, making small, manageable changes that gradually lead to a cleaner, more maintainable, and more scalable system.

The complete code for this chapter can be found within the `01-monolith_legacy` branch within the book's GitHub repository here: `https://github.com/PacktPublishing/Domain-driven-Refactoring/tree/01-monolith_legacy`.

Understanding before acting

If you take a look at the `01-monolith_legacy` branch of our ERP example, you'll notice that the code is somewhat messy. While the project names are clear, it's difficult to identify any architectural pattern, such as Onion Architecture, Clean Architecture, or even Hexagonal Architecture.

Dig deeper into the code. If you open the `program.cs` file in the `BrewUp.Rest` project, you will see that every service and endpoint is registered in this file. This means that whenever you need to add, remove, or modify a service or endpoint, you have to update the `program.cs` file, the entry point of your application. This approach is far from ideal!

The `SalesOrderService` and `WarehousesService` files, located in the `Services` folder, serve as the `façade` of the underlying infrastructure. Placing these files directly in the `BrewUp.Rest` project creates a tight coupling with the underlying system. As a result, if you ever need to move one of these services out of the application as a standalone application, you will have to heavily modify the nt project once again and you will probably not be able to achieve that.

> **façade**
>
> A `façade` class offers a simplified interface to a complicated subsystem made up of many interconnected components. Although it simplifies access, a `façade` class may only offer partial functionality compared to interacting directly with the subsystem.

Challenges of Tight Coupling in Sales and Warehouse Services

Now, let's focus on SalesOrderService in BrewUp.Domain\Services, which is invoked by SalesOrderService in BrewUp.Rest\Services. In this class' constructor, as shown in the code that follows, you will notice the injection of two different instances of the IRepository interface: one for handling sales and the other for warehouse operations. This setup is necessary because when a request for a new order arrives, you need to check the beer availability before confirming the order. However, this approach creates a tight coupling between the Sales and Warehouses contexts. As you can see, any change within the warehouse context, beginning with the database schema, inevitably impacts the sales context. As a result, any modification to one service impacts the other, making it impossible to split these services into separate APIs due to their interdependence.

The following code demonstrates this:

```
public async Task CreateSalesOrderAsync(SalesOrderId salesOrderId,
SalesOrderNumber salesOrderNumber, OrderDate orderDate, CustomerId
customerId, CustomerName customerName, IEnumerable<SalesOrderRowJson>
rows, CancellationToken cancellationToken)
{
    List<SalesOrderRowJson> beersAvailable = new();
    foreach (var row in rows)
    {
var availability = await warehouseRepository.GetByIdAsync<Shared.Entities.
Availability>(row.BeerId.ToString(), cancellationToken);
        if (availability!=null)
            beersAvailable.Add(row);
    }

    var aggregate = SalesOrder.CreateSalesOrder(salesOrderId,
salesOrderNumber, orderDate, customerId, customerName, beersAvailable);

await saleRepository.InsertAsync(aggregate.MapToSharedDto(),
cancellationToken);
}
```

A major challenge with refactoring lies in the intricate web of dependencies between objects. When you modify one object, these dependencies often force you to make changes in others, creating a cascading effect. Therefore, before diving into refactoring, it's crucial to identify the boundaries within different contexts. Understanding these boundaries equips you with the tools needed for effective refactoring.

Figure 5.1 illustrates the ripple effect that any modification, regardless of the layer, has on the entire solution. This is one of the biggest challenges in maintaining and evolving a code base. Every time you need to introduce a new feature, you are forced to modify the entire solution. Given that no one fully understands the entire code base, there is a constant fear of introducing regressions or bugs. This fear often becomes a constraint, leading developers to resist making necessary changes.

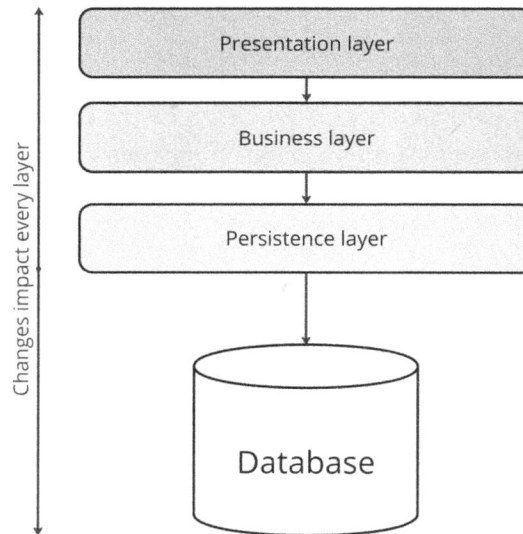

Figure 5.1 – How changes impact all the monolith's layers

Attempting to transform a monolithic architecture into something different, such as a microservices architecture, in just one step will surely backfire on you. Gall's law reminds us that complex systems evolve from simpler ones, emphasizing the importance of gradual transformation:

> *"A complex system that works is invariably found to have evolved from a simple system that worked. The inverse proposition also appears to be true: a complex system designed from scratch never works and cannot be made to work. You have to start over, beginning with a working simple system."*

The key to a successful evolution of your monolithic application relies on proceeding with small, incremental steps. This evolution starts by reorganizing your code base into modules applying architectural modularity. This is a stepping stone to architectural quantum, as you will see in the coming chapters.

However, what is a module? Modular architecture is based on the idea of breaking down a system into smaller, independent components, or modules, that can be developed, tested, and maintained separately. Within a module, objects can have dependencies on each other, but in this case, we are talking about cohesion rather than coupling.

Coupling versus cohesion

Cohesion refers to the degree of relation of the elements within a module, or component of a software system, that work together to achieve a common purpose. On the other hand, coupling refers to the degree of interdependence between different modules in a software system.

The primary goal of modularity is to enable teams to make changes to one part of the system without impacting others. This approach minimizes the risk of changes cascading through the system and causing unexpected issues.

After adopting a modular architecture, it's crucial to establish clear communication methods between modules. Since your goal is to eliminate dependencies, implementing **Consumer-Driven Contracts (CDCs)** is essential. CDCs are agreements between service providers and consumers that specify how services should interact. These contracts are versioned and validated to ensure backward compatibility, allowing services to evolve independently without disrupting consumers. By explicitly defining and testing these interactions, CDCs support safe and incremental changes.

Incremental change involves making small, manageable adjustments to the system, rather than implementing large, sweeping modifications all at once. By breaking down changes into smaller increments, the scope of potential failure is significantly reduced, which makes it easier to isolate, test, and resolve issues before they escalate. This methodical approach allows for a more thorough understanding of the impact of each change, minimizing the risk of introducing new bugs or disruptions.

Moreover, incremental changes align well with continuous delivery and deployment practices. By integrating and deploying smaller updates frequently, teams can quickly roll out new features and fixes in a controlled manner. This reduces the time between development and production, allowing teams to respond swiftly to feedback and adapt to evolving requirements. The ability to make safe, incremental changes is crucial in maintaining system stability and ensuring that software can evolve over time without compromising quality or performance.

Before making any changes to your code base, it's crucial to prepare the necessary tests to ensure your modifications don't disrupt existing functionality. Automated testing involves creating and maintaining a suite of tests that cover various aspects of the application, such as unit, integration, **End-to-End (E2E)**, and performance tests. Although it may not be feasible to cover all types of tests at this stage, prioritizing E2E tests is essential. The primary goal of refactoring is to improve the internal structure of the code without changing its external behavior. Automated testing acts as a safety net, helping to identify any regressions or issues that arise during the refactoring process, thereby ensuring that changes do not introduce new bugs or break existing features.

Establishing CI/CD and Observability in Refactoring

Another key aspect of the refactoring process is implementing **Continuous Integration and Continuous Deployment (CI/CD)**. Legacy applications often lack these automated processes, so one of your goals should be to establish them. CI/CD pipelines automate the building, testing, and deployment of software. CI ensures that changes are frequently integrated, while CD automates the release of those changes to production. These practices shorten the time between making a change and seeing its impact in production, promoting rapid feedback and minimizing the risks associated with deploying updates.

Last but not least, once you have automated all the processes to build and deploy your application, you need to observe and monitor it. Observability involves the tools and processes to monitor the health and performance of the system in real time. The fundamental pillars of observability include logging, metrics, and tracing. Observability allows teams to detect and respond to issues quickly, minimizing the impact of any problems that arise from changes. It also provides insights into the behavior of the system, which can inform future changes.

These pillars work together to create a framework that supports the safe evolution of software systems. By adhering to these principles, teams can make changes with confidence, knowing that they have mechanisms in place to catch issues early and mitigate risks. This approach is essential in complex, distributed environments where changes are frequent, and the impact of failures can be significant.

During a refactor, developers often feel tempted to implement new patterns or frameworks they have learned, driven by both their ego (who hasn't been there?) and the belief that patterns are the key to writing better code. However, this approach can be a double-edged sword. The following chart illustrates the idea that the more senior a developer becomes, the less complex their code tends to be.

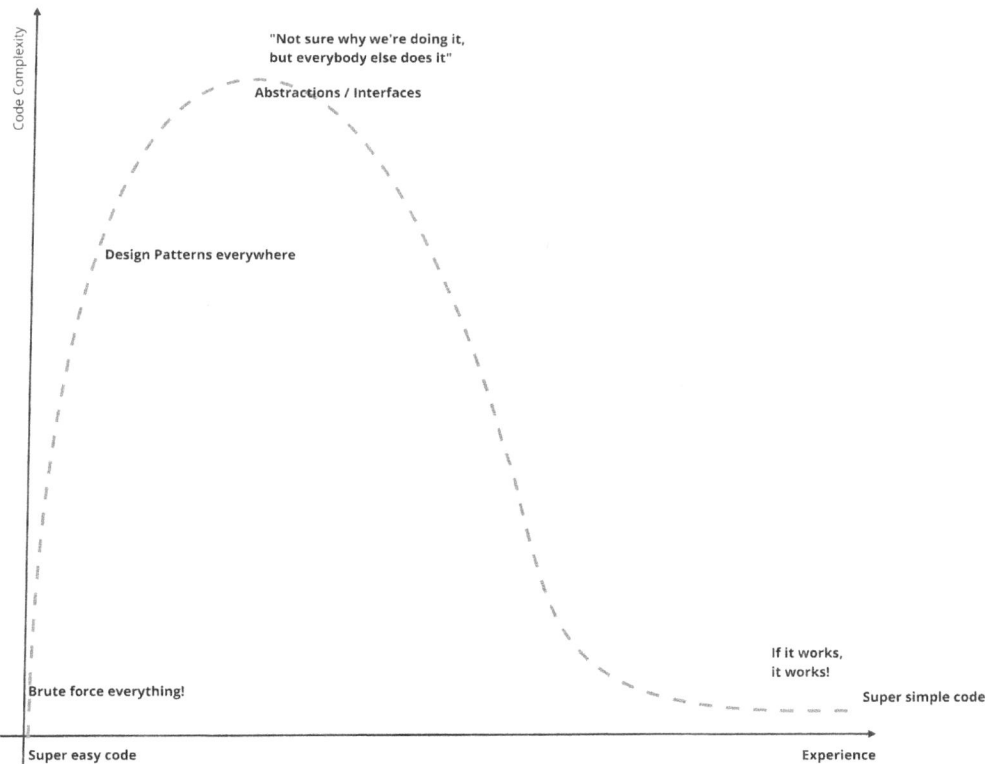

Figure 5.2 – Code complexity versus experience

You should have noticed that at the beginning of the **Experience** axis, we wrote **Super easy code**, while at the end, it says **Super simple code**. That's because writing easy code is in no way the same as writing simple code. The former just works but it is not well structured, maintainable, or readable while the latter tends to be all of them while maintaining simplicity.

As stated by Neal Ford in his book *The Productive Programmer*, "*Developers are drawn to complexity, like moths to a flame, often with the same outcome.*"

The pillars of safe change

It is now time to implement some solutions for the problems exposed in the previous paragraphs. As discussed, modularizing a monolithic system is an essential first step toward achieving a more flexible and maintainable architecture. Refactoring within this context requires a careful approach that aligns with the principles of modularity and incremental change. Our goal is to decouple tightly interwoven components so that they can evolve independently, reducing the risk of cascading changes and enhancing the system's overall stability.

Exploring the solution structure

Let's start by exploring how our project was initially developed by looking at the solution structure inside Visual Studio in *Figure 5.3*.

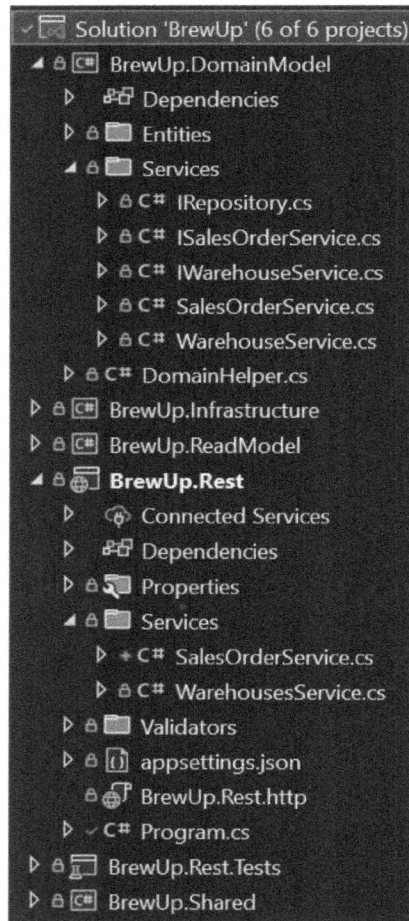

Figure 5.3 – The initial solution structure

As you can see, there is a little bit of DDD in it. As you should have already spotted, there is lots of coupling because everything is inside single folders of specific common projects. For example, BrewUp.DomainModel contains a folder named Services with both sales and warehouse services.

We know that we could do so much better with a bit of moving around, but before we dive deep into it and discover too late that we broke something, let's try to apply the design and architectural principles introduced in previous chapters at the code level.

You can apply these principles by examining SalesService in BrewUp.Rest.Services. You can immediately see that SalesOrderService is tightly coupled with WarehouseService:

```
public sealed class SalesOrderService(
    [FromKeyedServices("sale")] IRepository saleRepository,
    [FromKeyedServices("warehouse")] IRepository warehouseRepository) :
ISalesOrderService
{
    public async Task CreateSalesOrderAsync(SalesOrderId salesOrderId,
SalesOrderNumber salesOrderNumber, OrderDate orderDate,
        CustomerId customerId, CustomerName customerName,
IEnumerable<SalesOrderRowJson> rows, CancellationToken cancellationToken)
    {
        List<SalesOrderRowJson> beersAvailable = new();
        foreach (var row in rows)
        {
            var availability = await warehouseRepository.
GetByIdAsync<Entities.Warehouses.Availability>(row.BeerId.ToString(),
cancellationToken);
            if (availability != null)
                beersAvailable.Add(row);
        }

        var aggregate = SalesOrder.CreateSalesOrder(salesOrderId,
salesOrderNumber, orderDate, customerId, customerName, beersAvailable);

        await saleRepository.InsertAsync(aggregate.MapToReadModel(),
cancellationToken);
    }
}
```

Here, `SalesOrderService` is not only aware of the existence of `WarehouseService` but is also directly responsible for managing interactions with it. This tight coupling creates a situation where any changes to `WarehouseService`—even changes as minor as altering the method signature—could have ripple effects throughout `SalesOrderService`, thus violating the principles of modularity (remember the impact of changes as shown in *Figure 5.1*).

These services are bound together, making it difficult to modify one without affecting the other. To move toward a modular architecture, we need to break this dependency, enabling each service to operate independently and making it easier to adapt the system incrementally.

However, before tackling the refactoring process head-on, it's crucial to understand the role that tests play in ensuring a smooth and safe process. Refactoring, by its very nature, involves altering the internal structure of your code without changing its external behavior. However, this can be risky if not done with due care. This is where the concept of a safety net of tests comes into play.

Establishing comprehensive tests ensures that our changes do not inadvertently break existing functionality.

Understanding tests and their role in refactoring

At its core, a test is a piece of code that checks whether another piece of code (the system under test) behaves as expected. When you refactor an application, you inevitably change the code base, sometimes significantly. Without a robust set of tests, you have no reliable way to confirm that your changes haven't introduced new bugs or altered the system's behavior unintentionally.

Tests act as your first line of defense. They give you the confidence to make changes because you know that if something goes wrong, the tests will catch it. This is particularly important in a DDD context, where the alignment between the business domain and the code is critical. Any misalignment introduced during refactoring could have significant consequences on the overall design and functionality of the application.

Before reviewing the specific types of tests, it's essential to grasp the variety available and how each serves a unique purpose in maintaining your application's health.

In *Figure 5.4*, you can see the famous **pyramid of tests**, a concept that visualizes the optimal distribution of different types of tests in your code base.

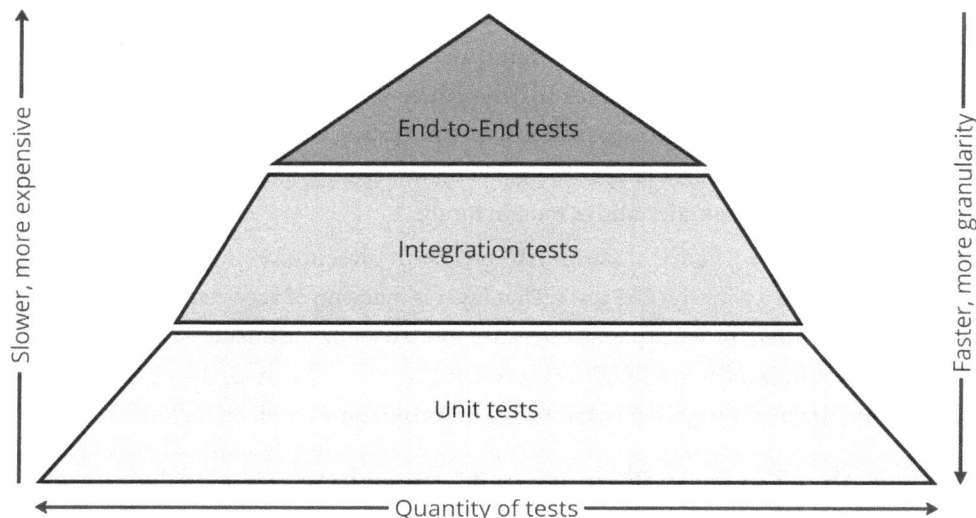

Figure 5.4 – The pyramid of tests

As you can see, the pyramid categorizes tests into three different layers: Unit tests, Integration tests, and E2E tests. Let's discuss each of these and acceptance tests next:

- **Unit tests**: Unit tests lie at the base of the pyramid and focus on individual units of code, typically functions or methods, verifying that they perform as expected in isolation. Unit tests are the fastest to run and are usually abundant in well-tested code bases. Their speed and granularity make them ideal for covering the smallest units of your application. They provide the foundation of your safety net and allow you to refactor with the confidence that the fundamental building blocks of your application will continue to function correctly.

- **Integration tests**: In the middle layer, you have integration tests. They check how different modules or services work together. Unlike unit tests, they don't isolate individual pieces of code but instead focus on the interactions between them. They are fewer in number and slower than unit tests but crucial for ensuring that the various parts of your system interact correctly. When refactoring, integration tests ensure that changes in one module don't break its interactions with others. They provide a broader safety net, catching issues that unit tests might miss.

- **E2E tests**: At the top layer lie E2E tests that simulate real user scenarios, testing the entire application from the user interface down to the database. These are the least numerous but the most comprehensive, testing the entire system as a user would interact with. While they are slower and more expensive to maintain, their ability to validate complete user flows makes them indispensable. When refactoring, E2E tests assure you that the application's core functionalities remain intact.

- **Acceptance tests**: There is also a fourth layer not represented in the original pyramid that tends to overlap with the E2E tests. That layer is made up of acceptance tests. These tests are often written from the perspective of the end user or the business. They validate that the system meets the specified requirements. As already stated, they overlap with E2E tests but are usually more focused on business outcomes than on technical correctness.

Applying the Testing Pyramid: A complete example

Each layer of the testing pyramid has its strengths and weaknesses. Unit tests, for example, are fast and easy to write, but they only cover individual components. If you refactor a significant portion of your code, unit tests alone might not be enough to guarantee that everything still works as intended.

Integration tests, while slower and more complex, give you confidence that different parts of your system interact correctly. However, they can be more challenging to maintain, especially if the integration points change during refactoring.

E2E tests provide the highest level of assurance but at the cost of speed and maintenance overhead. They are often brittle, meaning small changes in the code base can cause them to fail, even if the underlying functionality hasn't been affected.

In conclusion, the simplicity and essence of the pyramid provide a couple of rules of thumb for choosing how many and which tests to write:

- Write tests with different granularity
- High-level tests should be significantly fewer in proportion to tests at lower levels

Let's go back to the scenario explained in the *Exploring the solution structure* subsection at the beginning of this section. We could write unit tests that validate the interaction between SalesOrderService and WarehouseService, such as the following:

```
public class SalesOrderServiceTests
{
    [Fact]
```

```
    public void ProcessOrder_ShouldReserveInventory()
    {
        // Arrange
        var warehouseServiceMock = new Mock<IWarehouseService>();
        var salesOrderService = new
SalesOrderService(warehouseServiceMock.Object);
        var order = new Order { BeerId = 1, Quantity = 10 };

        // Act
        salesOrderService.ProcessOrder(order);

        // Assert
        warehouseServiceMock.Verify(ws => ws.ReserveInventory(order.
BeerId, order.Quantity), Times.Once);
    }
}
```

Writing many unit tests provides a foundation that allows you to refactor with confidence, knowing that any regression will be caught early.

Mock library

A **mock library** is a tool used in unit testing to simulate the behavior of real objects, allowing you to isolate and test specific parts of your code without relying on external systems. It helps ensure your tests are reliable, consistent, and fast by controlling the behavior of dependencies, making it easier to verify how your code interacts with other components. For this book, we choose to use *Moq* (https://github. com/devlooped/moq), a popular mock library for C# that makes it easy to create and configure mock objects for your tests.

Another set of tests you should consider writing before starting to apply any change to the code base are those on the presentation layer. To reference our pyramid, we should also write some integration tests. The following code should give you an idea:

```
[Fact]
public async Task Can_Create_SalesOrder()
{
    DateTime now = DateTime.UtcNow;
```

```
SalesOrderJson body = new(Guid.NewGuid().ToString(),
    $"{now.Year:0000}{now.Month:00}{now.Day:00}-{now.Hour:00}{now.
Minute:00}",
    Guid.NewGuid(), "Customer",
    now, new List<SalesOrderRowJson>
    {
        new()
        {
            BeerId = Guid.NewGuid(),
            BeerName = "BrewUp IPA",
            Quantity = new(10, "Lt"),
            Price = new(5, "EUR")
        }
    });

var stringJson = JsonSerializer.Serialize(body);
var httpContent = new StringContent(stringJson, Encoding.UTF8,
"application/json");
var postResult = await integrationFixture.Client.PostAsync("/v1/
sales", httpContent);

Assert.Equal(HttpStatusCode.Created, postResult.StatusCode);
}
```

In this test, we are making sure that the payload that arrives at our service is handled as it should be without bothering the internal working. What matters is that the result does not change. For this very reason, we did not call the specific method mapped to the /v1/sales/ endpoint as you would normally do with unit tests and a mock library. Instead, we emulated an HTTP call to be as abstract as possible.

By writing these tests in both the domain and application layers, we end up with the safety net we were talking about at the beginning of this section. We can finally move on to reorganizing our code base so that it relates to the bounded contexts already explained in *Chapter 3, Strategic Patterns*.

Towards cleaner and more maintainable code

At the end of our journey, our goal is to refactor the application toward an architecture such as that in *Figure 5.5*.

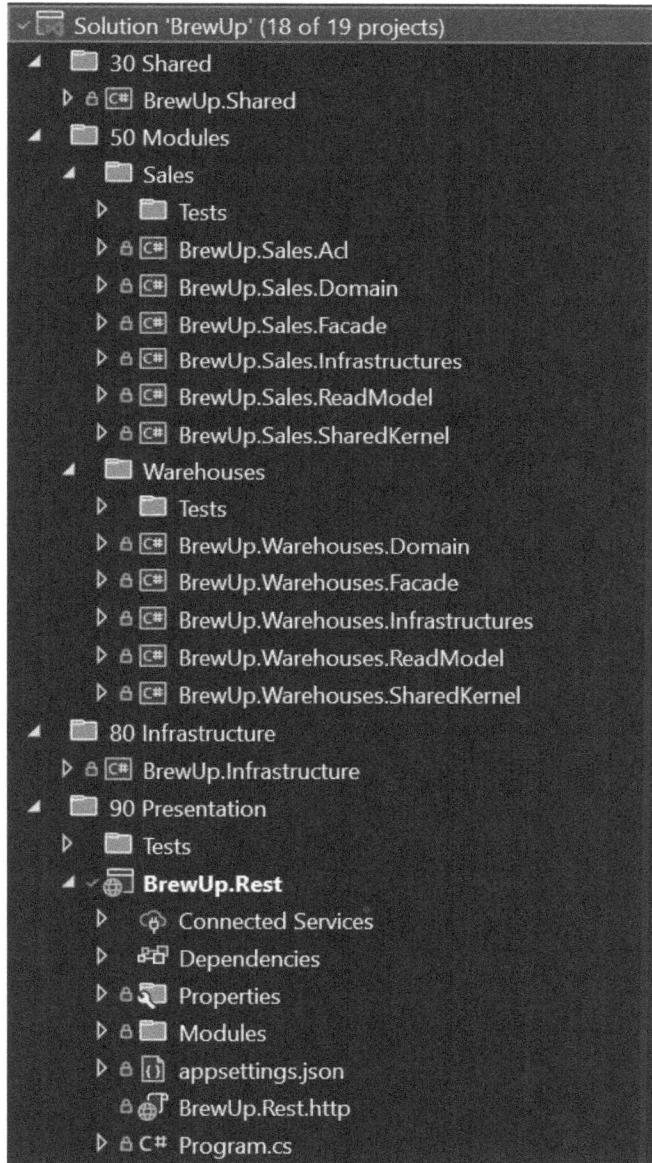

Figure 5.5 – The end result of our refactoring process

This is a well-organized code base. You should have already noticed that we used numbers in the solution folders' names. We usually do this to clearly indicate the level of every layer of our application and, in our opinion, this follows the Onion Architecture pattern more closely. The solution folder we are referring to is just a logical folder that you can create to organize your projects inside IDEs such as Microsoft Visual Studio or JetBrains Rider. Obviously, you can easily achieve the same result with other frameworks and languages by using physical folders instead of logical ones.

A well-organized code base benefits all team members, including newcomers. It immediately clarifies the separation of concerns when opening the solution, making it easier to identify which component or module needs to be touched to introduce a new feature or solve a bug. Additionally, the presence of tests at every level reduces the fear of introducing regressions.

Also, an important thing you should have noticed right away is how the modules folder clearly represents the bounded contexts we defined and created in *Chapter 3*.

Last but not least, *Figure 5.5* represents an event-driven approach paired with **Command Query Responsibility Segregation (CQRS)**.

The term CQRS was coined by Greg Young in 2010. This architectural pattern is based on the principle of separating the responsibilities of commands (which modify state) and queries (which retrieve data) within a system. Young's introduction of CQRS built upon **Command Query Separation (CQS)**, which was originally defined by Bertrand Meyer in his 1988 book, *Object-Oriented Software Construction*.

In our specific case, the commands are found in BrewUp.Sales.Domain and BrewUp.Warehouses. Domain, while the queries part are handled by BrewUp.Sales.ReadModel and BrewUp.Warehouses. ReadModel.

CQRS is often used in conjunction with event sourcing to enhance system architecture by providing clear boundaries between read and write operations, thereby improving scalability and maintainability, hence the definition of **CQRS+ES**.

In *Figure 5.6*, you can see how a CQRS+ES system works.

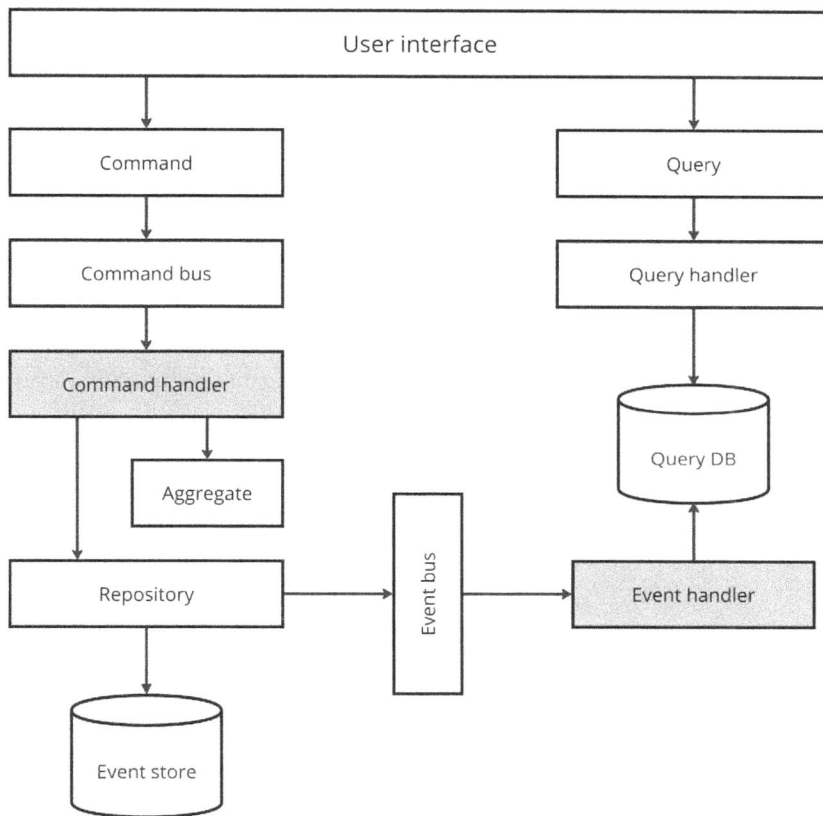

Figure 5.6 – CQRS+ES diagram

In *Chapter 7, Integrating Events with CQRS*, we will start the refactoring process by implementing CQRS and then add events for communication between bounded contexts.

As with all things in life, to be able to solve or work on large complex problems, you must break them down into smaller ones. As far as our architecture is concerned, it is not advisable to refactor directly to CQRS+ES in one step, but instead, as reiterated multiple times throughout this book, take small steps.

To conclude our tour of the tools we need in our toolbox to be able to do what we described, we must review the last principles essential to successful refactoring. These design patterns play a pivotal role in ensuring that the system remains flexible, maintainable, and scalable.

Single responsibility principle

One of the foundational principles is the **Single Responsibility Principle (SRP)**. The SRP states that a class or module should have only one reason to change, meaning it should be responsible for only one aspect of the system's functionality. This is different from the common misconception that SRP means a class should simply 'do one thing.' Instead, it means that all the responsibilities of the class should align with a single, well-defined reason for change. When your code adheres to the SRP, it becomes easier to understand, test, and maintain because each component has a clear purpose. In the context of DDD, this principle ensures that your code reflects the distinct concepts of the domain, making the system more intuitive and aligned with business needs. It is essential for refactoring because it helps to break down complex, monolithic classes into smaller, more manageable pieces. Each class handles a specific aspect of the functionality, making the system easier to maintain and extend.

Using `SalesOrderService` and `WarehouseService`, as shown earlier in this chapter, we could refactor them as follows:

```
public class SalesOrderService
{
    private readonly IWarehouseService _warehouseService;

    public SalesOrderService(IWarehouseService warehouseService)
    {
        _warehouseService = warehouseService;
    }

    public void ProcessOrder(Order order)
    {
        if (_warehouseService.IsBeerAvailable(order.BeerId, order.
Quantity))
        {
            // Process the order
        }
        else
        {
            // Handle out-of-stock scenario
        }
    }
}
```

```
}

public interface IWarehouseService
{
    bool IsBeerAvailable(int beerId, int quantity);
}

public class WarehouseService : IWarehouseService
{
    public bool IsBeerAvailable(int beerId, int quantity)
    {
        // Check availability in the warehouse
        return true; // or false
    }
}
```

Now, SalesOrderService is only responsible for processing orders, while WarehouseService only handles inventory checks, adhering to the SRP.

Open/closed principle

Another critical principle is the **Open/Closed Principle (OCP)**, which posits that software entities should be open for extension but closed for modification. This means that the behavior of a class can be extended without modifying its source code. By adhering to the OCP during refactoring, you protect your system from the unintended consequences that often come with modifying established code. This approach not only preserves the integrity of your application but also facilitates the gradual introduction of new features.

Imagine we need to add a discount feature to SalesOrderService. Instead of modifying the existing code, we can extend the service using the OCP:

```
public class SalesOrderService
{
    private readonly IWarehouseService _warehouseService;
    private readonly IDiscountStrategy _discountStrategy;

    public SalesOrderService(IWarehouseService warehouseService,
IDiscountStrategy discountStrategy)
```

```csharp
    {
        _warehouseService = warehouseService;
        _discountStrategy = discountStrategy;
    }

    public void ProcessOrder(Order order)
    {
        if (_warehouseService.IsBeerAvailable(order.BeerId, order.
Quantity))
        {
            decimal discount = _discountStrategy.CalculateDiscount(order);
            // Apply discount and process the order
        }
        else
        {
            // Handle out-of-stock scenario
        }
    }
}


public interface IDiscountStrategy
{
    decimal CalculateDiscount(Order order);
}


public class NoDiscountStrategy : IDiscountStrategy
{
    public decimal CalculateDiscount(Order order)
    {
        return 0;
    }
}


public class SeasonalDiscountStrategy : IDiscountStrategy
{
    public decimal CalculateDiscount(Order order)
```

```
    {
        // Implement seasonal discount logic
        return 10; // Placeholder discount value
    }
}
```

Here, we've introduced an `IDiscountStrategy` interface and implemented different discount strategies. We can now easily introduce new discount types without modifying the existing `SalesOrderService` logic.

Dependency inversion principle

The **Dependency Inversion Principle (DIP)** is another powerful tool in your refactoring arsenal. The DIP suggests that high-level modules should not depend on low-level modules; instead, both should depend on abstractions. This principle helps in decoupling your code, making it more modular and flexible. During refactoring, applying the DIP allows you to isolate changes to specific parts of the system, minimizing the ripple effect that modifications can have. This decoupling is particularly beneficial in large, complex systems where changes in one area should not unnecessarily impact others.

Consider a scenario where `SalesOrderService` directly depends on a concrete implementation of `WarehouseService`. This tight coupling makes it difficult to change or mock `WarehouseService` for testing.

Let's apply the DIP to improve this:

```
public class SalesOrderService
{
    private readonly IWarehouseService _warehouseService;

    public SalesOrderService(IWarehouseService warehouseService)
    {
        _warehouseService = warehouseService;
    }

    public void ProcessOrder(Order order)
    {
        if (_warehouseService.IsBeerAvailable(order.BeerId, order.
Quantity))
```

```
        {
            // Process the order
        }
        else
        {
            // Handle out-of-stock scenario
        }
    }
}


public interface IWarehouseService
{
    bool IsBeerAvailable(int beerId, int quantity);
}

public class WarehouseService : IWarehouseService
{
    public bool IsBeerAvailable(int beerId, int quantity)
    {
        // Check availability in the warehouse
        return true; // Placeholder logic
    }
}
```

The introduction of the IWarehouseService interface inside the constructor of SalesOrderService allows decoupling from the concrete implementation and allows us to create mock classes to fully unit test SalesOrderService.

Strategy pattern

The **Strategy pattern** defines a family of algorithms, encapsulates each one, and makes them interchangeable. The pattern allows the algorithm to vary independently from the clients that use it.

This matters because this pattern is valuable when you have multiple ways to perform a certain task and want to make the system easily extendable with new strategies without modifying existing code.

Let's expand our discount calculation logic using the Strategy pattern:

```csharp
public interface IDiscountStrategy
{
    decimal CalculateDiscount(Order order);
}

public class NoDiscountStrategy : IDiscountStrategy
{
    public decimal CalculateDiscount(Order order)
    {
        return 0;
    }
}

public class PercentageDiscountStrategy : IDiscountStrategy
{
    private readonly decimal _percentage;

    public PercentageDiscountStrategy(decimal percentage)
    {
        _percentage = percentage;
    }

    public decimal CalculateDiscount(Order order)
    {
        return order.TotalAmount * _percentage;
    }
}

public class SalesOrderService
{
    private readonly IWarehouseService _warehouseService;
    private readonly IDiscountStrategy _discountStrategy;

    public SalesOrderService(IWarehouseService warehouseService,
IDiscountStrategy discountStrategy)
    {
```

```
        _warehouseService = warehouseService;
        _discountStrategy = discountStrategy;
    }

    public void ProcessOrder(Order order)
    {
        if (_warehouseService.IsBeerAvailable(order.BeerId, order.
Quantity))
        {
            decimal discount = _discountStrategy.CalculateDiscount(order);
            // Apply discount and process the order
        }
        else
        {
            // Handle out-of-stock scenario
        }
    }
}
```

In the preceding example, `SalesOrderService` can work with any discount strategy without needing to know the specifics of how discounts are calculated.

By embracing the principles and techniques we have discussed in this section, you will be able to systematically transform your code into a cleaner, more maintainable state. Each refactoring effort will contribute to a code base that not only better supports the current business requirements but is also more resilient and adaptable to future changes. Ultimately, this approach ensures that your system remains agile, responsive, and closely aligned with the evolving needs of the business domain.

In addition, the modular architecture we are working on will lead to the possibility of moving to a microservices architecture with less effort (you will read about it in *Part 3* of this book).

Summary

This chapter has equipped you with a solid foundation in the principles and practices of refactoring within a DDD context. You learned that refactoring is not just about making code cleaner but also about aligning it more closely with the underlying business needs, enhancing its maintainability, and ensuring its resilience to future changes.

You learned about the importance of thoroughly analyzing your code base before taking any action, recognizing potential pitfalls, and selecting the appropriate tools for the job. The chapter highlighted the critical role of testing in the refactoring process, emphasizing how a robust suite of tests acts as a safety net, allowing you to make changes with confidence that your application's integrity will be preserved.

Furthermore, you explored the application of key design principles, such as the SRP, OCP, DIP, and Strategy pattern. These principles will guide you in making incremental, manageable changes that lead to a cleaner, more maintainable, and more scalable system. The practical examples provided showed you how to tackle common challenges in refactoring, such as reducing tight coupling between services and transitioning toward a modular architecture.

As you move forward, the skills you've acquired—critical code analysis, comprehensive testing strategies, and the application of design principles—will empower you to refactor your code base effectively. This will ensure that your system remains agile, adaptable, and aligned with the evolving needs of your business domain, setting the stage for continued success in software development.

In the next chapter, we will start to refactor our monolithic code base into a well-organized modular monolith.

Get this book's PDF version and more

Scan the QR code (or go to `packtpub.com/unlock`). Search for this book by name, confirm the edition, and then follow the steps on the page.

UNLOCK NOW

Note: Keep your invoice handy. Purchases made directly from Packt don't require an invoice.

6

Transitioning from Chaos

In the previous chapters, we explored the challenges of navigating a tightly coupled monolithic architecture, using the tangled interactions between `SalesOrderService` and `WarehouseService` as a prime example. Now, it is time to bring structure to this chaos.

In this chapter, you will start to refactor your monolithic code base into a well-organized modular monolith using DDD principles. This transformation will not only improve maintainability and scalability but also align your software more closely with the core business domains it serves. You will learn how to identify core business domains, establish clear boundaries between components, and refactor tightly coupled services. By the end of this chapter, you'll be equipped with practical techniques to create a more manageable and efficient architecture that reflects business needs while reducing complexity.

In this chapter, we will cover the following:

- Identifying core business domains in a monolithic application
- Decoupling tightly coupled services using clear domain boundaries
- Applying DDD principles to refactor a monolithic code base
- Implementing the facade and mediator patterns to simplify interactions and reduce dependencies
- Creating modular architecture with clearly defined interfaces and responsibilities
- Setting up automated tests and fitness functions to ensure architectural integrity during refactoring

This chapter will guide you through practical steps and real-world examples, preparing you to refactor complex systems and ensure your software evolves in a structured, maintainable way.

The complete code for this chapter can be found at the following branch in the book's GitHub repository: `https://github.com/PacktPublishing/Domain-driven-Refactoring/tree/02-monolith_with_cqrs`.

Identifying core domains

When embarking on the refactoring of a monolithic application, it is common to encounter a code base that lacks clear boundaries around domain-specific areas. This is where DDD can help, but it is crucial to avoid common pitfalls, especially for first-time practitioners. One of the biggest mistakes is focusing too early on technical implementation details rather than on the business domain and its underlying logic. You learned about the complexity and problem space in *Chapter 2, Understanding Complexity: Problem and Solution Space*.

At this stage, the key is to prioritize business strategies. Your goal should be to deeply understand the business and its various subdomains and let that inform your design. Consider our ERP system and the `Customer` entity as an example. If you attempt to use a single `Customer` entity across multiple subdomains such as `Sales`, `Warehouses`, and `Purchases`, you will create unnecessary interdependencies. Changes to the `Customer` entity in one context (such as `Sales`) could unintentionally affect how the entity behaves in others, such as `Warehouses` or `Purchases`. This results in ambiguity and hinders the maintainability of the system. Instead, recognize that different subdomains might need their own version of `Customer` to reflect the specific needs of that area without creating a ripple effect across the system.

Imagine the sales team changes how orders are tracked, but because you are sharing the same `Customer` model across domains, it disrupts how the warehouse manages stock. Properly separating the domains lets you customize models for each part of the business without causing unintended ripple effects.

If you carefully observe the code in our ERP example, you will notice a significant issue of coupling within the `SalesOrderService` class. This class depends on two separate instances of the `IRepository` interface, meaning it has dependencies on both the `Sales` and `Warehouses` components. As a result, any change to the `IRepository` implementation for `Warehouse` will likely affect this class, even if the change is unrelated to `Sales`. This kind of tight coupling between components makes the system fragile and harder to maintain. It is a clear sign that the service is overly dependent on both contexts, creating unnecessary complexity.

In the next section, we will address this issue by focusing on decoupling these components. But the first crucial step is to establish clear boundaries between the Sales and Warehouse domains, allowing them to evolve independently without causing unintended side effects.

Understanding the business landscape

Identifying the right boundaries between components is a challenging task. It is not something that can be solved purely from a technical perspective. In these situations, you have to adopt the mindset of a software architect, which means understanding the broader business drivers and applying all the necessary trade-offs, not just focusing on the technical details. DDD offers valuable patterns to help identify these boundaries, but its true power lies in understanding the problem space. DDD emphasizes collaboration with customers and stakeholders, ensuring that your solutions are aligned with the business's needs, not just its technical requirements.

Figure 6.1 shows the boundaries of the contexts discovered in *Chapter 3*, *Strategic Patterns*:

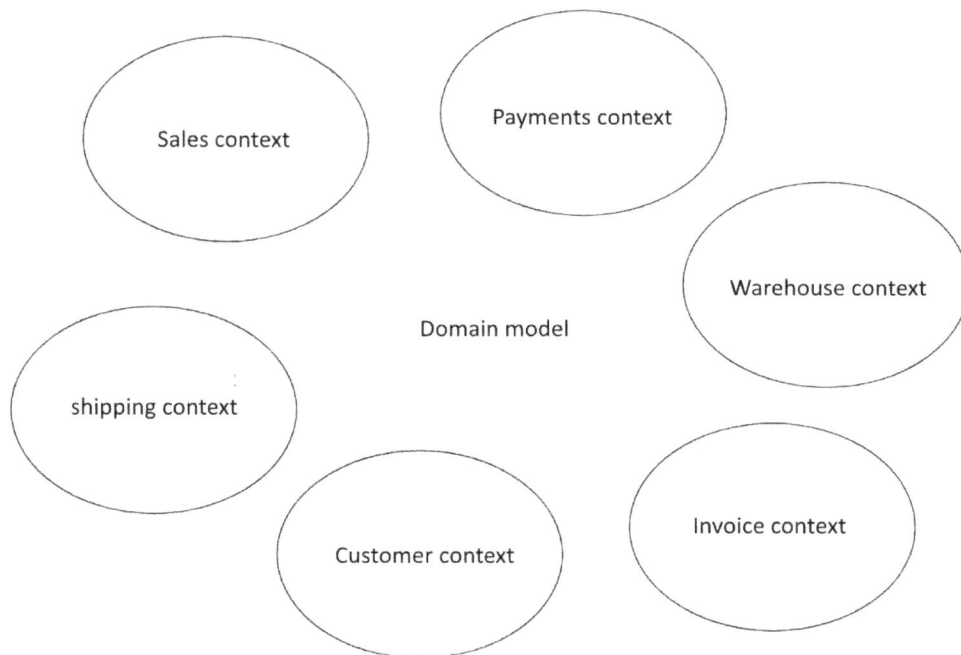

Figure 6.1 – Well-defined bounded contexts

The idea is to replicate in your code base the contexts that you discovered in your exploration phase.

To avoid common pitfalls, it is essential to leverage DDD to focus on the most critical and valuable parts of the domain. Identify the areas that deliver the highest business value and ensure your modeling aligns with the company's strategic objectives. Active collaboration with key business stakeholders is crucial for understanding their priorities and directing your efforts toward what matters most. By doing so, you ensure that your model accurately reflects the business's needs and contributes to achieving its strategic goals.

Equally important is establishing close collaboration with domain experts from the very first stages of the design and development process. Regular engagement with them ensures that your understanding of the domain remains accurate and aligned with business needs. Involving domain experts in discussions, design sessions, and model reviews allows you to gather critical insights that shape the model. Techniques such as EventStorming and Domain Storytelling are particularly effective for facilitating collaborative modeling, ensuring that the model genuinely reflects the domain and its intricacies.

When you run an EventStorming session, start by gathering key stakeholders—sales, warehouse, and IT leaders. Lay out the core business events from end to end. Have each stakeholder explain how their domain works and map their processes on a whiteboard. This gives you insight into where dependencies and bottlenecks are lurking in your code.

To foster collaborative discussions within your team and gain a comprehensive understanding of the core domain driving your system, it can be helpful to ask yourself these questions:

- **What are the primary functions of the systems?**: This question clarifies the essential capabilities the system must deliver, ensuring alignment with the system's core purpose.
- **Which business processes are most crucial?**: By identifying the most important business processes, you can prioritize system features that support the organization's key objectives.
- **How do different components interact to meet business requirements?**: Understanding the interaction between system components ensures that they work together harmoniously to fulfill the business's overall needs.

For instance, in our example, the key domains could include the following:

Sales: Responsible for managing customer orders, pricing, and promotions

Inventory: Focused on tracking stock levels and managing warehouse operations

Shipping: Handles the coordination of deliveries and logistics

By clearly defining these domains, you create a structure that mirrors the business's core processes. This approach not only makes the code base more organized but also ensures that each part of the system aligns with the specific business area it supports.

Mapping the current code base

Once you have identified the core domains, the next step is to analyze your existing code base to find bottlenecks and areas where the architecture needs improvement. To do this effectively, follow these guidelines:

- **Code analysis**: Review classes, methods, and modules to evaluate how well they align with newly identified domains
- **Dependency mapping**: Use visualization tools to map out dependencies between components and identify areas of tight coupling
- **Responsibility assessment**: Assess whether modules adhere to the single responsibility principle or whether they handle multiple, unrelated concerns

The goal at this stage is to decouple the logical connections in your current code base and design a new architecture that better reflects the business processes and requirements. As a software architect, you must continuously balance business needs with technology choices. This is where the importance of establishing a shared language and model becomes clear, ensuring that everyone, from developers to stakeholders, understands and operates within the same context.

So far, you may discover that `SalesOrderService` not only handles order processing but also updates inventory levels directly, indicating a violation of domain boundaries.

Identifying bounded contexts

In DDD, bounded contexts define the boundaries within which a particular domain model is valid. They help manage complexity by isolating domain models that might have overlapping concepts but different implementations.

One of the essential tools that DDD offers is the concept of **Ubiquitous Language**, which helps in defining clear boundaries around domain areas. The first step is learning to actively listen to your stakeholders and paying attention to the language they use to describe their business processes. Terminology disparities between the business and technical teams often lead to misunderstanding, misaligned implementations, and a need for constant synchronization to ensure accurate translation of business logic into code.

Thanks to Ubiquitous Language, you can do the following:

Define contexts: Establish the bounded contexts within each domain. For example, the `Sales` domain might have contexts such as `Order Management` and `Customer Relations`.

Clarify terminology: Ensure that within each context, terms and concepts are used consistently. This is known as establishing a ubiquitous language.

By identifying bounded contexts, you can prevent the accidental mixing of domain logic and maintain clarity in your code base.

Another aspect that we want to reiterate is that the model you will come up with is not a copy of reality but an unavoidable simplification of it. This is because humans tend to try to simplify complex matters.

As we dive into code refactoring, it is important to first understand the value of having tests in place. Tests act like a safety net; they make sure that as we clean up and improve the structure of the code, we are not unknowingly breaking things.

However, for simplicity, we will not dive into the details of test creation right now. We will cover all the necessary tests at the end of this chapter. For now, let us stay focused on the main task (code refactoring), which is all about making the code more readable, maintainable, and efficient without changing its functionality.

Establishing clear interfaces

Now, we can start to decouple `SalesOrderService` and `WarehouseService`. To do so, we need to apply the concepts reviewed in *Chapter 5, Introducing Refactoring Principles* and in the previous section, such as defining clear interfaces for the services so that we can encapsulate all their work to the outside world.

We want to restructure our project to reflect the domain boundaries. To do so, we need to do the following:

Physical separation: Organize code into separate directories or namespaces per domain

Logical separation: Ensure that classes and methods within a module pertain only to that domain

To achieve this, we can start by creating a *solution folder* named `Modules` with two subfolders named `Sales` and `Warehouses` in which we will create all the projects for the two bounded contexts.

In the Sales folder, we create a project named BrewUp.Sales.Domain, and the same in the Warehouses folder, this time named BrewUp.Warehouses.Domain. In these two projects, we move our aggregates and services as shown in *Figure 6.2*:

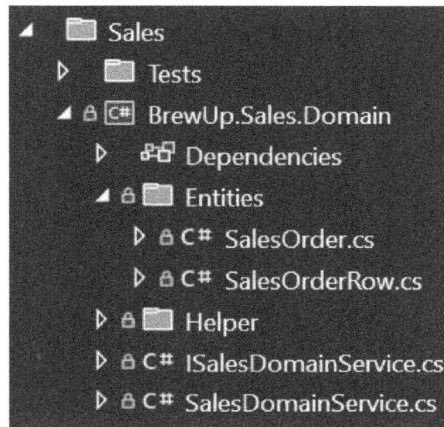

Figure 6.2 – The new Sales project

The same changes must be applied to the Warehouses module as shown in *Figure 6.3*:

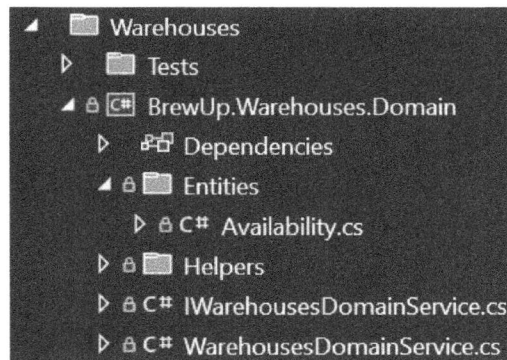

Figure 6.3 – The new Warehouses project

We moved the classes and interfaces from the generic BrewUp.DomainModel to two specific projects to start to isolate sales and warehouses and, of course, we also updated their namespaces.

So far so good, but what about persistence? Shall we remain with the generic BrewUp.Infrastructure project? That's right; of course, we cannot!

Every bounded context, as you already know, should be like a black box. It needs to have its own persistence. Let us start by creating the infrastructure projects for both `sales` and `warehouses` and move the relative repositories in them.

Basically, we want to move from the project of `01-monolith_legacy` (https://github.com/ PacktPublishing/Domain-driven-Refactoring/tree/01-monolith_legacy) in *Figure 6.4*:

Figure 6.4 –The old infrastructure project

To the ones in *Figure 6.5*:

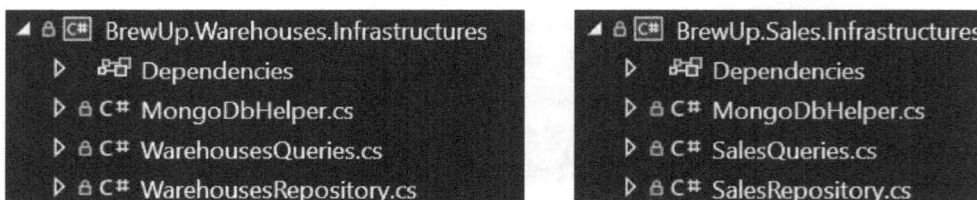

Figure 6.5 – The new infrastructure projects

This organization enhances readability and enforces the separation of concerns. Now that we have two well-defined groups of projects that map our bounded contexts, the next step will be to refactor the code base to create clear, well-defined interfaces.

We start by decoupling interdependencies. That is, identify tight couplings where one module depends heavily on the internal workings of another. In our case, `SalesOrderService` is calling methods deep within `WarehouseService`. It is time to introduce abstraction:

- **Introduce interfaces**: Define interfaces that expose only the necessary functionalities. Replace direct dependencies with interface implementations.

- **Apply the dependency inversion principle**: High-level modules should not be dependent on low-level modules; both should be dependent on abstraction.

This decoupling allows modules to evolve independently and reduces the risk of changes causing widespread issues.

To achieve this, we should create a *facade* for Sales and Warehouses so that the domain is not exposed outside, as shown for sales in *Figure 6.6*:

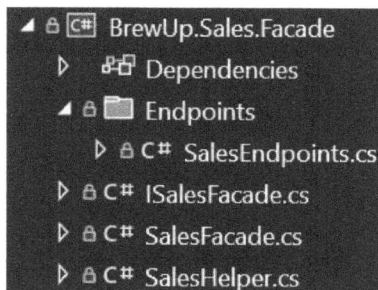

Figure 6.6 – The facade project for sales

And we will do the same for the Warehouses module.

Facade pattern

The **facade pattern** is a structural design pattern that provides a streamlined interface to a complex subsystem. It acts as a front-facing interface masking more complex underlying or structural code. At its core, the facade pattern is about simplification and abstraction, offering a higher-level interface that makes the subsystem easier to use while abstracting its complexities behind a single interface. This pattern is particularly useful when you need to provide a simple interface to a complex subsystem. By implementing a facade, you can significantly reduce the complexity that clients have to deal with, shielding them from the intricacies of subsystem components. The facade pattern shares some similarities with other design patterns. For instance, while the adapter pattern converts one interface to another, the facade pattern defines a new interface. The mediator pattern is also similar, but its primary purpose is to abstract communication between objects.

Let us look at the SalesFacade.cs code:

```
public sealed class SalesFacade(ISalesDomainService salesDomainService,
    ISalesQueryService salesQueryService) : ISalesFacade
{
```

```csharp
    public async Task<string> CreateOrderAsync(SalesOrderJson body,
CancellationToken cancellationToken)
    {
        if (body.SalesOrderId.Equals(string.Empty))
            body = body with { SalesOrderId = Guid.NewGuid().ToString() };

        await salesDomainService.CreateSalesOrderAsync(new
SalesOrderId(new Guid(body.SalesOrderId)),
            new SalesOrderNumber(body.SalesOrderNumber), new
OrderDate(body.OrderDate),
            new CustomerId(body.CustomerId), new CustomerName(body.
CustomerName),
            body.Rows, cancellationToken);

        return body.SalesOrderId;
    }

    public async Task<PagedResult<SalesOrderJson>>
GetOrdersAsync(CancellationToken cancellationToken)
    {
        return await salesQueryService.GetSalesOrdersAsync(0, 30,
cancellationToken);
    }
}
```

In the preceding code, we expose CreateOrderAsync and GetOrderAsync for the other components of the systems to encapsulate the inner working and domain models.

The last thing that is missing is a helper to register the module's services in the application.

We can easily do that by creating SalesHelper.cs with the following code:

```csharp
public static class SalesHelper
{
    public static IServiceCollection AddSales(this IServiceCollection
services)
    {
        services.AddFluentValidationAutoValidation();
```

```
            services.AddScoped<ISalesFacade, SalesFacade>();
            services.AddScoped<ISalesDomainService, SalesDomainService>();
            services.AddScoped<ISalesQueryService, SalesQueryService>();
            services.AddScoped<IQueries<SalesOrder>, SalesOrderQueries>();

            return services;
        }


        public static IServiceCollection AddSalesInfrastructure(this
    IServiceCollection services)
        {
            services.AddSalesMongoDb();

            return services;
        }
    }
```

The preceding code is straightforward and as simple as it could be; it grants a cleaner organization of components and their infrastructure initialization. We created two methods that register the services of the module for the dependency injection that we will instantiate in the startup of our application.

Because we are talking about modules, in our startup project called BrewUp.Rest, which exposes the endpoints to interact with our application, we decided to write a little helper that has the responsibility of loading all the modules and keeping the code tidy.

Basically, we define a module class that has the responsibility of calling all the startup code of the model it refers to, such as the one defined in SalesHelper.cs.

These modules implement our interface named IModule:

```
public interface IModule
{
    bool IsEnabled { get; }
    int Order { get; }

    IServiceCollection Register(WebApplicationBuilder builder);
    WebApplication Configure(WebApplication app);
}
```

The two properties, in the preceding code, are there to control the call order between modules (sometimes it needs to be instantiated before others) and whether that module should be loaded or not.

The two methods are called by the `ModuleExtensions` class, which has the responsibility of discovering all the classes that implement the `IModule` interface and call `Register` and `Configure`:

```
public static class ModuleExtensions
{
    private static readonly IList<IModule> RegisteredModules = new
List<IModule>();

    public static WebApplicationBuilder RegisterModules(this
WebApplicationBuilder builder)
    {
        var modules = DiscoverModules()
                .Where(m => m.IsEnabled)
                .OrderBy(m => m.Order);

        foreach (var module in modules)
        {
            module.Register(builder);
            RegisteredModules.Add(module);
        }

        return builder;
    }

    public static WebApplication ConfigureModules(this WebApplication app)
    {
        foreach (var module in RegisteredModules)
            module.Configure(app);

        return app;
    }
}
```

```
    private static IEnumerable<IModule> DiscoverModules()
    {
        return typeof(IModule).Assembly
                .GetTypes()
                .Where(p => p.IsClass &&
 p.IsAssignableTo(typeof(IModule)))
                .Select(Activator.CreateInstance)
                .Cast<IModule>();
    }
}
```

All the magic happens in the `DiscoverModules` method whereby, using reflection, we search all the classes that implement the `IModule` interface and create their instances.

With this code, we can instantiate all the module classes that we need without worrying about any startup file or configuration to update.

As a result, we will end up with a `program.cs` file without any kind of clutter, as in the following:

```
using BrewUp.Rest.Modules;

var builder = WebApplication.CreateBuilder(args);

builder.RegisterModules();

var app = builder.Build();

app.ConfigureModules();

app.Run();
```

What we are implementing can already be called **architectural quanta**. Because we are no longer focusing only on the code within the domain, we are already maintaining the infrastructure part. Databases, service buses, and so on are fundamental elements of our bounded context and, therefore, our module because they represent the operational part of it.

Architectural quanta

This concept refers to the smallest cohesive and autonomous unit within a software architecture that encapsulates a set of related functionalities. Each quantum has well-defined boundaries, a clear responsibility, and can operate independently or with minimal dependencies on other quanta. This concept aligns with the design principles of modularity, encapsulation, and separation of concerns. In DDD, a quantum often maps to a bounded context where each quantum can evolve independently, offering scalability, resilience, and flexibility in large, distributed systems, such as microservices. Quanta are the building blocks of a system's architecture, allowing for isolated changes and independent deployment. You can read more on the topic in the book *Fundamentals of Software Architecture* by Mark Richards and Neal Ford.

Now that everything is set up, we can start writing the glue that will hold all the components cohesively by using the mediator pattern.

Building the modular monolith

Since the modules are independent and decoupled from each other, we need to create something to orchestrate the calls between them. This is where the mediator pattern comes in.

The **mediator pattern** encourages the decoupling of components that need to work together by eliminating direct communication between them. Instead of interacting directly, these components communicate through a mediator that is responsible for coordinating their interactions. This approach reduces dependencies between components as they no longer need to know about each other and rely solely on the mediator. As a result, the system becomes more flexible and maintainable, with each component depending only on the mediator rather than being tightly coupled to several others. *Figure 6.7* shows a representation of the mediator pattern.

Figure 6.7 – The mediator pattern

Before diving into the code, let's take a quick look at how the mediator pattern differs from the facade pattern so as to understand when it is best to use one or the other.

Mediator versus facade

In a tightly coupled monolithic system, SalesOrderService needs to directly call methods in WarehouseService, leading to messy, fragile code. By applying the mediator pattern, you ensure that these services communicate through a centralized interface, reducing direct dependencies and making the code easier to maintain.

First, the **facade** and **mediator** patterns are both used to simplify and manage interactions between objects, but they serve distinct purposes and have different characteristics, especially when applied to DDD.

Purpose

From the *purpose* point of view, the facade pattern provides a simplified, unified interface to a set of subsystems or complex components. Its main goal is to reduce the complexity for clients by providing a higher-level abstraction. It does not control the communication between the subsystems; instead, it just makes the system easier to use by hiding complexity. The mediator pattern focuses on controlling and coordinating interactions between multiple objects or components. It centralizes the communication between components, so they do not communicate directly with each other but through the mediator. This leads to reduced coupling between components.

Applied to the DDD context, the facade could serve as a high-level interface that wraps multiple domain services, repositories, or even application services. It simplifies the way external clients interact with the domain without exposing its internals. The mediator, instead, can manage interactions between domain objects or between domain services. It orchestrates the flow of information between various entities, aggregates, or modules in a way that decouples them. This can be useful in complex domains where multiple aggregates need to collaborate to fulfill a business operation.

Interaction

Moving to the interaction between components, the facade could be seen as a one-way abstraction that simplifies the interaction for the client. The subsystems behind the facade are still independent, and the facade does not control or mediate communication between them. It is simply an entry point that hides the underlying complexity. The mediator, on the other hand, controls bidirectional communication between components. It ensures that components do not talk directly to each other, reducing dependencies between them. Instead, they interact with the mediator, which decides how to propagate actions and responses.

Decoupling

Lastly, the facade does not decouple the internal components or systems it represents. It is an entry point to a complex system that does not change how the subsystems interact with each other. The purpose is to decouple the client from the complexity of the underlying subsystems, not to decouple the subsystems from each other.

The mediator decouples the components it coordinates by making them communicate only through the mediator. This results in less direct dependency between components, making the system easier to modify, extend, or maintain.

In *Table 6.1*, we summarize the main differences between the facade and mediator patterns.

Aspect	Facade	Mediator
Purpose	Simplifies the interface for clients by hiding complexity	Centralizes and controls communication between components
Decoupling	Decouples the client from subsystems' complexity	Decouples components by mediating their communication
Interaction	One-way abstraction; does not control the interaction between components	Bidirectional interaction; controls the communication flow
Usage in DDD	Used in the application layer to simplify client access to domain services or APIs	Used in the domain layer to orchestrate interactions between aggregates, domain objects, or modules

Table 6.1 – A summary of differences between the facade and mediator patterns

Going back to our code, let us create a new solution folder named `Mediator` inside the `modules` folder. After that, we should start by defining an interface named `IBrewUpMediator.cs` as in the following:

```
public interface IBrewUpMediator
{
    Task<string> CreateOrderAsync(SalesOrderJson body, CancellationToken cancellationToken);
}
```

The concrete implementation would be like the following:

```
public class BrewUpMediator(ISalesFacade salesFacade, IWarehousesFacade warehouseFacade) : IBrewUpMediator
{
    public async Task<string> CreateOrderAsync(SalesOrderJson body, CancellationToken cancellationToken)
    {
        List<BeerAvailabilityJson> availabilities = new();

        foreach (var row in body.Rows)
        {
            var availability = await warehouseFacade.GetAvailabilityAsync(row.BeerId, cancellationToken);
```

```
        if (availability.TotalRecords > 0)
            availabilities.Add(availability.Results.First());
    }


        // Prepare the list of rows that are available for sale
        List<SalesOrderRowJson> rowsForSale = (from row in body.Rows
                                        let beerAvailability =
availabilities.Find(a => a.BeerId == row.BeerId.ToString())
                                        where beerAvailability !=
null && beerAvailability.Availability.Available >= row.Quantity.Value
                                        select row).ToList();


        if (rowsForSale.Count == 0)
        {
            return "No beer available for sale";
        }


        body = body with { Rows = rowsForSale };
        return await salesFacade.CreateOrderAsync(body,
cancellationToken);
    }
}
```

In this way, we expose the method for creating an order so that `sales` and `warehouse` remain isolated and decoupled.

However, for everything to work, we must add one last thing. We need to create a couple of resources for our API endpoints so that the external clients can call our mediator's methods.

We can do that by creating `MediatorEndpoints.cs` in the `BrewUp.Mediator` project:

```
public static class MediatorEndpoints
{
    public static WebApplication MapMediatorEndpoints(this WebApplication
app)
    {
        var group = app.MapGroup("/v1/brewup/")
            .WithTags("BrewUp");
```

```
        group.MapPost("/", HandleCreateOrder)
            .Produces(StatusCodes.Status400BadRequest)
            .Produces(StatusCodes.Status201Created)
            .WithName("OrderBeers");

        return app;
    }


    public static async Task<IResult> HandleCreateOrder(
        IBrewUpMediator mediator,
        IValidator<SalesOrderJson> validator,
        ValidationHandler validationHandler,
        SalesOrderJson body,
        CancellationToken cancellationToken)
    {

        await validationHandler.ValidateAsync(validator, body);
        if (!validationHandler.IsValid)
            return Results.BadRequest(validationHandler.Errors);

        var orderId = await mediator.CreateOrderAsync(body,
cancellationToken);

        return Results.Created($"/v1/brewup/orders/{orderId}", orderId);
    }
}
```

In this class, other than exposing the endpoints, we also validate the inbound payload. We will not cover in detail how we do this because it is out of the scope of this book, but just know that we used the FluentValidation library that leverages all the invariants in a fluent approach. You can find the complete implementation in 02-monolith_with_cqrs in this book's GitHub repository (https://github.com/PacktPublishing/Domain-driven-Refactoring/tree/02-monolith_with_cqrs).

With everything in place, you should have a project like the one in *Figure 6.8*.

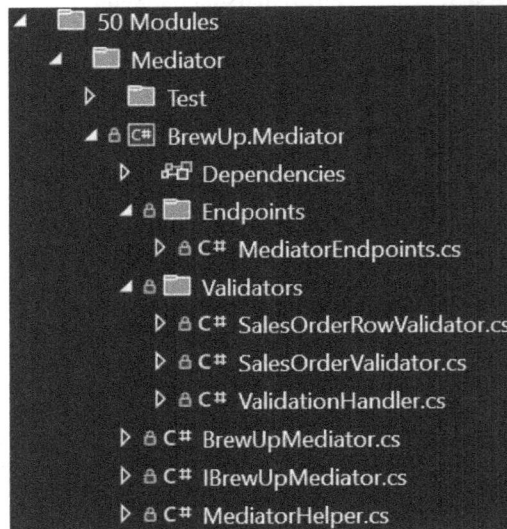

Figure 6.8 – The complete Mediator project

As stated at the beginning of this chapter, we chose to focus first on the refactoring of the code and then move to the testing part, but keep in mind that before starting with refactoring, it is mandatory to create the safety net that guarantees that we are not altering any functionality during the process.

Testing and stabilizing

Before starting refactoring, it is essential to have established **end-to-end (E2E)** tests to ensure the stability of the code base and to prevent introducing regressions or bugs.

In *Chapter 5*, within the *Understanding tests and role in refactoring* section, you can find a detailed explanation of the E2E tests. The purpose of these tests is to verify that when you invoke an endpoint, the response matches your expectations. As outlined in *Chapter 5*, these tests play a crucial role in ensuring that refactoring does not introduce unintended side effects. You can see an example of this approach here:

```
[Fact]
public async Task Can_Create_SalesOrder()
{
```

```
    DateTime now = DateTime.UtcNow;
    SalesOrderJson body = new(Guid.NewGuid().ToString(),
        $"{now.Year:0000}{now.Month:00}{now.Day:00}-{now.Hour:00}{now.
Minute:00}",
        Guid.NewGuid(), "Customer",
        now, new List<SalesOrderRowJson>
        {
            new()
            {
                BeerId = Guid.NewGuid(),
                BeerName = "BrewUp IPA",
                Quantity = new(10, "Lt"),
                Price = new(5, "EUR")
            }
        });

    var stringJson = JsonSerializer.Serialize(body);
    var httpContent = new StringContent(stringJson, Encoding.UTF8,
"application/json");
    var postResult = await integrationFixture.Client.PostAsync("/v1/
sales", httpContent);

    Assert.Equal(HttpStatusCode.Created, postResult.StatusCode);
}
```

This is the behavior that your system exhibits before starting the code refactoring, and you must ensure that remains the behavior after you complete your work.

However, as you make architectural decisions, such as choosing modularity, it is equally important to protect these decisions as your system evolves. To achieve this, you need to ensure that everyone on your team maintains architectural integrity and avoids creating unnecessary coupling or technical debt. Since your goal is to evolve incrementally, the next critical step is to establish tests at the architectural level. These tests will ensure that the design principles and structure you have implemented remain intact as the system grows and changes.

An evolutionary architecture thrives on guided incremental changes. In a physics analogy, software systems resemble complex systems that naturally drift toward disorder, much like physical systems tend toward entropy. Just as energy is needed to maintain order in a physical system, software systems also require continuous effort. Software architects must consistently invest time and resources to maintain the structural integrity of the system, as it will not stay organized on its own.

As an architect, it is your responsibility to provide tools that ensure this guidance, and to be truly effective, these tools need to be automated. In the book titled *Building Evolutionary Architectures* authored by Neal Ford, Rebecca Parsons, and Patrick Kua, the authors describe a family of techniques, called **fitness functions**, which are used to automate many aspects of architectural governance. Fitness functions are essential in helping you monitor and enforce architectural principles as the system evolves, ensuring the architecture stays aligned with its intended goals.

Fitness functions

Fitness functions describe how well an architecture aligns with its intended goals. In test-driven development, you write tests to verify that features meet desired outcomes. Similarly, in fitness function-driven development, you write tests to measure how closely the system adheres to architectural objectives. These tests help you verify that your architecture continues to meet its intended purpose as the system evolves.

Fortunately, there are libraries available to help you implement fitness functions directly in your code without effort. For Java developers, ArchUnit (https://www.archunit.org/) offers a robust solution, while .NET developers can use NetArchTest (https://github.com/BenMorris/NetArchTest). These libraries allow you to define and enforce architectural rules, ensuring that your system remains modular and follows the intended design principles.

Here is an example from our ERP system, demonstrating how to ensure that the Sales module does not depend on any other modules. The following fitness function helps protect the module's isolation and ensures that no unintended dependencies are introduced over time:

```
[Fact]
public void Should_SalesArchitecture_BeCompliant()
{
```

```
    var types = Types.InAssembly(typeof(SalesFacade).Assembly);

    var forbiddenAssemblies = new List<string>
    {
        "BrewUp.Warehouses.Domain",
        "BrewUp.Warehouses.Infrastructures",
        "BrewUp.Warehouses.ReadModel",
        "BrewUp.Warehouses.SharedKernel"
    };

    var result = types
        .ShouldNot()
        .HaveDependencyOnAny(forbiddenAssemblies.ToArray())
        .GetResult()
        .IsSuccessful;

    Assert.True(result);
}
```

This test demonstrates how to implement a fitness function using NetArchTest to ensure that the Sales module in our ERP system does not have any unintended dependencies on another module, such as the Warehouse module.

The preceding piece of code can be broken down as follows:

- Types.InAssembly(typeof(SalesFacade).Assembly); selects all types within the Sales module's assembly, which, in this case, is the assembly where SalesFacade is defined.
- forbiddenAssemblies is the list of assemblies that the Sales module should not depend upon, such as Warehouses.Domain, Warehouses.Infrastructure, Warehouses.ReadModel, and Warehouses.SharedKernel
- ShouldNot().HaveDependencyOnAny(forbiddenAssemblies.ToArray()) asserts that the types in the Sales module should not have dependencies on any of the forbidden assemblies listed.
- GetResult().IsSuccessfull evaluates the result of the dependency check to determine whether the test passed or not.

- `Assert.True(result)` finally asserts that the result is true, meaning the `Sales` module is free from unwanted dependencies. If there are dependencies, the test fails, flagging a violation of the architecture.

Refactoring is not complete until the new structure is robust and reliable. Introducing a modular architecture ensures that each module within your code base operates independently. The system's entry points, such as REST endpoints, should avoid direct dependencies on any module's internal logic. Such dependencies increase complexity and maintenance overhead by necessitating adjustments to the REST layer when modifying modules. To ensure independence, a fitness function can test that the REST project, `BrewUp.Rest`, relies solely on each module's facade. Here is an example of such a fitness function:

```
[Fact]
public void Should_BrewUpArchitecture_BeCompliant()
{
    var types = Types.InAssembly(typeof(Program).Assembly);

    var forbiddenAssemblies = new List<string>
    {
        "BrewUp.Sales.Domain",
        "BrewUp.Sales.Infrastructures",
        "BrewUp.Sales.ReadModel",
        "BrewUp.Sales.SharedKernel",
        "BrewUp.Warehouses.Domain",
        "BrewUp.Warehouses.Infrastructures",
        "BrewUp.Warehouses.ReadModel",
        "BrewUp.Warehouses.SharedKernel"
    };

    var result = types
        .ShouldNot()
        .HaveDependencyOnAny(forbiddenAssemblies.ToArray())
        .GetResult()
        .IsSuccessful;

    Assert.True(result);
}
```

As you can see, in the preceding example, `forbiddenAssemblies` is the list of the projects inside each module, and the test asserts that there are no direct dependencies with them.

Summary

In this chapter, you tackled the challenge of transforming a chaotic monolithic code base into a well-organized modular monolith using DDD principles. You learned how to identify core domains and establish clear boundaries between components such as `Sales` and `Warehouse`, addressing issues of tight coupling and improving maintainability.

You explored the process of mapping the current code base, identifying bounded contexts, and establishing clear interfaces. You were also introduced to the concept of architectural quanta and showed how to implement it in your project structure. You learned about the differences between the facade and mediator patterns, and how to apply them effectively in your architecture.

The chapter guided you through building a modular monolith, demonstrating how to create a mediator to orchestrate communication between decoupled modules. You saw practical examples of how to implement these patterns in code, including the creation of endpoints for your API.

And last but not least, you learned about the critical role of testing in the refactoring process. The chapter emphasized the importance of end-to-end tests as a safety net before refactoring, and introduced you to the concept of fitness functions. You saw how to use tools such as `NetArchTest` to create automated tests that enforce architectural principles and prevent unintended dependencies between modules.

You acquired valuable skills in refactoring complex systems, implementing modular architectures, and using automated tests to maintain architectural integrity. These skills will help you create more maintainable, scalable, and robust software systems as you continue to develop your expertise in software development and architecture.

In the next chapter, you will start to implement **Command Query Responsibility Segregation (CQRS)**, at first, without events, and then you will implement them too. You will also learn how to start testing event-driven architecture.

7

Integrating Events with CQRS

In this chapter, you will explore how to effectively integrate events into your system using the **Command Query Responsibility Segregation (CQRS)** pattern. As software architectures shift from monolithic designs to more modular, distributed systems, adopting event-driven communication becomes essential. This approach offers scalability, decoupling, and resilience, but also brings complexity and challenges such as eventual consistency, fault tolerance, and infrastructure management.

The primary goal of this chapter is to guide you through the implementation of event-driven mechanisms within the context of a CQRS architecture. By the end of this chapter, you will have a clear understanding of how events and commands operate in tandem to manage state changes, communicate between services, and optimize both the reading and writing of data.

In this chapter, you will learn about the following:

- The benefits and trade-offs of transitioning from synchronous to asynchronous communication
- How event-driven architectures improve system scalability and decoupling
- The difference between commands (which trigger state changes) and events (which signal that something has happened)
- How to apply proper message-handling patterns for both
- The principles of CQRS and understanding why separating read and write models enhances performance and scalability
- How to implement the separation of command and query responsibilities with a focus on read and write optimization
- How to introduce a message broker for handling asynchronous communication

- How to capture and replay the history of state changes with event sourcing
- A way to test event-driven systems, ensuring the stability and correctness of aggregates through specification testing

This chapter will provide you with a comprehensive understanding of integrating events into your CQRS architecture, allowing you to build robust, scalable, and decoupled systems.

The complete code for this chapter can be found within the `02-monolith_with_cqrs` branch (`https://github.com/PacktPublishing/Domain-driven-Refactoring/tree/02-monolith_with_cqrs`) and the `03-monolith_with_cqrs_and_event_sourcing` branch (`https://github.com/PacktPublishing/Domain-driven-Refactoring/tree/03-monolith_with_cqrs_and_event_sourcing`) within the book's GitHub repository.

Understanding the role of messages in a modular monolith

One of the fundamental steps in moving from a monolithic architecture to a microservice-based solution is to adopt events to facilitate communication between different modules. Introducing events into a modular architecture can significantly enhance the design by enabling systems to be more loosely coupled, scalable, and reactive. Of course, as discussed in previous chapters, every architectural change comes with trade-offs. Replacing synchronous communication with asynchronous event-based messaging introduces a new set of challenges, which can be summarized as shown in *Table 7.1*:

Aspect	Event-Driven	Direct Communication
Communication	Asynchronous Decoupled	Synchronous Tightly coupled
Scalability	Highly scalable	Easier to optimize for low-latency, real-time use
Consistency	Eventual consistency Complex synchronization	Immediate consistency but tightly coupled
Fault tolerance	More resilient Fault isolation	Real-time feedback but prone to cascading failures
Complexity	Complex infrastructure and eventual consistency	Simpler to implement but complex for scaling

Table 7.1 – Event-driven versus direct communication

As you can see, introducing events into an application requires careful consideration of the pros and cons, since this choice fundamentally alters how different parts of your system interact. Your code base will evolve to accommodate these changes, which can affect the way you handle data consistency, fault tolerance, and scalability.

But before diving into the code to see how events reshape your application, it is important to understand the different types of messages and their specific purpose within this architecture.

Commands versus events

It is crucial to distinguish between the different types of messages in your system, as each serves a distinct purpose and requires different handling patterns. **Commands** are messages that change the state of an aggregate. These are direct instructions that typically represent user actions or business requests, such as placing an order or updating its state. On the other hand, **events** are messages that notify other parts of the system that something has happened, such as an order being placed or a payment being accepted, but they do not alter the aggregate's state.

While we will dive deeper into these concepts in the following sections, it is important to understand the different messaging patterns you need to apply depending on the message type. Commands usually follow a **fire-and-forget pattern**. A command is sent to a specific component that is responsible for executing it, ensuring that the requested action is performed.

To ensure reliable processing of commands—especially in asynchronous systems—the **send-receive pattern** or the **producer-consumer pattern** is often used. In this pattern, a producer sends a command message, which is then consumed and processed by one or more consumers. *Figure 7.1* illustrates this pattern.

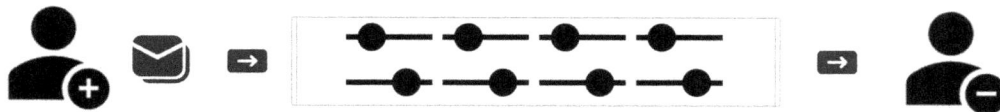

Figure 7.1 – Producer-consumer pattern

In contrast, events are handled using a **publish-subscribe pattern**, where the event is published and multiple components interested in this event can subscribe and react to it independently. *Figure 7.2* shows the *publish-subscribe* pattern. Each published message is made available to each subscription registered with the topic.

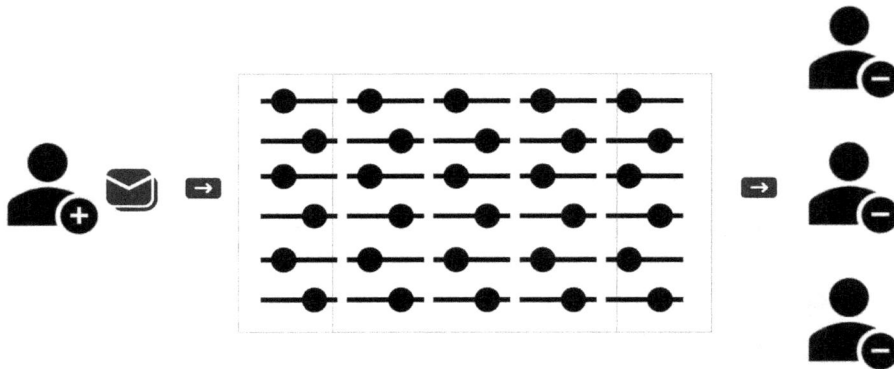

Figure 7.2 – Publish-subscribe pattern

Recognizing these differences will help you select the appropriate messaging pattern for each scenario, ensuring your system is designed efficiently and operates in a predictable manner.

Understanding the different types of messages in your system is crucial, as they directly reflect the business intent in your code, as you discovered in the *EventStorming* subsection in *Chapter 2, Understanding Complexity: Problem and Solution Space.*

By appropriately using message types, you replicate the business intent within your application architecture, enabling a clearer alignment between the business process and the code. For instance, implementing commands ensures that actions are executed as intended, while events allow for the decoupling of components, facilitating communication across the system. Recognizing the *publish-subscribe pattern* for events will help maintain a robust and responsive system that mirrors the underlying business logic.

When designing a system using commands and events, it is essential that the naming of each message clearly conveys its business intent. The name of a message should instantly communicate whether it is meant to trigger an action or report a past occurrence, ensuring your code is easy to understand and maintain.

For commands, the name should be in the imperative form, as they represent requests or instructions for actions that need to be executed. A command tells the system what the user or business process wants to happen. Look at the following command from our ERP example project:

```
public class CreateSalesOrder(SalesOrderId aggregateId,
    Guid commitId,
    SalesOrderNumber salesOrderNumber,
    OrderDate orderDate,
```

```
        CustomerId customerId,
        CustomerName customerName,
        IEnumerable<SalesOrderRowDto> rows)
        : Command(aggregateId, commitId)
{
    public readonly SalesOrderId SalesOrderId = aggregateId;
    public readonly SalesOrderNumber SalesOrderNumber = salesOrderNumber;
    public readonly OrderDate OrderDate = orderDate;

    public readonly CustomerId CustomerId = customerId;
    public readonly CustomerName CustomerName = customerName;

    public readonly IEnumerable<SalesOrderRowDto> Rows = rows;
}
```

The name of the command, CreateSalesOrder, makes the intent clear: The user wants to create a new order. Other than that, there are other important aspects in this class, but for now, it is important to pay attention to its name.

For events, the name should be in the past tense because they represent something that has already happened in the system. Events notify other parts of the system that a particular business operation has been completed. The following is the event related to the command shown before:

```
public sealed class SalesOrderCreated(SalesOrderId aggregateId,
    Guid commitId,
    SalesOrderNumber salesOrderNumber,
    OrderDate orderDate,
    CustomerId customerId,
    CustomerName customerName,
    IEnumerable<SalesOrderRowDto> rows) : DomainEvent(aggregateId,
commitId)
{
    public readonly SalesOrderId SalesOrderId = aggregateId;
    public readonly SalesOrderNumber SalesOrderNumber = salesOrderNumber;
    public readonly OrderDate OrderDate = orderDate;

    public readonly CustomerId CustomerId = customerId;
    public readonly CustomerName CustomerName = customerName;
```

```
    public readonly IEnumerable<SalesOrderRowDto> Rows = rows;
}
```

The name of the event, `SalesOrderCreated`, clearly indicates that the action has already occurred, allowing subscribers to react accordingly. This makes the event's purpose explicit and easy to understand.

By using the imperative form for commands and the past tense form for events, you not only make the business intent explicit in your code but you also create a common language between developers and domain experts, ensuring consistency and clarity throughout the system. Remember what we discussed about ubiquitous language in the section titled *Defining terms clearly will solve half of the problem* in *Chapter 3, Strategic Patterns*.

Domain and integration events

Now that you understand the difference between commands and events, it is time to take things a step further. While the primary purpose of an event is to notify other parts of the system that a particular business operation has been completed, not all parts of the system should receive this notification. Because an event carries important business information, it must be treated carefully. Specifically, we need to differentiate between events that belong within a bounded context and those that can be shared across contexts.

A **domain event** is an event that captures something meaningful that happened within a specific bounded context. These events express business intent and are often tied closely to the internal logic and rules of that context. Since each bounded context operates with its ubiquitous language and domain model, domain events are typically meant to stay within the boundaries of that context, ensuring that the integrity of the model is preserved without unnecessary coupling to the other parts of the system.

However, some events need to be shared between bounded contexts, especially when the actions in one context impact another. In this case, we use **integration events**. These events are designed to share information across contexts or even systems, without tightly coupling them. An integration event should contain only the essential data needed by other contexts to react to it while keeping the contexts independent. By carefully identifying which events should stay local (domain events) and which can be shared (integration events), you can avoid unnecessary coupling and ensure that the boundaries between contexts are respected.

Domain and integration events

A domain event remains within the boundaries of a single bounded context and reflects business operations relevant to that domain. On the other hand, an integration event is used to communicate with other bounded contexts or systems, enabling them to stay loosely coupled while still reacting to important changes.

Understanding this distinction helps ensure that your system stays modular and scalable and maintains a clear separation of concerns.

When transitioning your code base to asynchronous communication, it becomes necessary to introduce a message broker into your system. In an event-driven architecture, the broker acts as an intermediary that ensures events are properly delivered to the appropriate consumers, enabling components to communicate asynchronously without needing direct interaction.

We will dive deeper into this topic in *Chapter 11, Dealing with Events and Their Evolution* .

Separating command and query responsibilities

Before jumping to the implementation of events in the monolith, let's look at **CQRS**. This concept was introduced in the *Towards cleaner and more maintainable code* section in *Chapter 5, Introducing Refactoring Principles*. To review the flow of CQRS, you can refer to *Figure 5.6* in the same section. So, if you need a refresher on its origin and fundamental workings, go back for a quick review before reading further.

In *Chapter 6, Transitioning from Chaos*, we started refactoring our monolith, and the last thing missing is to implement CQRS without events yet.

The key concept of CQRS is the separation of responsibilities of reading and writing data within a system. In a typical application, the same model is often used for both querying (reading) and updating (writing) data. However, with CQRS, these concerns are separated into distinct models; the command model (write model) is responsible for handling commands, which are operations that change the state of the system (e.g., creating, updating, or deleting records) and the query model (read model) is optimized for reading data and retrieving information. The query model can be structured differently from the write model to support efficient queries, often focusing on the performance and scalability of read operations.

By separating these responsibilities, CQRS allows each model to be optimized independently. For example, the read model might denormalize data to make querying faster, while the write model can remain normalized to ensure consistency during updates. So, CQRS encourages the use of distinct models for reads and writes, which can lead to better scalability, maintainability, and performance in complex systems. *Figure 7.3* shows how a CQRS application works.

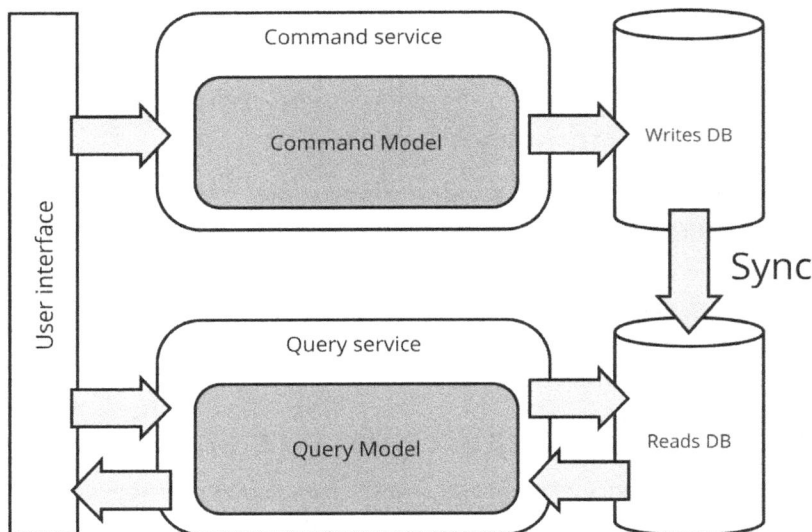

Figure 7.3 – A CQRS application's working

What you should have noticed immediately is that we have two distinct databases (schemas): one for the write model and one for the read model. Be aware that this does not mean that you should also have two distinct database instances. You could have just one instance of your database server with two different schemas in it (the databases).

Another important thing to keep in mind is the choice of the synchronization option between the two models. There are various ways to achieve that and, maybe, the most efficient is by using **event sourcing**. Using events to communicate the domain's state changes allows us to achieve better scalability and performance in a distributed or high-traffic system. The trade-off, because you know there is no silver bullet, is called **eventual consistency**. Eventual consistency means that we accept that data may be temporarily inconsistent between the write and read models but guarantees that all parts of the system will eventually reflect the latest state.

There are several strategies to synchronize the write and read models, each with its own trade-offs in terms of complexity, consistency, and performance. Before introducing event-based synchronization, let's first explore simpler approaches—starting with direct database synchronization—before moving on to options like database polling, materialized views, shared databases, and database triggers.

Direct database synchronization

Direct database synchronization involves synchronous dual writes, where the write model (command handler) directly updates both the write store and the read store at the same time when processing a command. For example, when a command updates the state (e.g., changing a user profile), the system can immediately update both the write database and the read database.

To maintain consistency, both the write and read models must be updated atomically in the same transaction, or compensating actions (rollback) should be implemented in case one update fails. There can still be a slight lag between these updates if they are processed in sequence or through separate database connections, resulting in eventual consistency.

The challenge here is that the write model becomes more complex because it must handle two updates directly, potentially slowing down the command handling process.

If one update succeeds and the other fails, you need robust error handling and rollback mechanisms.

Database polling

Database polling is an approach where the read model periodically polls the write model or the write database for changes. This involves checking for new or updated data at regular intervals (e.g., every few seconds or minutes) and updating the read-optimized views or caches accordingly.

This process introduces eventual consistency because the read model will eventually get the updated data, but there will be a delay between the write operation and when the read side reflects the changes. The tricky part of this solution is determining how often to poll the write model, as the polling interval introduces a time lag. If the interval is too long, the read model might be outdated for longer periods. On the other hand, polling too frequently could increase database load and performance overhead.

Materialized views

Materialized views are essentially snapshots of query results stored as actual tables, and they can be periodically refreshed to reflect changes in the write model. So, the read model could be derived as a materialized view in the database, where the read store automatically reflects changes made to the write store.

In this case, the database itself maintains the read side by listening for changes to the write model and updating the read model accordingly.

Materialized views depend on the underlying database technology, and it is not updated in real time but only reflects changes after a refresh. The databases update materializes views asynchronously, which results in eventual consistency rather than strong consistency.

Keep in mind that, as per the polling approach, refreshing materialized views frequently can add extra load to the database. On top of that, scaling this approach can become difficult if you have complex read models or if the underlying database is under heavy load.

Shared database

Shared database is an approach where both the write and read models use the same database, but the query layer is optimized differently for each model. The read model queries the same tables as the write model, but the queries are optimized using indexes, denormalization, or caching strategies to ensure fast reads.

As a result, this approach doesn't involve distinct synchronization, because the read and write models are working on the same underlying data. Beware that since both models share the same database, there is less separation of concerns, which reduces the benefits of CQRS in terms of scalability and flexibility.

Database triggers

Database triggers are a replication technique where the write and read databases are synchronized through the database system itself. Triggers automatically propagate changes from the write model's database to the read model, handling synchronization whenever data is updated.

The only advantage of this solution is that you demand the burden of updating the read model to the database without requiring explicit logic in the application.

As with the materialized views, you are heavily depending on the database technology, which could also lead to performance bottlenecks if overused and delays in the update process.

More importantly, issues in triggers can be hard to debug compared to explicit application code. That's why you should be discouraged from following this path except for some really niche cases during your refactoring process.

Before we move on, let us look at *Table 7.2* which summarizes the pros and cons of all the approaches we have discussed in this section.

Method	Pros	Cons
Direct database synchronization	Immediate consistency Simple to implement	Performance overhead Complex error handling and rollback
Database polling	Loose coupling Less immediate complexity	Data staleness due to polling interval Increased load on the database from frequent polling
Materialized views	Read optimization Simplified synchronization process	Refresh lag between updates Frequent refreshes can add database load
Shared database	No data synchronization needed Query optimization for performance	Lack of decoupling Reduces the separation of concerns inherent in CQRS
Database triggers	Automatic synchronization Consistent state as long as trigger fires	Database-dependent Harder to debug compared to application-level logic

Table 7.2 – Pros and cons of different synchronization options

Going back to our ERP application, it is time to add the missing piece to complete the first step of our refactoring journey: the read model. Let us see how we implemented it in 02-monolith_with_ cqrs of our application. To do that, let's start with a new project in the Sales folder named BrewUp. Sales.ReadModel and in the Warehouses folder named BrewUp.Warehouses.ReadModel. Inside these projects, we will create Data Transfer Objects (DTOs) and services to query the read model.

As usual, during the refactoring process, to keep complexity at bay, you should opt for the simplest solution possible in your context. For this first step, we opted for the **shared database** option to not touch the database yet. You will see the strategies to better approach database refactoring in *Chapter 8, Refactoring the Database*.

That said, we want to create classes and services for the Sales bounded context, as shown in *Figure 7.4*.

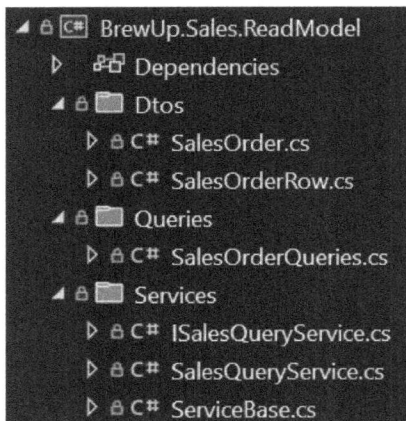

Figure 7.4 – Sales read model

We also want to do this for the Warehouses bounded context, as shown in *Figure 7.5*.

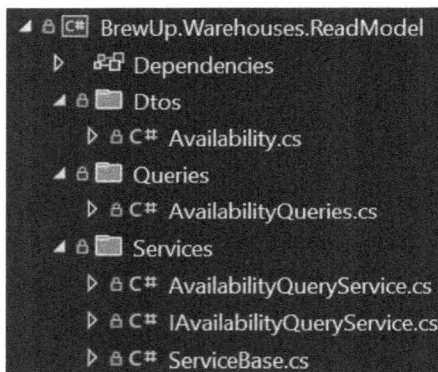

Figure 7.5 – Warehouses read model

For starters, we created a DtoBase class in BrewUp.Shared.ReadModel and then specific DTOs named SalesOrder, SalesOrderRow, and Availability in the Dtos folders.

These classes are mirroring the ones in the domain model folder for both Sales and Warehouses.

The code is straightforward. Let's just look at availability.cs as an example:

```
public class Availability : DtoBase
{
    public string BeerId { get; private set; } = string.Empty;
```

```
    public string BeerName { get; private set; } = string.Empty;

    public Quantity Quantity { get; private set; } = new(0, string.Empty);

    protected Availability()
    {
    }

    public static Availability Create(BeerId beerId, BeerName beerName,
Quantity quantity)
    {
        return new Availability(beerId.Value.ToString(), beerName.Value,
quantity);
    }

    private Availability(string beerId, string beerName, Quantity
quantity)
    {
        Id = beerId;

        BeerId = beerId;
        BeerName = beerName;
        Quantity = quantity;
    }

    public BeerAvailabilityJson ToJson() => new(Id, BeerName, new Shared.
CustomTypes.Availability(0, Quantity.Value, Quantity.UnitOfMeasure));
}
```

This DTO mirrors the structure of the corresponding domain entity but is designed for the read model. It simplifies data transfer by focusing solely on the properties needed for querying, without the complexity of domain behavior.

Next, we moved the queries and services to their respective folders and changed the using clauses from BrewUp.Shared.Entities to BrewUp.Shared.ReadModel to use the new DTO classes.

This allowed us to switch from the domain model to the read model without changing the underlying service and query logic.

By doing so, we achieved a CQRS-like structure that clearly separates the read and write concerns. It is now time to move to the next step and explore how to implement event sourcing.

Capturing state changes with events

So far, you have learned about the differences between commands and domain events. Now, let's dive deeper into the impact of choosing an event-driven aggregate solution instead of a more traditional CRUD approach.

Before starting, a quick disclaimer: as you saw earlier, using CQRS does not necessarily require using event sourcing. However, incorporating event sourcing into your design can give your application a significant boost. But it also brings extra complexity; like everything in software architecture, it is a trade-off.

The key benefit of an event-driven approach lies in how you manage state changes. In a traditional CRUD system, you are storing only the current state of the aggregate. Each time an update occurs, the new state overwrites the previous one. While this is simple, you are losing all the information on how your aggregate has arrived at its current state.

In *Figure 7.6*, you can observe the usual behavior of a CRUD system. A customer places an order, and at the beginning, its state is Pending with the amount the customer owes, which is €500.00.

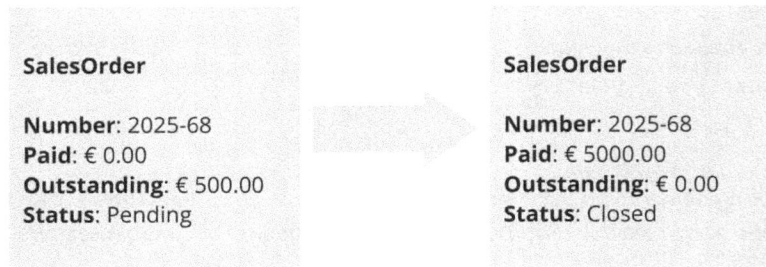

SalesOrder	SalesOrder
Number: 2025-68	**Number**: 2025-68
Paid: € 0.00	**Paid**: € 5000.00
Outstanding: € 500.00	**Outstanding**: € 0.00
Status: Pending	**Status**: Closed

Figure 7.6 – Example of CRUD

After the customer's payment, the SalesOrder status is Closed and the amount the customer owes is €0.00.

In an event-sourced system, the status change would be captured as an event, as in *Figure 7.7*.

SalesOrder

Number: 2025-68
Paid: € 0.00
Outstanding: € 500.00
Status: Pending

SalesOrder

Number: 2025-68
Paid: € 5000.00
Outstanding: € 0.00
Status: Closed

SalesOrderPaymentReceived

Number: 2025-68
Amount: € 500.00
Status: Closed

Figure 7.7 – Event-sourced system

Because the change of state has been captured, you not only have the same result but also the business action that you applied to obtain it.

With domain events, you shift from merely recording the last known state of the aggregate to capturing each meaningful change over time. Instead of storing just the result, you are saving the entire history of state changes through domain events. Each event is an important piece of something that happened within your domain and that composes the aggregate's story. This makes it easier to track the lifecycle of the aggregate, understand its business decisions, and even rewind or audit changes. Now you have the movie of the aggregate, not just the picture!

Capturing a historical record through domain events makes both traceability and auditability possible, especially in systems where legal compliance, financial auditing, or business transparency is essential. **Traceability** refers to the ability to track the sequence of changes and understand how the system reached its current state, while **auditability** ensures that every change can be verified and justified for compliance or regulatory purposes.

Now that we've seen how capturing domain events enhances traceability and auditability, it's important to understand how this fits into the overall system architecture.

Integrating Event Sourcing into CQRS Architecture

Event sourcing transforms how the system handles state changes, particularly when combined with the CQRS pattern. This integration ensures not only reliable data handling but also consistent, verifiable state transitions.

Figure 7.8 illustrates how CQRS architecture evolves when event sourcing is introduced. While this architectural flow was briefly discussed in *Chapter 5*, it's crucial to revisit it now in the context of how domain events shape the system's behavior and data flow.

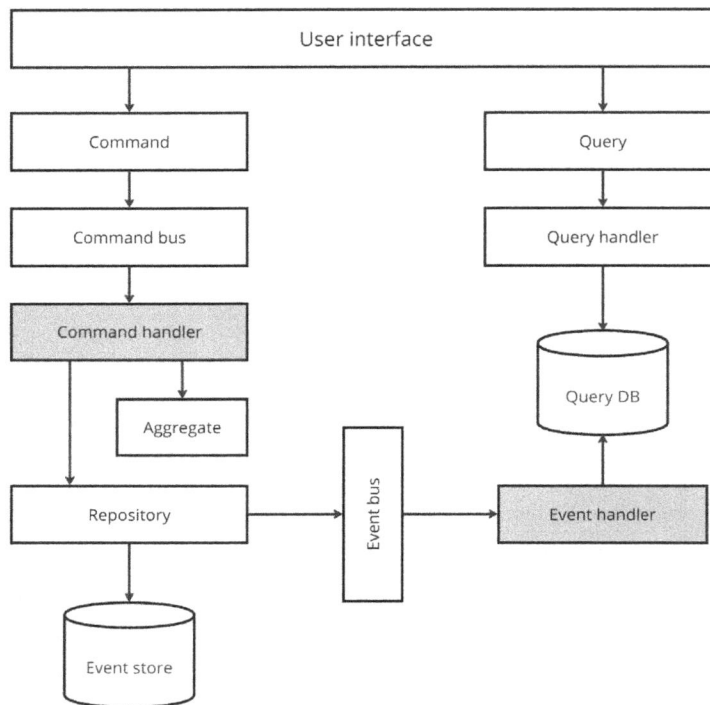

Figure 7.8 – CQRS with event sourcing

The preceding scenario is the evolution of the one in *Figure 7.3*. The aggregate, when it receives a command, validates the domain rules, checks the invariants, and raises one or more domain events. These domain events are stored in an event store and are then published on an event bus. The event store becomes the source of truth of your system. That is because it stores all the domain events that have occurred, and you can rewind them to rebuild your read model or create completely new projections. If you do not remember what a projection is, do not worry—it is nothing more than a denormalized and optimized view inside the read model.

Once the domain events have been published, one or more event handlers can subscribe to them to update the projections inside the read model, create and publish integration events, send emails, and so on.

Implementing the CQRS pattern is simpler than it may look, and to make the process even more approachable, we developed our own open source library, Muflone. Our goal was to eliminate unnecessary complexity and repetitive coding often associated with CQRS. Muflone achieves this by reducing boilerplate code and streamlining implementation. If you explore Muflone, you'll see how straightforward it is to use, and we hope it inspires you to build your own implementation without much effort. CQRS doesn't have to be intimidating; with the right tools and mindset, it can be both practical and accessible.

Muflone

Muflone is an open-source library that simplifies the implementation of the CQRS pattern in .NET projects. It provides boilerplate code to streamline the handling of commands, events, and other CQRS components. The library includes built-in components for integrating with service buses (*RabbitMQ* and *Azure*), handling persistence (EventStoreDB and MongoDB), and building sagas.

You can find more details on the project repository here:

```
https://github.com/CQRS-Muflone/Muflone
```

Two classes in this library need to be explained in detail to help you understand the code in 03-monolith_with_cqrs_and_event_sourcing, which represents the result of the refactoring at the end of this chapter. The first is the AggregateRoot class, which, as the name suggests, represents the entity root of an aggregate. You learned about the aggregate pattern in *Chapter 4, Tactical Patterns*.

The following code is just a portion of the AggregateRoot class, and it focuses on the _ uncommittedEvents property. This property holds the list of domain events raised by the aggregate that have yet to be persisted in an event store. Whenever something significant happens within the aggregate, you need to call the RaiseEvent method to create a domain event to apply it to the aggregate and add it to _uncommittedEvents.

The repository will use this property to persist the events. Since the domain layer is unaware of persistence concerns, when you call the Save method of the repository (explained later in this section), you pass the entire aggregate. The IRepository implementation can then either persist events for an event-sourced approach by reading _uncommittedEvents or save the whole aggregate in a traditional CRUD manner.

Here is the code just described:

```
public abstract class AggregateRoot : IAggregate, IEquatable<IAggregate>
{
    private readonly ICollection<object> _uncommittedEvents = new
LinkedList<object>();

    public IDomainId Id { get; protected set; } = default!;
    public int Version { get; protected set; }

    void IAggregate.ApplyEvent(object @event)
    {
        RegisteredRoutes.Dispatch(@event);
        Version++;
    }

    ICollection IAggregate.GetUncommittedEvents() => (ICollection)_
uncommittedEvents;

    void IAggregate.ClearUncommittedEvents() => _uncommittedEvents.
Clear();

    protected void RaiseEvent(object @event)
    {
        ((IAggregate)this).ApplyEvent(@event);
        _uncommittedEvents.Add(@event);
    }


}
```

The other important class is `Repository`. In the core package of the `Muflone` library, you can find its `IRepository` interface.

Here is the code:

```
public interface IRepository : IDisposable
{
    Task<TAggregate?> GetByIdAsync<TAggregate>(IDomainId id,
CancellationToken cancellationToken = default) where TAggregate : class,
IAggregate;
```

```
    Task<TAggregate?> GetByIdAsync<TAggregate>(IDomainId id, long version,
CancellationToken cancellationToken = default) where TAggregate : class,
IAggregate;
    Task SaveAsync(IAggregate aggregate, Guid commitId,
Action<IDictionary<string, object>> updateHeaders, CancellationToken
cancellationToken = default);
    Task SaveAsync(IAggregate aggregate, Guid commitId, CancellationToken
cancellationToken = default);
}
```

The IRepository interface, which forms the basis of the *Repository* pattern, exposes only two methods: Save and GetById, available in both synchronous and asynchronous versions. This design optimizes the write model for write operations, meaning it does not support running queries. Instead, you use GetById to load the aggregate (or rebuild it, as you will see later) from a store and Save to persist the aggregate. Nothing more.

In the following code, which is part of the EventStoreRepository implementation of IRepository in the Muflone.Eventstore.gRPC package, you can see the two methods implemented:

```
namespace Muflone.Eventstore.gRPC.Persistence;


public class EventStoreRepository : IRepository
{

    public async Task<TAggregate?> GetByIdAsync<TAggregate>(IDomainId
id, long version, CancellationToken cancellationToken = default) where
TAggregate : class, IAggregate
    {
        if (version <= 0)
            throw new InvalidOperationException("Cannot get version <= 0");

        var streamName = aggregateIdToStreamName(typeof(TAggregate), id);
        var aggregate = ConstructAggregate<TAggregate>();

        var readResult = eventStoreClient.ReadStreamAsync(Direction.
Forwards, streamName, StreamPosition.Start, maxCount: version,
cancellationToken: cancellationToken);

        if (await readResult.ReadState != ReadState.Ok)
```

```
            throw new AggregateNotFoundException(id, typeof(TAggregate));

        await foreach (var @event in readResult)
            aggregate!.ApplyEvent(DeserializeEvent(@event));

        if (aggregate!.Version != version && version < int.MaxValue)
            throw new AggregateVersionException(id, typeof(TAggregate),
aggregate.Version, version);

        return aggregate;
    }

    private static TAggregate? ConstructAggregate<TAggregate>()
    {
        return (TAggregate)Activator.CreateInstance(typeof(TAggregate),
true)!;
    }

    private static object DeserializeEvent(ResolvedEvent resolvedEvent)
    {
        var eventClrTypeName = JObject.Parse(Encoding.
UTF8.GetString(resolvedEvent.Event.Metadata.ToArray())).
Property(EventClrTypeHeader)!.Value;
        return JsonConvert.DeserializeObject(Encoding.UTF8.
GetString(resolvedEvent.Event.Data.ToArray()), Type.GetType(((string)
eventClrTypeName)!)!)!;
    }

    public async Task SaveAsync(IAggregate aggregate, Guid commitId,
Action<IDictionary<string, object>> updateHeaders, CancellationToken
cancellationToken = default)
    {
        var commitHeaders = new Dictionary<string, object>
        {
            { CommitIdHeader, commitId },
            { CommitDateHeader, DateTime.UtcNow},
            { AggregateClrTypeHeader, aggregate.GetType().
AssemblyQualifiedName! }
```

```
        };
        updateHeaders(commitHeaders);

        var streamName = aggregateIdToStreamName(aggregate.GetType(),
    aggregate.Id);
        var newEvents = aggregate.GetUncommittedEvents().Cast<object>().
    ToList();
        var eventsToSave = newEvents.Select(e => ToEventData(Uuid.
    NewUuid(), e, commitHeaders)).ToList();

        var originalVersion = aggregate.Version - newEvents.Count;
        var expectedVersion = originalVersion == 0 ? ExpectedVersion.
    NoStream : originalVersion - 1;

        await eventStoreClient.AppendToStreamAsync(streamName, StreamState.
    Any, eventsToSave, cancellationToken: cancellationToken);

        aggregate.ClearUncommittedEvents();
    }
}
```

The GetById method reads the events from the beginning of the events stream in the event store by calling eventStoreClient.ReadStreamAsync and then applies them to the aggregate by invoking its ApplyEvent method. In this way, it rebuilds the aggregate's latest state.

The core of this method is an asynchronous operation that processes a stream of events. For each event, aggregate!.ApplyEvent(…) applies the event to the aggregate to rebuild its state. The DeserializeEvent(@event) method converts the event from its serialized format into an object that can be applied to the aggregate.

The Save method retrieves the domain events from the aggregate via the GetUncommittedEvents method, checks the version for optimistic locking, and appends the events to the stream using the eventStoreClient.AppendToStreamAsync method.

Now that you know how events work coupled with CQRS, we can implement events in our code base.

Adding events to our ERP

Before starting to refactor, remember that the complete code base can be found in 03-monolith_
with_cqrs_and_event_sourcing of the book's repository. We begin by working on the Sales
bounded context. For starters, we refactor the SalesOrder aggregate as shown in the following
code:

```
public class SalesOrder : AggregateRoot
{
    internal SalesOrderNumber _salesOrderNumber;
    internal OrderDate _orderDate;

    internal CustomerId _customerId;
    internal CustomerName _customerName;

    internal IEnumerable<SalesOrderRow> _rows;

    protected SalesOrder()
    {
    }

    internal static SalesOrder CreateSalesOrder(SalesOrderId salesOrderId,
Guid correlationId, SalesOrderNumber salesOrderNumber,
        OrderDate orderDate, CustomerId customerId, CustomerName
customerName, IEnumerable<SalesOrderRowDto> rows)
    {
        // Check SalesOrder invariants

        return new SalesOrder(salesOrderId, correlationId,
salesOrderNumber, orderDate, customerId, customerName, rows);
    }

    private SalesOrder(SalesOrderId salesOrderId, Guid correlationId,
SalesOrderNumber salesOrderNumber, OrderDate orderDate,
        CustomerId customerId, CustomerName customerName,
IEnumerable<SalesOrderRowDto> rows)
    {
        RaiseEvent(new SalesOrderCreated(salesOrderId, correlationId,
salesOrderNumber, orderDate, customerId, customerName, rows));
```

```
    }

    private void Apply(SalesOrderCreated @event)
    {
        Id = @event.SalesOrderId;
        _salesOrderNumber = @event.SalesOrderNumber;
        _orderDate = @event.OrderDate;
        _customerId = @event.CustomerId;
        _customerName = @event.CustomerName;
        _rows = @event.Rows.MapToDomainRows();
    }
}
```

Based on what we have explained in the chapter, you will already have noticed the things we changed.

Firstly, we derived the class from Muflone's AggregateRoot, because this class is our aggregate entry point. Then, we modified the constructor using RaiseEvent to precisely raise the SalesOrderCreated event. Finally, we defined the Apply method for the same event to update the necessary properties of the aggregate. The Apply method is called by the repository's GetById when reading the stream and encountering an event of this type. Similarly, for other event types, the repository will invoke the corresponding Apply method within SalesOrder for each event it finds in the stream.

But now who will call the constructor? Because we are implementing CQRS with event sourcing, we need to change how things work inside our application. As you know, changes are fired by a command, so we need to create the CreateSalesOrder command and its handler. The command will be created in the Commands folder of the BrewUp.Sales.SharedKernel project while the handler will be added to the new CommandHandlers folder within the BrewUp.Sales.Domain project.

The command is straightforward:

```
public class CreateSalesOrder(SalesOrderId aggregateId, Guid commitId,
SalesOrderNumber salesOrderNumber,
        OrderDate orderDate, CustomerId customerId, CustomerName
customerName,
        IEnumerable<SalesOrderRowDto> rows)
    : Command(aggregateId, commitId)
{
```

```
    public readonly SalesOrderId SalesOrderId = aggregateId;
    public readonly SalesOrderNumber SalesOrderNumber = salesOrderNumber;
    public readonly OrderDate OrderDate = orderDate;

    public readonly CustomerId CustomerId = customerId;
    public readonly CustomerName CustomerName = customerName;

    public readonly IEnumerable<SalesOrderRowDto> Rows = rows;
}
```

The only thing to point out in the preceding code is that the CreateSalesOrder class is derived from Muflone's Command class and if you take a look at it, you will see it is only composed of a bunch of constructors, nothing fancy.

The real work is made by the command handler that is the consumer for the CreateSalesOrder command:

```
public sealed class CreateSalesOrderCommandHandler :
CommandHandlerAsync<CreateSalesOrder>
{
    public CreateSalesOrderCommandHandler(IRepository repository,
ILoggerFactory loggerFactory) : base(repository, loggerFactory)
    {
    }

    public override async Task HandleAsync(CreateSalesOrder command,
CancellationToken cancellationToken = default)
    {
        var aggregate = SalesOrder.CreateSalesOrder(command.SalesOrderId,
command.MessageId, command.SalesOrderNumber,
            command.OrderDate, command.CustomerId, command.CustomerName,
command.Rows);
        await Repository.SaveAsync(aggregate, Guid.NewGuid());
    }
}
```

What matters in the preceding code is HandleAsync. It is this method that calls the constructor of SalesOrder passing by its factory.

Inside the constructor, the event is raised and added to the UncommittedEvents list that will be persisted by the call to Repository.SaveAsync.

Aggregate's factory

Using a static constructor for `AggregateRoot` offers several advantages over directly calling the constructor. Firstly, it encapsulates important business rules and validations, ensuring they are applied consistently when creating the aggregate. This prevents bypassing key domain logic that might occur with a direct constructor call. Secondly, it provides clarity of intent by emphasizing that the creation process involves more than just object instantiation—it reflects a domain action. The factory method also allows for controlled instantiation, ensuring that internal invariants are respected and that complex setup is handled properly. Lastly, the approach offers flexibility for future changes, as any modifications to the creation logic can be made in one place without affecting the rest of the code base. This approach aligns well with DDD principles by promoting maintainability and clarity.

Now that we have completed the handling of the command, it is time to move to the other side of the aggregate. We need to handle the events.

We know that the aggregate constructor, upon verifying the invariants, will raise an event called `SalesOrderCreated` (remember the past tense because something has happened). We then need to create the event in the `Events` folder of `BrewUp.Sales.SharedKernel` and its handler in the `EventHandlers` folder of the `BrewUp.Sales.ReadModel` project.

The code for the event is as follows:

```
public sealed class SalesOrderCreated(SalesOrderId aggregateId, Guid
commitId, SalesOrderNumber salesOrderNumber,
    OrderDate orderDate, CustomerId customerId, CustomerName customerName,
    IEnumerable<SalesOrderRowDto> rows) : DomainEvent(aggregateId,
commitId)
{
    public readonly SalesOrderId SalesOrderId = aggregateId;
    public readonly SalesOrderNumber SalesOrderNumber = salesOrderNumber;
    public readonly OrderDate OrderDate = orderDate;

    public readonly CustomerId CustomerId = customerId;
    public readonly CustomerName CustomerName = customerName;

    public readonly IEnumerable<SalesOrderRowDto> Rows = rows;
}
```

As you can see, the `SalesOrderCreated` event, just like a command, is a simple message that carries information. However, as an event that remains within the bounded context, it is derived from the `DomainEvent` class rather than the `IntegrationEvent` class.

As you can already imagine, we need to create its respective handler, which is one of what could be many **subscribers** for the event:

```
public sealed class SalesOrderCreatedEventHandlerAsync(ILoggerFactory
loggerFactory, ISalesOrderService salesOrderService)
    : DomainEventHandlerAsync<SalesOrderCreated>(loggerFactory)
{
    public override async Task HandleAsync(SalesOrderCreated @event,
CancellationToken cancellationToken = new())
    {
        try
        {
            await salesOrderService.CreateSalesOrderAsync(@event.
SalesOrderId, @event.SalesOrderNumber, @event.CustomerId,
                @event.CustomerName, @event.OrderDate, @event.Rows,
cancellationToken);
        }
        catch (Exception ex)
        {
            Logger.LogError(ex, "Error handling sales order created
event");
            throw;
        }
    }
}
```

Again, everything is relatively simple; the handler reacts to the event and passes the information to our service, which will update the projection with the new `SalesOrder`.

The last piece of the puzzle is how to deliver messages throughout the system. We need to eliminate the mediator project that we no longer need and, in the infrastructure project, add a service bus that will replace the mediator in communicating with the various parts of the system.

As explained earlier, the service bus will be responsible for receiving and delivering messages to the command and event handlers. We will not delve into the code because the `Mulfone.Trasport.RabbitMQ` package will solve all the implementation details of the *RabbitMQ* service bus (this is the service bus we chose for our application) and it is not in the scope of this book. Anyway, all the source code is publicly available if you want to understand the inner workings of this package.

> **RabbitMQ**
>
> **RabbitMQ** is a popular open source message broker that facilitates communication between different parts of an application by sending and receiving messages through queues. Common use cases include task scheduling, load balancing, and managing background processes. *RabbitMQ* supports multiple messaging protocols and features such as message acknowledgment, retries, and flexible routing via exchanges, making it suitable for both simple and complex messaging scenarios in distributed systems (`https://www.rabbitmq.com`).

An event-sourced system offers many advantages other than those you discovered until now. For example, one of the most challenging aspects of designing a system is accurately reflecting the business intent within your solution. Domain events are powerful because they mirror actual business actions. Rather than only storing the final state of an aggregate, events capture the sequence of actions that lead to that state. This gives you a deeper understanding of the business processes at play, providing critical insights into how and why specific outcomes were reached. With this visibility, you are able to make more informed decisions, as your system isn't just tracking data, it is also aligned with the intent and reasoning behind each change.

It is now time for the last, but no less important, part of this chapter: testing an event-sourced aggregate

Testing the event-driven modular monolith

Now that we have implemented the events, before moving on to the next topic, it is important to understand how to effectively test aggregates with events.

It is good to remember the safety net principle from *Chapter 5*. Without comprehensive tests in place, you risk breaking critical functionalities, making the system unstable during refactoring. Especially in a CQRS+ES architecture, where commands and events shape the system's state, robust tests are your guardrails. Testing becomes more intricate than in traditional systems because you need to verify not just the behavior of individual components but also how events ripple through the system.

In this context, **specification testing** emerges as the ideal approach.

Specification tests

Unlike unit tests, which focus on isolated methods or classes, specification tests target the entire lifecycle of an aggregate by simulating real-world scenarios. This is crucial because your refactoring will likely impact how aggregates generate and react to events, especially across modular boundaries. Unit tests, while useful for small, isolated pieces of logic, simply cannot capture the complex interplay of commands, events, and eventual consistency that defines a modular monolith leveraging CQRS and event sourcing.

When testing the state changes of an aggregate, **specification tests** allow you to model the expected flow. Given a certain initial state, when a command is issued, you assert that specific events are emitted and you verify that the resulting state aligns with your expectations. This mirrors how the system will function in production, making specification tests highly reliable for detecting unintended side effects caused by your refactoring efforts.

To approach this systematically, we test the aggregate by defining the initial state through a sequence of events that brought the aggregate to the state we want to test. Then, by issuing a command, we can observe which events are emitted. The key advantage is that we are not just verifying the isolated outcome of a single method but also testing how the entire aggregate responds to a series of actions. This offers a holistic view of the business process, ensuring that refactoring maintains the integrity of the aggregate's lifecycle and its interactions with the broader system.

But what better way to demonstrate what you just read if not with some code?

Example 1: Creating a Sales Order

So, let's start by examining a simple first test:

```
public sealed class CreateSalesOrderSuccessfully :
CommandSpecification<CreateSalesOrder>
{
    private readonly SalesOrderId _salesOrderId = new(Guid.NewGuid());
    private readonly SalesOrderNumber _salesOrderNumber = new("20240315-
1500");
    private readonly OrderDate _orderDate = new(DateTime.UtcNow);

    private readonly Guid _correlationId = Guid.NewGuid();

    private readonly CustomerId _customerId = new(Guid.NewGuid());
```

```
    private readonly CustomerName _customerName = new("Muflone");

    private readonly IEnumerable<SalesOrderRowDto> _rows = Enumerable.
Empty<SalesOrderRowDto>();

    protected override IEnumerable<DomainEvent> Given()
    {
        yield break;
    }

    protected override CreateSalesOrder When()
    {
        return new CreateSalesOrder(_salesOrderId, _correlationId, _
salesOrderNumber, _orderDate, _customerId, _customerName, _rows);
    }

    protected override ICommandHandlerAsync<CreateSalesOrder> OnHandler()
    {
        return new CreateSalesOrderCommandHandler(Repository, new
NullLoggerFactory());
    }

    protected override IEnumerable<DomainEvent> Expect()
    {
        yield return new SalesOrderCreated(_salesOrderId, _correlationId,
_salesOrderNumber, _orderDate, _customerId, _customerName, _rows);
    }
}
```

The first thing to notice in the preceding code is the base class, CommandSpecification<Creat
eSalesOrder>. This class is part of the Muflone.SpecificationTests library. Without delving
into trivial implementation details, we will quickly describe the code's functionality, making it
easier to understand how this type of test works.

The CommandSpecification<CreateSalesOrder> class orchestrates the testing process by
requiring the implementation of four key methods: Given, When, OnHandler, and Expect. These
methods collectively establish the test's framework, detailing the setup, action, handling, and
expected outcomes.

The following portion of the `CommandSpecification` code shows that these methods are simply defined as abstract:

```
public abstract class CommandSpecification<TCommand> where TCommand :
Command
    {
        protected Exception ExpectedException { get; set; } = default!;

        protected InMemoryEventRepository Repository { get; set; }
        protected CommandSpecification()
        {
            Repository = new InMemoryEventRepository();
        }

        protected abstract IEnumerable<DomainEvent> Given();

        protected abstract TCommand When();

        protected abstract ICommandHandlerAsync<TCommand> OnHandler();

        protected abstract IEnumerable<DomainEvent> Expect();
```

Everything happens inside the `SetUp` method. `Given` is called to retrieve and apply the initial events (recall the `Apply` method in the aggregate that responds to `RaiseEvent` from the *Adding events to our ERP* section earlier in this chapter), setting the aggregate to the desired starting state. `OnHandler` is then called with the command from `When`. Next, we retrieve the list of expected events from `Expected` and compare them. As you can see, the code is not complicated at all. As a bonus, it can be further improved, for example, with a function to output some sort of self-documentation based on the events and the command passing through it:

```
[Fact]
    public async Task SetUp()
    {
        Repository.ApplyGivenEvents(Given().ToList());
        var handler = OnHandler();
        try
        {
            await handler.HandleAsync(When());
            var expected = Expect().ToList();
```

```
                    var published = Repository.Events;
                    CompareEvents(expected, published);
                }
                catch (Exception exception) //Otherwise should be something
expected
                {
                    if (ExpectedException == null)
                        Assert.True(false, $"{exception.GetType()}:
{exception.Message}\n{exception.StackTrace}");
                    Assert.True(exception.GetType() == ExpectedException.
GetType(),
                        $"Exception type {exception.GetType()} differs from
expected type {ExpectedException.GetType()}");
                    Assert.True(exception.Message == ExpectedException.
Message,
                        $"Exception message \"{exception.Message}\" differs
from expected message \"{ExpectedException.GetType()}\"");
                }
            }
```

The last piece of code to analyze is `CompareEvents`. This function does the heavy lifting in our test class comparing each event by type and property values.

If just one of them differs from the ones expected, it fails the test. This is easily achieved thanks to the `CompareNETObjects` package:

```
        private static void CompareEvents(IEnumerable<DomainEvent>
expected, IEnumerable<DomainEvent> published)
        {
            if (published == null)
                published = new List<DomainEvent>();

            Assert.True(expected.Count() == published.Count(), "Different
number of expected/published events.");

            var config = new ComparisonConfig();
            config.MembersToIgnore.Add("Headers");
            config.MembersToIgnore.Add("MessageId");
```

```
                var compareObjects = new CompareLogic(config);
                var eventPairs = expected.Zip(published, (e, p) => new {
    Expected = e, Published = p });
                foreach (var eventPair in eventPairs)
                {
                    var result = compareObjects.Compare(eventPair.Expected,
    eventPair.Published);
                    Assert.True(result.AreEqual,
                        $"Events {eventPair.Expected.GetType()}
    and {eventPair.Published.GetType()} are different: {result.
    DifferencesString}");
                }
            }
        }
```

Going back to our test, you should immediately notice that the Given method returns an empty list. That is because we are testing the creation of a SalesOrder and there are no starting events for something that does not exist yet. As we will see in the next example, in this method, you should put all the events that bring your aggregate to the starting state for your test.

The When and OnHandler methods are straightforward; they just return, respectively, the CreateSalesOrder command and the command handler (CreateSalesOrderCommandHandler) needed by the base class to ignite the test as explained before. The nice thing about this is that we are not mocking anything, and we are working with the aggregate's code. We obviously mock the repository, but it is already done by the class itself.

The last thing to do is declare the event or events we expect as the aggregate's output in reaction to the CreateSalesOrder command in the Expect method.

In this specific case, we are saying that after sending the command to the aggregate (handled by our command handler), in the uncommitted events list of our aggregate, we expect to find just one SalesOrderCreated with the same data as the command.

As you can see, this test does not focus on lines of code or a specific method of the aggregate but tests the aggregate as a whole, observing how its state changes in response to a specific command. This state, as explained in the previous section, is represented by the events that describe what happened in the aggregate.

Now, we can move to a slightly more complex scenario, a scenario where we need to put the aggregate in a specific state before testing it.

Example 2: Updating Availability

Let's look at the following code for the warehouse's domain:

```csharp
public class UpdateAvailabilityDueToProductionOrderAfterAggregateCreation
: CommandSpecification<UpdateAvailabilityDueToProductionOrder>
{
    private readonly BeerId _beerId = new(Guid.NewGuid());
    private readonly BeerName _beerName = new("Muflone IPA");
    private readonly Quantity _quantity = new(100, "Lt");

    private readonly Quantity _newQuantity = new(200, "Lt");

    private readonly Guid _correlationId = Guid.NewGuid();

    protected override IEnumerable<DomainEvent> Given()
    {
        yield return new AvailabilityUpdatedDueToProductionOrder(_beerId,
_correlationId, _beerName, _quantity);
    }

    protected override UpdateAvailabilityDueToProductionOrder When()
    {
        return new UpdateAvailabilityDueToProductionOrder(_beerId, _
correlationId, _beerName, _quantity);
    }

    protected override
ICommandHandlerAsync<UpdateAvailabilityDueToProductionOrder> OnHandler()
    {
        return new
UpdateAvailabilityDueToProductionOrderCommandHandler(Repository, new
NullLoggerFactory());
    }

    protected override IEnumerable<DomainEvent> Expect()
    {
```

```
        yield return new AvailabilityUpdatedDueToProductionOrder(_beerId,
_correlationId, _beerName, _newQuantity);
    }
}
```

In this specific case, we want to test that the quantity to be produced of a specific beer is correctly updated following a second command to increase its production by 100 liters. What changes from the previous example is only the Given method. In this method, we have defined that the initial sequence of events consists of one AvailabilityUpdatedDueToProductionOrder, which declares that the quantity was previously set to 100 liters. This means we are setting the aggregate in a specific state (i.e., a state in which it has already handled a quantity update due to a production order). Therefore, what we expect as a result of the test is that the quantity to be produced becomes 200 liters, as specified in the event returned by the Expect method.

Remember, in a modular architecture, the flow of events between modules can introduce subtle yet impactful changes. Specification tests help you catch these as you refactor, providing immediate feedback if something breaks. By focusing on state transitions and event emissions, you ensure that your system's domain logic remains intact, even as you break down your monolith into well-encapsulated modules.

In essence, specification testing becomes your primary safety net during this phase. It guarantees that refactoring your modular monolith will preserve the integrity of your event-driven system, giving you the confidence to proceed without sacrificing correctness.

Summary

In this chapter, you learned about the integration of events with CQRS, gaining a comprehensive understanding of how to implement and manage an event-driven architecture in a modular system. You started by exploring the fundamental shift from direct, synchronous communication to asynchronous messaging, emphasizing the trade-offs in terms of consistency, scalability, and fault tolerance. You learned about the distinct roles of commands and events: commands trigger actions that change the state of the system, while events notify other parts of the system about these changes without altering the state directly.

You then learned how to implement CQRS, which separates the responsibilities of reading and writing data. By designing distinct read and write models, you saw how this approach optimizes performance and scalability, allowing you to handle high-traffic systems more efficiently. You also explored different methods of synchronizing these models, from direct database updates to more complex strategies such as materialized views and database polling.

You then explored event sourcing, a powerful technique that captures state changes over time by storing domain events rather than the current state of aggregates. This approach enhances traceability, auditability, and flexibility, enabling you to rebuild state or create new projections as needed. You also learned how to leverage event stores and message brokers to facilitate asynchronous communication between components in your system.

Finally, you focused on testing event-driven systems. More precisely, you were introduced to specification testing, which allows you to test the full lifecycle of aggregates by validating commands and their corresponding events. This method ensures that your system's behavior remains consistent and correct as you refactor or scale your architecture.

You have now acquired the skills to understand and apply asynchronous, event-driven communication in a CQRS architecture; use event sourcing to capture business processes and ensure data consistency over time; and implement and test CQRS and event-driven systems, maintaining robustness and alignment with business needs.

You are now equipped to refactor your applications into scalable, loosely coupled systems that leverage the power of events and CQRS to meet the demands of modern software architecture.

In the next chapter, you will learn some strategies to refactor the database. As your system transitions to a more modular, event-driven architecture, choosing the right strategy for database refactoring is crucial. You'll explore different approaches to restructuring the database, ensuring it aligns with your new architecture without compromising performance or data consistency. Understanding the importance of selecting the correct refactoring strategy will be key to successfully completing your transition to a scalable, maintainable system.

Get this book's PDF version and more

Scan the QR code (or go to `packtpub.com/unlock`). Search for this book by name, confirm the edition, and then follow the steps on the page.

UNLOCK NOW

Note: Keep your invoice handy. Purchases made directly from Packt don't require an invoice.

8

Refactoring the Database

In the previous chapters, we explored how to use CQRS and event sourcing to break apart a monolithic application, allowing services to align with specific bounded contexts in a microservices architecture. However, while separating application logic is a crucial step, the database itself often remains a bottleneck, tightly coupled and shared across services. For a true transition to microservices, database refactoring is essential to ensure that each service has control over its own data and operates independently.

In this chapter, you'll learn about the primary patterns for database refactoring, each addressing different strategies for managing and partitioning database tables to support service-specific ownership. We are going to cover how to do the following:

- Clearly identify and align domain boundaries to support independent service evolution
- Apply common table ownership strategies to manage data shared across multiple services effectively
- Implement single table ownership for assigning exclusive data control to individual services
- Navigate joint table ownership scenarios, ensuring distinct services clearly define their data boundaries
- Gradually migrate stored procedures into your application code, reducing coupling and enhancing testability and maintainability

Additionally, many legacy systems rely on stored procedures to handle complex logic within the database. While stored procedures can be efficient, they also create a tight coupling between the application code and the database, making them difficult to maintain and test in a microservices context. This chapter will also guide you through patterns for migrating stored procedures into your code base, ensuring cleaner service boundaries and improved maintainability.

By the end of this chapter, you'll have a strong foundation in database refactoring strategies, enabling you to move confidently toward a fully decoupled microservices architecture.

The complete code for this chapter can be found in the `01-monolith_legacy` branch within the book's GitHub repository: `https://github.com/PacktPublishing/Domain-driven-Refactoring/tree/01-monolith_legacy`.

Modular services and the need for database refactoring

Modular services form the core of the transformation from a monolithic architecture to a more flexible, maintainable, and scalable system. As you already learned in previous chapters, modular services are built around specific business domains and function as independent units that can evolve separately. This independence fosters agility, allowing teams to make changes in one service without having to worry about impacting other services. Each service owns its data, logic, and specific responsibilities, making it easier to manage complexity.

In practice, modular services are often designed around the principles of DDD, where each service represents a **bounded context**—a clearly defined area of the business. By aligning the database schema with these bounded contexts, we can significantly reduce the coupling between different parts of the system and ensure that each service interacts only with the data it needs. This eliminates the need for complex joins and relationships that are typical in monolithic databases and makes the services more autonomous.

For example, consider our ERP system where `Orders`, `Customers`, and `Warehouses` each represent a distinct bounded context. In a monolithic setup, a single database might store tables for all these domains, with intricate foreign key relationships linking them together. In a modular architecture, however, each of these domains could have its own service with its own database or schema. The `Orders` service would handle only order data, while the `CustomerManagement` service would manage customer-related data independently. This separation means that changes in customer information do not directly impact order processing, and vice versa, minimizing the risk of cascading failures.

Another key aspect of modular services is data ownership and autonomy. Each service should be responsible for the data it needs to fulfill its role. This ownership is critical in ensuring that services remain loosely coupled and can operate independently of each other. In our previous example, WarehouseService is the only service that has the authority to modify beer's availability. OrdersService can inform WarehouseService of an order event, but it cannot directly modify inventory data. This separation of concerns helps maintain clear boundaries and prevents unintended side effects that are common in tightly coupled systems.

By understanding and implementing modular services effectively, the database refactoring process becomes much more manageable. The database is refactored to align with individual service domains, reducing complexity and making future changes more straightforward. Each modular service becomes a self-contained unit, capable of evolving without introducing significant risks to the overall system. This approach ultimately sets the foundation for a distributed system, where each service can scale, be updated, or even be replaced independently, providing a robust pathway toward microservices if the business needs to evolve in that direction.

As our software architecture evolves from a monolithic legacy system to a modular monolith with CQRS and event sourcing, the role of the underlying database becomes increasingly critical. The transformation toward a modular architecture inevitably demands that the database structure evolve as well, aligning more closely with new, separated application components. This chapter focuses on why refactoring the database is crucial during this transition, and how the database itself must shift to reflect the changes made at the application level.

While we frequently reference SQL databases in our discussions, the same principles apply to NoSQL systems—simply think in terms of collections instead of tables, and you'll find that most patterns remain just as relevant.

Monolithic databases, which are typically characterized by tightly coupled tables, global relationships, and shared schemas, often grow in complexity as the system evolves, leading to poor maintainability, significant technical debt, and increased fragility. As application components move toward a more modular design—decoupling responsibilities through CQRS and implementing event sourcing to handle state transitions—the underlying database needs to follow suit. Without corresponding changes to the database structure, the benefits of a modular application layer are limited. The persistence layer remains a bottleneck, restricting the flexibility and independence that modular services need.

Hidden business rules in the data schema

Legacy databases commonly embed business logic implicitly within the data schema, particularly through constraints such as foreign keys. For instance, a foreign key constraint between an order table and a customer table often enforces business rules, such as ensuring an order cannot exist without a valid customer. While technically useful, these constraints represent embedded business logic that can make changes or refactoring difficult, as the business rules are maintained implicitly and scattered throughout the database structure. This implicit embedding of business logic can significantly hinder refactoring efforts.

The purpose of refactoring the database is twofold: to maintain consistency with the refactored modular application, and to reduce the coupling and complexity that often plague monolithic databases. For instance, in the previous chapter, the refactoring we carried out allowed application components to function independently, using CQRS to separate read and write responsibilities and event sourcing to provide a more traceable and resilient state mechanism. Now, our challenge is to ensure that the database schema and architecture adequately reflect these changes—enabling modularity at both the data and application levels.

The database refactoring must tackle several key areas:

- **Aligning domain boundaries:** The goal is to ensure the database aligns with the DDD boundaries we defined during the modularization process. Tables and other database structures that originally spanned multiple business contexts may need to be broken down or reorganized to reflect new, more granular services. As an example, imagine a table called `SalesOrders` that stores not only the order information but also customer details such as address and contact information. In a modular approach, customer information belongs in a separate domain, such as `CustomerManagement`, while `SalesOrders` focuses purely on order data. Thus, the `SalesOrders` table should be split into two tables: one for `SalesOrders` and another for `CustomerDetails`, which reside in separate schemas aligned with their respective domains.

- **Managing data consistency across services**: In a modular architecture, data that was previously centralized might now belong to multiple separate domains. It is critical to identify how to manage consistency across these domains while avoiding overly tight coupling—a challenge especially pertinent when moving toward CQRS and distributed data models. To be more clear, consider the situation where you need to ensure consistency between Warehouse and SalesOrders. In a monolithic database, these might have been joined directly in queries. Now, with modular services, Warehouse and SalesOrders are separate services, potentially with different data stores. To maintain consistency, you could use an event-driven approach where a SalesOrderCreated event triggers WarehouseService to update stock levels, ensuring eventual consistency without tightly coupling the services.

- **Transitioning while ensuring performance**: During the transition period, the legacy monolith must continue to serve existing business operations without a drop in performance or reliability. This often means supporting a dual schema—maintaining parts of the old schema while introducing the new one, until the transition is complete. For example, suppose we have refactored a Payments table to separate payment processing from payment history. During the transition, both Payments (original) and PaymentProcessing (new) tables may coexist. Any updates to the payment data need to be synchronized across both tables until all dependent services are updated to use the new PaymentProcessing structure. This could be achieved using database triggers or a background synchronization script.

By addressing the database refactoring alongside the refactoring of the application components, we can ensure that our modular monolith is truly modular from top to bottom—paving the way for easier maintenance, greater agility in responding to changing requirements, and a smoother path forward to future service extraction or migration to a fully distributed system.

Finally, it is crucial to clearly communicate these choices to the business, as their need for real-time updates can often be met with eventual consistency. As architects, it is our responsibility to explain these choices and collaboratively decide with business experts which approach to adopt, ensuring a smooth transition.

Principles of database refactoring and identifying domain boundaries

A shared database introduces strong coupling across different bounded contexts, limiting flexibility, and making each change ripple across the entire system. While this approach simplifies consistency management by offloading it to the database rather than handling it directly in code, in legacy applications, this structure often leads to unintended side effects whenever updates or changes are made to accommodate new requirements. For example, if a new feature needs to be added to the warehouse context in our ERP, altering the database schema may inadvertently disrupt the sales context, causing errors or requiring additional refactoring.

This entanglement between contexts opposes the principle of modularity central to DDD. By splitting the database into smaller, context-specific databases, each subdomain can evolve independently. Each bounded context should manage its own data model, enabling each team to independently refine, extend, and optimize their database structures without impacting others.

We are confident that many of you have heard this sentence at least once:

"I assumed the database structure would be thoroughly defined and finalized from the beginning."

In traditional development, teams often start with a fixed, predefined database schema and then they build code on top of it. This approach assumes that database requirements will remain static, which rarely aligns with real-world project dynamics. The principles of DDD challenge these dynamics by emphasizing that system design should evolve, starting with deep collaboration with stakeholders and using the Ubiquitous Language that reflects the business context. DDD recommends iterating the design of both the code and the database, evolving the system in small steps to stay aligned with changing requirements and insights.

This approach requires us to move away from a rigid database schema toward what is known as **evolutionary database development**.

Evolutionary database development

This concept was introduced by Pramod J. Sadalage and Scott W. Ambler in their book *Refactoring Databases – Evolutionary Database Design*. The approach adapts Agile and test-driven development practices, traditionally used in software development, to the database layer. Just as software code is continuously refactored and tested, the database can be incrementally designed and updated to mirror the ongoing evolution of the application and its requirements.

With evolutionary database development, teams can adapt the database structure as the project progresses, aligning it more closely with the actual needs of each bounded context. This avoids the common pitfall of early, rigid database decisions that constrain flexibility and force developers to work around outdated structures. This approach also encourages using techniques such as database migration, automated tests, and version control for the database schema. Together, these tools make it safer and simpler to modify the database incrementally without breaking the system. By evolving the database alongside the code, teams can respond to change more effectively, ensuring that both the application and the database remain relevant, efficient, and aligned with the business goals over time.

Adopting this evolutionary approach in database development offers multiple benefits. Its key advantages include the following:

- **Minimizing waste**: Avoids unnecessary work on detailed requirements and design artifacts that may become obsolete as requirements evolve
- **Reducing rework**: Enables early identification of major issues without prematurely diving into minor details, thereby lowering the risk of costly rework
- **Ensuring functionality**: Frequent deployment of working versions, even in demo environments, helps teams consistently validate that the system operates as expected, reducing project risk
- **Enhancing database quality**: Regular, incremental database refactoring ensures the schema evolves and maintains high-quality design over time
- **Aligning with developers' workflow**: An evolutionary approach ensures data professionals work compatibly with developers using Agile methods
- **Reducing effort**: Focuses only on essential, immediate tasks, avoiding unnecessary work and lowering overall development effort

Of course, because you are an architect and you know the first architecture law (there is always a trade-off), here are some disadvantages to evolutionary database development:

- **Cultural barriers**: Many data professionals are accustomed to a sequential approach, preferring detailed, upfront data modeling. However, modern methodologies favor an agile, evolutionary approach, which some professionals, particularly those trained in older methods, may resist.
- **Learning curve**: Shifting from a serial to an evolutionary mindset requires time and a willingness to learn new techniques.

- **Limited tool support**: While refactoring tools for code are widely available, similar tools for database refactoring are still developing, though efforts such as the Eclipse Data Tools Platform (`https://projects.eclipse.org/projects/tools.datatools`) aim to bridge this gap.

Before introducing the patterns you can use in database refactoring, it's important to remember that the goal is to improve the structure while preserving the database's behavioral and informational semantics. That means database refactoring is conceptually more challenging than code refactoring because it requires maintaining not only behavioral consistency but also informational accuracy. This complexity is compounded by the high degree of coupling often present in database architectures, where multiple parts of the system depend on shared data structures. Achieving what we explained requires treating database structure changes with the same rigor as code changes, following principles of testing, versioning, and incremental updates.

The benefits can be summarized as follows:

- **Thorough testing**: Both data teams and developers should thoroughly test schema changes to ensure stability and compatibility. If an ORM tool is used, fitness functions (introduced in *Chapter 6, Transitioning from Chaos*) can be helpful for keeping schema mappings in sync with database structures.
- **Version control**: Database schemas should be versioned in sync with the code that depends on them, as each relies on the other to function correctly. Separating code and schema management often introduces unnecessary complexity and inefficiencies.
- **Incremental updates**: Like code, schema changes should be gradual and incremental to support system evolution. Automated migration tools are favored for updating schemas, avoiding the risks and delays associated with manual changes.

As you should already know, it is important to understand and analyze the problem before attempting to refactor the database. For example, if multiple services or applications access your database, you cannot refactor it and then deploy all of these services simultaneously. You need a transition period, called **deprecation mode**, until the schema changes take place in all the services. For a detailed explanation, you can read the paper *The Agile Database: Tutorial Notes*, by Pramod Sadalage and Peter Schuh (2002).

Figure 8.1 shows three typical scenarios to consider before splitting the database.

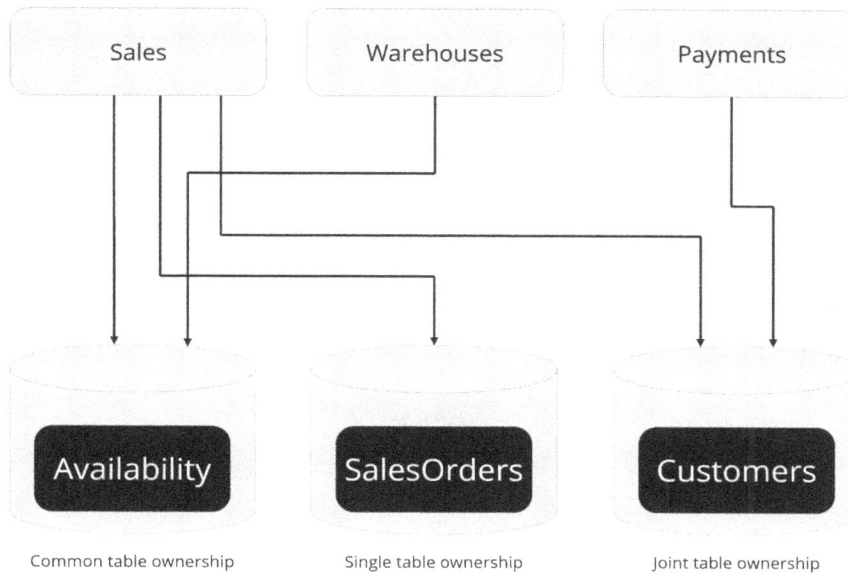

Figure 8.1 – Database splitting

Patterns for database refactoring

There are at least three key patterns you can apply during database refactoring, each with its own advantages and limitations. The following explanations highlight these essential patterns, showcasing how each offers a targeted approach to improving database design and functionality:

- **Common table ownership**: In this situation, multiple services access the same table for both reading and writing data. Before separating the table, it is important to clarify which module, or bounded context, has responsibility for write operations and which modules have read-only access.

- **Single table ownership**: This is the simplest scenario, where only one service accesses the table for all read and write operations. Here, you can move the table into a dedicated database that aligns with this bounded context, as there are no conflicting ownership issues.

- **Joint table ownership**: In this scenario, different services are responsible for managing different sets of properties within the same table. To split the table, you need to follow domain-specific rules and patterns, separating properties according to the responsibilities of each module.

Common table ownership is the scenario you will frequently find in projects, and it is also used in our ERP. *Figure 8.2* shows the starting step of our refactoring process and where it is used as an integration point.

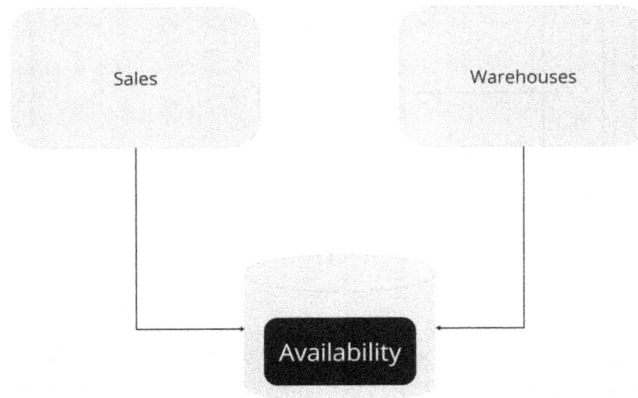

Figure 8.2 – The database as an integration point

As you can see in *Figure 8.2*, `Sales` and `Warehouse` use the same database, but what if their features start to diverge so much that the database will become a burden?

In the book *Refactoring Databases*, by Pramod Sadalage and Scott Ambler, the authors suggest using the **expand/contract pattern**. *Figure 8.3* represents this pattern.

Figure 8.3 – The expand/contract pattern

With this approach, developers start with an initial state and move to a final state, keeping both the previous and updated states available during the transition. This intermediate state supports backward compatibility and allows other services within the system adequate time to adapt to changes. There isn't a constraint on the duration of this transition. It could be a few days or several months.

During the *Start* phase, developers implement the refactoring; in the *Transition* phase, both schemas, old and new, exist, and finally, in the *End* phase, the refactoring is completed.

Firstly, in the *Start* phase, both `Sales` and `Warehouse` bounded contexts access the same `Availability` collection in the same database. `Warehouses` owns the collection, but `Sales` needs read access to check availability when processing an order.

Secondly, during the *Transition* phase, we duplicate the `Availability` table (or collection if using a NoSQL database) into two distinct databases and `Sales` still reads data from the table in the original database.

Finally, during the *End* phase, `Sales` is refactored to read the `Availability` data from its own database (the one we created during the *Transition* phase). At the end of this phase, only the `Warehouse` bounded context retained ownership of the `Availability` table. *Figure 8.4* shows the result of our refactoring in which you can notice that there are two different databases, with the same table, but with different responsibilities.

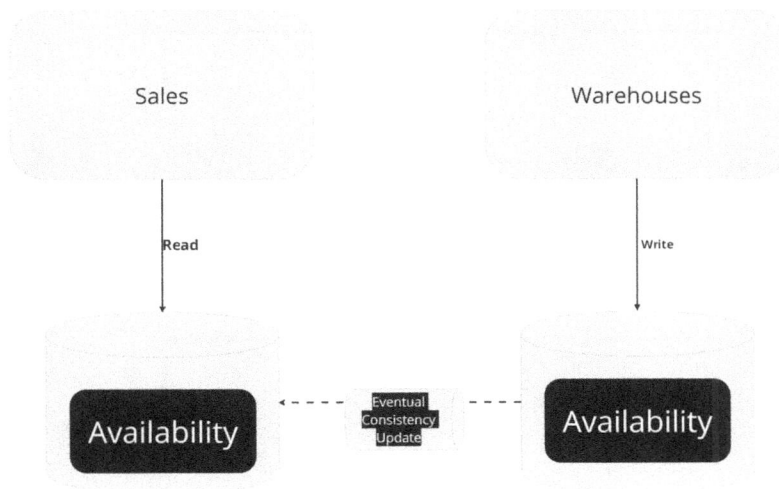

Figure 8.4 – Two databases with eventual consistency

As you can see, after the *End* phase, only the `Warehouse` bounded context has ownership of the `Availability` table of the original database. The same table, in the `Sales` database, is eventually consistently updated, and the `Sales` bounded context can just be read from it.

After applying this operation, you need to synchronize data from the original database to the newly created one. For this purpose, **Data Duplication through Event-Based Data Synchronization** is the recommended pattern. We'll go deeply into it in the next chapter.

An essential aspect of database refactoring involves reworking stored procedures, which are written in the database's native SQL. While stored procedures offer a powerful and efficient way to manipulate data, they are challenging to test and often lead to tight coupling between modules because separating behaviors across them is difficult.

To address this, the native SQL code should be migrated into the module's application code. You must use the same Extract/Contract pattern applied before. *Figure 8.5* shows the steps to follow.

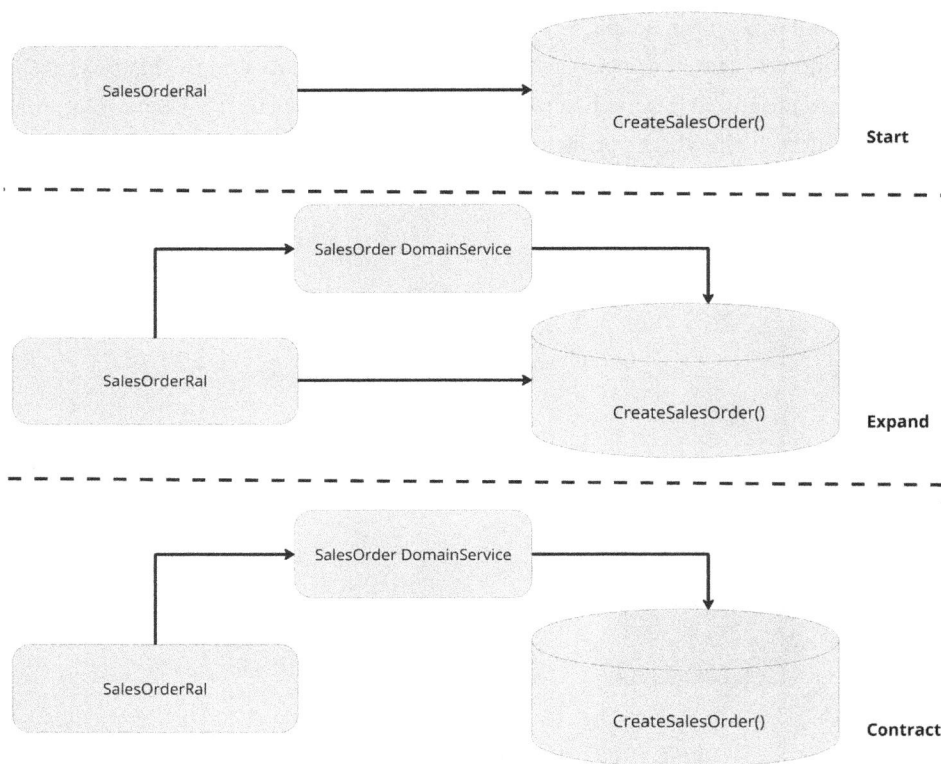

Figure 8.5 – Steps to extract stored procedures

As you learned with table extraction, extracting a stored procedure isn't as simple as moving the script directly into your code base. This process requires a step-by-step approach, with thorough testing at each stage to ensure stability and accuracy before proceeding. Here's an explanation of the pattern applied to stored procedures to guide you through this careful extraction process:

1. **Start:** At the beginning, the layer used to access the database calls the stored procedure directly within the database. It is a common scenario in many legacy systems. Your goal is to remove this stored procedure.

2. **Expand**: It is impossible to move the stored procedure's script directly in your code in just one step. That's because you don't know how many services are calling it. So, you prepare your code in SalesOrderDomainService and move the calls to the database into this new domain service, without removing the stored procedure.

3. **Contract**: Finally, when no services are calling the stored procedure, you can safely remove it from the database.

This operation often requires additional refactoring, especially when the data in question is no longer housed in a single database. In such cases, processing mechanisms such as the **saga pattern** may be necessary to coordinate actions across modules, but we'll explore this in more detail in the next chapter.

Extracting services and managing data consistency

Going back to the 01-monolith_legacy branch, you can observe the original database used in our ERP. *Figure 8.6* shows the original database with both the SalesOrder and Availability collections:

Figure 8.6 – Common table ownership

As you can see, in the beginning, we had a situation where multiple services relied on a single database to store and access all the collections they needed—for instance, services such as SalesQueryService or AvailabilityQueryService in the ERP code base. In this scenario, any of these services can modify the data in each collection, which creates several risks. Because all services have direct access to the same collections, there is a high risk of tight coupling.

Just as all collections are in the same database, all the services are in the same code base. In our ERP, we have just one module that is responsible for updating all the collections, BrewUp.DomainModel. *Figure 8.7* shows the project with all the necessary services.

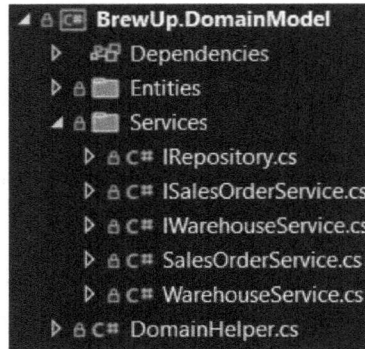

Figure 8.7 – All the services are in the same module

In this scenario, when a new order is processed, we check for the availability of the beer using warehouseRepository, which is an implementation of IRepository for the Availability collection. Because all the collections rely on the same database, we can have multiple implementations in the same modules. The side effect is that we are creating tight coupling inside the CreateSalesOrderAsync method:

```
public sealed class SalesOrderService(
    [FromKeyedServices("sale")] IRepository saleRepository,
    [FromKeyedServices("warehouse")] IRepository warehouseRepository) :
ISalesOrderService
{
    public async Task CreateSalesOrderAsync(SalesOrderId salesOrderId,
SalesOrderNumber salesOrderNumber, OrderDate orderDate,
        CustomerId customerId, CustomerName customerName,
IEnumerable<SalesOrderRowJson> rows, CancellationToken cancellationToken)
    {
        List<SalesOrderRowJson> beersAvailable = new();
        foreach (var row in rows)
        {
            var availability = await warehouseRepository.
GetByIdAsync<Entities.Warehouses.Availability>(row.BeerId.ToString(),
cancellationToken);
            if (availability!=null)
                beersAvailable.Add(row);
        }

        var aggregate = SalesOrder.CreateSalesOrder(salesOrderId,
salesOrderNumber, orderDate, customerId, customerName, beersAvailable);
```

```
        await saleRepository.InsertAsync(aggregate.MapToReadModel(),
    cancellationToken);
        }
    }
```

In a simple example such as this one, it is not a big problem, but when the application grows, the number of services in this module will grow, and adding new features will be increasingly complicated.

To avoid this scenario, we moved the Availability collection within the Warehouse module, and of course, in a separate database. At the end of the migration, the solution will look like the one shown in *Figure 8.8*.

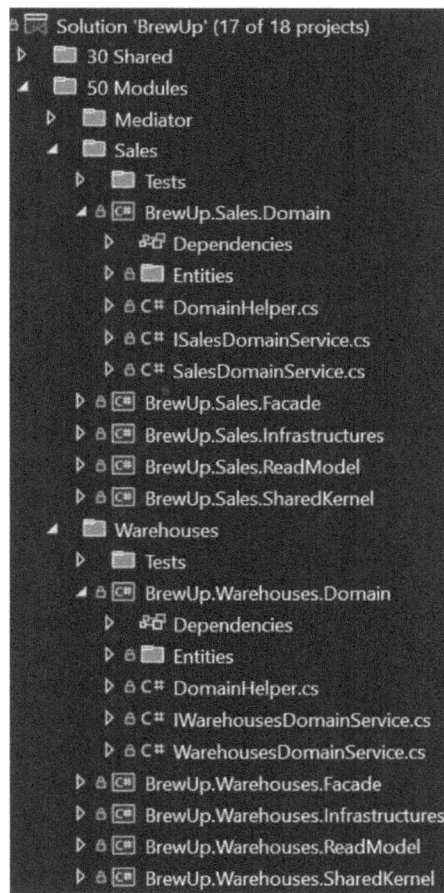

Figure 8.8 – Solution after migrating the collection and services

Having the `Availability` collection in two different databases implies the problem of keeping them synchronized. `Warehouse` is the bounded context that has the ownership of this data, but Sales needs to read the availability when processing a new order. We applied the *Data Duplication through Event-Based Data Synchronization* pattern introduced in the previous section. When the `Warehouse` domain receives a command to update `Availability`, because the beer production is over, it raises the `AvailabilityUpdatedDueToProductionOrder` domain event. As this is a domain event, it has be to managed inside the `Warehouse` bounded context. We have two event handlers for this purpose within the `BrewUp.Warehouses.ReadModel` project: the first one has the responsibility to update the read model, and the second one has to publish the `Availabilit yUpdatedForNotification` integration event. This event is caught by the `Sales` bounded context, inside the anti-corruption layer represented by the `BrewUp.Sales.Acl` project, and used to update the copy of the data into the `Availability` collection of the `BrewUpSales` database.

Here is the code to publish the integration event:

```
namespace BrewUp.Warehouses.ReadModel.EventHandlers;

public class AvailabilityUpdatedDueToProductionOrderFor
IntegrationEventHandler(ILoggerFactory loggerFactory,
    IEventBus eventBus) : DomainEventHandlerBase<AvailabilityUpdated
DueToProductionOrder>(loggerFactory)
{
    public override async Task HandleAsync
(AvailabilityUpdatedDueToProductionOrder @event,
        CancellationToken cancellationToken = new())
    {
        cancellationToken.ThrowIfCancellationRequested();

        var correlationId =
            new Guid(@event.UserProperties.FirstOrDefault(u => u.Key.
Equals("CorrelationId")).Value.ToString()!);


        AvailabilityUpdatedForNotification
availabilityUpdatedForNotification = new(@event.BeerId, correlationId, @
event.BeerName, @event.Quantity);
        await eventBus.PublishAsync(availabilityUpdatedForNotification,
cancellationToken);
    }
}
```

As you can see, this handler in the BrewUp.Warehouses namespace receives the AvailabilityU pdatedDueToProductionOrder domain event and publishes the AvailabilityUpdatedForNoti fication integration event.

Moving to the BrewUp.Sales bounded context, you can find the BrewUp.Sales.Acl anti-corruption layer project with the following handler:

```
namespace BrewUp.Sales.Acl;

public sealed class
AvailabilityUpdatedForNotificationEventHandler(ILoggerFactory
loggerFactory, IServiceBus serviceBus) : IntegrationEventHandlerAsync
<AvailabilityUpdatedForNotification>(loggerFactory)
{
    public override async Task HandleAsync
(AvailabilityUpdatedForNotification @event,
        CancellationToken cancellationToken = new())
    {
        cancellationToken.ThrowIfCancellationRequested();

        var correlationId =
            new Guid(@event.UserProperties.FirstOrDefault(u => u.Key.
Equals("CorrelationId")).Value.ToString()!);

        UpdateAvailabilityDueToWarehousesNotification command = new(@event.
BeerId, correlationId, @event.BeerName, @event.Quantity);
        await serviceBus.SendAsync(command, cancellationToken);
    }
}
```

The responsibility of the preceding piece of code is to receive the integration event and prepare the command to update the internal read model.

Using different events, as in this example, is a best practice to avoid coupling between the bounded contexts. In this way, you can modify the domain event to introduce new features into the Warehouse bounded context, without changing the integration event used to communicate with the other bounded contexts. *Figure 8.9* shows the solution on the Warehouse side after the refactor:

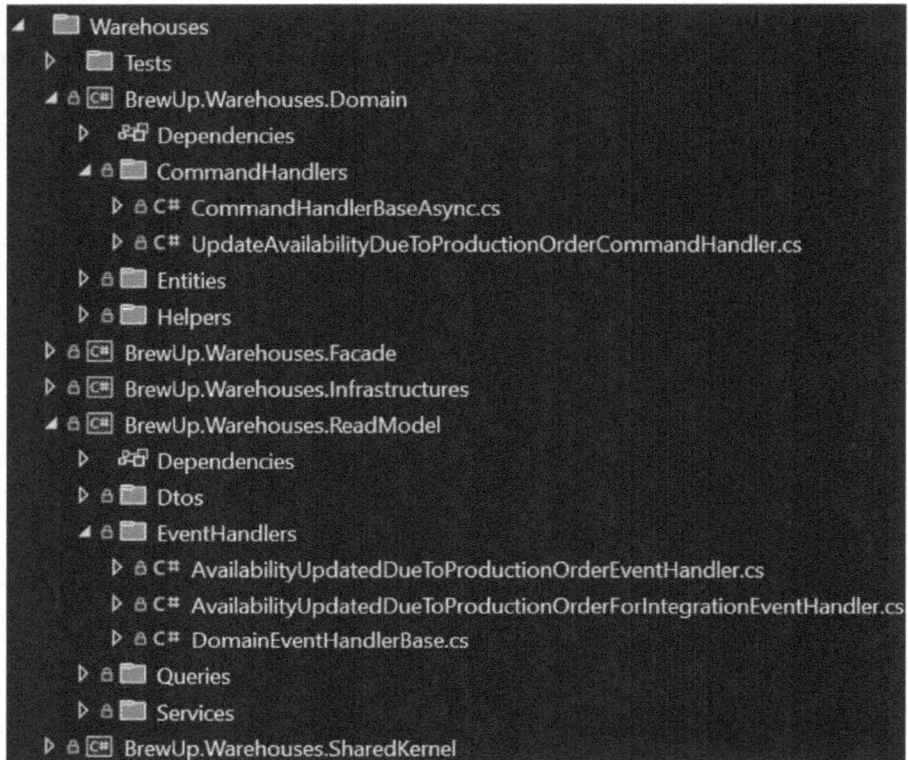

Figure 8.9 – The Warehouse bounded context after the refactor

The solution's organization highlights the separation of concerns inside the bounded context itself.

Figure 8.10 shows the same solution for the Sales bounded context:

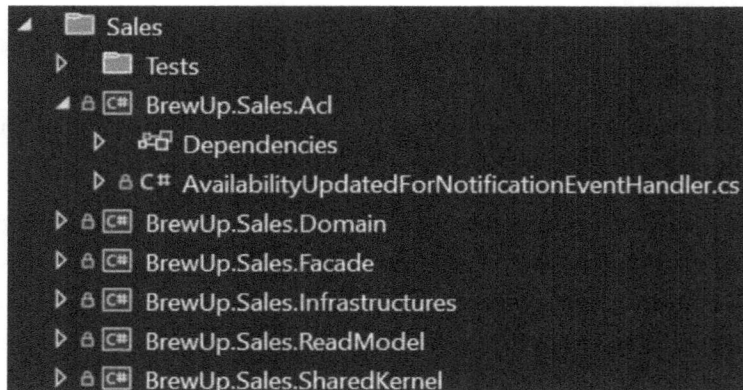

Figure 8.10 – The Sales bounded context after the refactor

In the preceding figure, you can see the anti-corruption layer implemented via the `BrewUp.Sales.Acl` project. This layer aims to translate the language used by the `Warehouse` bounded context into the language used inside the `Sales` bounded context. This is the ACL pattern, which we introduced in *Chapter 3, Strategic Patterns*.

Transitioning to the new architecture and ensuring performance

Now that we have made the first attempt to divide the database into smaller ones more aligned with our modules (or bounded contexts), we should start thinking about the various performance considerations involved during the transition from a monolithic database into a modular architecture, especially in distributed systems where asynchronous communication and eventual consistency are implemented. The challenge lies in optimizing performance while ensuring that the system's data remains consistent, particularly in scenarios where certain services are loosely coupled and rely on asynchronous operations for updates. Let's break down the steps involved in analyzing performance bottlenecks and implementing optimizations with the `SalesOrder` and `Warehouse` services.

We can summarize the potential performance bottlenecks as follows:

- **Network latency**: Direct service-to-service calls across the network add latency
- **Data synchronization delays**: Ensuring consistent data across services can be complex, particularly with asynchronous updates
- **Scalability issues**: Some patterns may scale poorly if data volumes or update rates increase

By identifying these bottlenecks, we can select appropriate optimization strategies tailored for performance in distributed systems.

Distributed data access patterns

To ensure the `SalesOrder` and `Warehouse` services operate efficiently with access to inventory data, three distributed data access patterns can be considered: replicated caching, synchronous interservice communication, and column schema replication.

Replicated caching

The **replicated caching pattern** uses an in-memory cache where each service maintains a synchronized cache of essential data, such as stock levels. The `Warehouse` service manages inventory data, while `SalesOrder` holds a read-only replica, updated asynchronously, as shown in *Figure 8.11*.

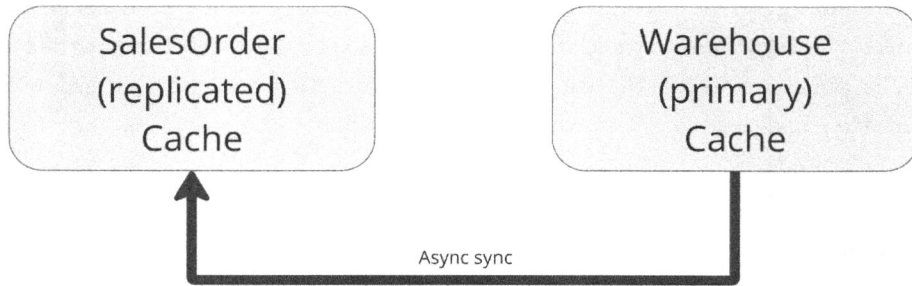

Figure 8.11 – Replicated caching architecture

This pattern minimizes network calls, reduces latency, and allows SalesOrder to remain operational even if Warehouse experiences downtime. Replicated caching is optimal for relatively static or low-frequency data updates but may struggle with high update rates.

Synchronous interservice communication

The **synchronous interservice communication pattern** is used in scenarios where immediate inventory accuracy is essential, where SalesOrder may query Warehouse directly. This is probably the most common pattern for accessing data in a distributed system. When a service needs to read data that it cannot access directly, it asks the owning service for it by using a remote access protocol (i.e., RPC or REST). However, this approach introduces latency from network roundtrips and dependency on Warehouse availability. It could also introduce security latency depending on the security level of the endpoint being accessed. Lastly, do not forget the data latency that you could have due to multiple database calls to retrieve the data requested.

So, while straightforward, this pattern scales poorly under high loads and tight consistency requirements due to its synchronous nature.

Column schema replication

Column schema replication is a strategy for services requiring high data responsiveness, where specific fields (or columns), such as availability, are duplicated from one service's database into the local tables of SalesOrder to enable immediate access without remote calls. This approach trades consistency for performance and requires a mechanism to synchronize changes from Warehouse via events or queues.

There are different solutions to achieve this async alignment between services. The first one is the **event-based pattern**. With event sourcing, the Warehouse service broadcasts stock updates asynchronously whenever the inventory changes, which SalesOrder listens to and updates locally. This pattern ensures that SalesOrder is eventually consistent with the latest stock levels while keeping performance high due to the decoupled nature of event handling. *Figure 8.10* shows the event stream that originates from Warehouse and is subscribed by SalesOrder.

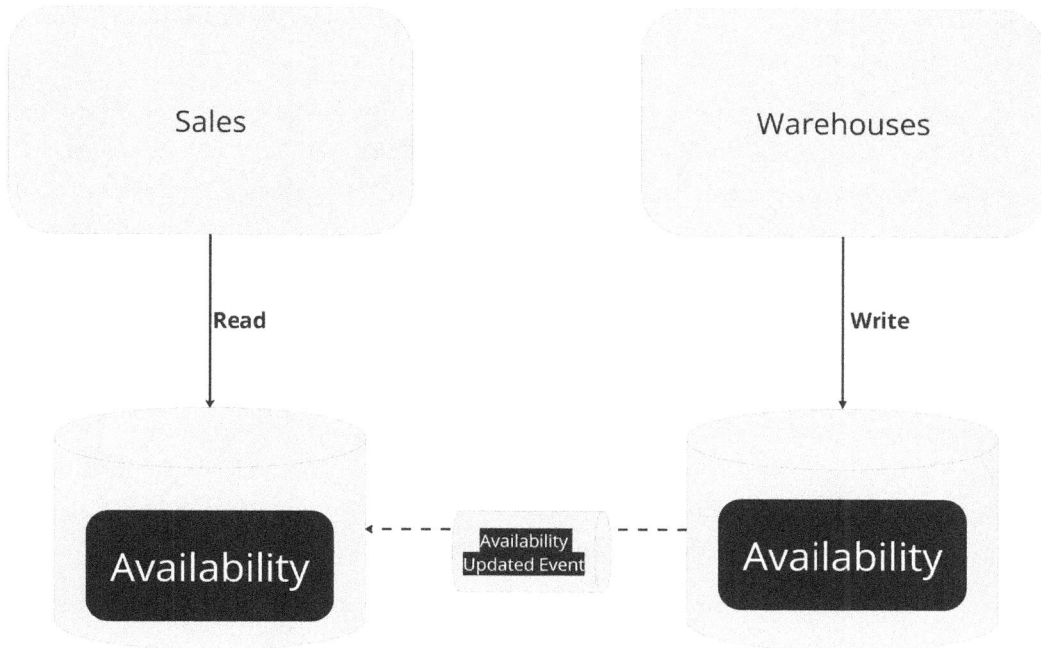

Figure 8.12 – Event-based pattern

The alternative is to go with **Background Synchronization**. For scenarios where immediate consistency is less critical, background synchronization processes can periodically update inventory records in SalesOrder. This method minimizes the real-time load on Warehouse but introduces a lag between updates, making it suitable for non-critical stock-level data.

Lastly, the **Orchestrated Request-Based Pattern** involves an orchestrator service that manages transactions between SalesOrder and Warehouse. This synchronous pattern ensures consistency but can become a bottleneck if the orchestrator's performance degrades under heavy loads. As such, this pattern is best suited for critical operations where strict data integrity is required.

Optimizing query performance with caching and indexing

There are other simple steps to consider in maintaining high performance that are often overlooked (at least in our experience). These are as follows:

- **Caching**: Utilize in-memory caches for frequently accessed data
- **Indexing**: Carefully index frequently queried fields, such as stock levels, in `SalesOrder`
- **Data duplication**: For critical data, duplication allows `SalesOrder` to function independently without frequent remote calls

By adopting a combination of distributed access patterns, eventual consistency, and strategic synchronization methods, the transition from monolithic to modular architecture becomes smoother and more performant. These strategies ensure that `SalesOrder` and `Warehouse` remain loosely coupled, maintain performance, and support the agility required in modular architecture.

Testing and deployment

As we transition to a modular architecture, testing and deploying the database becomes critical in ensuring that refactored services and their data schemas function correctly and remain resilient. In a distributed system with a refactored database, this process is more complex than in a monolithic setup. Each module's data is now independently managed and synchronized, requiring careful testing for consistency, reliability, and performance across services. Deployment practices must also ensure smooth updates without downtime or data loss.

Keep in mind that testing a distributed database in a modular architecture involves validating both the data integrity and the behavior of services that interact with it. With each bounded context now managing its own data, testing must account for consistency, failover handling, and compatibility.

Testing strategies

So, let's look at some strategies for effectively testing and deploying the database during this transition, ensuring stability as we move toward a fully modular and distributed system:

- **Unit testing for schema integrity and changes**: Each service should include unit tests that validate its individual schema, ensuring that changes to one module's schema do not inadvertently impact others. Unit tests should verify that tables are correctly indexed, have the right constraints, and adhere to the designed schema structure. For instance, tests on the `SalesOrder` service schema can ensure that fields such as `orderId` and `availability` maintain their expected data types and relationships.

- **Integration testing with mocked services:** Since multiple services may rely on data from other modules, integration tests are essential for verifying interactions between SalesOrder, Warehouse, and other related services. By using mocks or stubs for external services, we can isolate and verify database behavior within each service's context, simulating the full data flow without impacting live data. For example, integration tests should verify that SalesOrder can read stock levels accurately from the Warehouse cache or database replica.

- **Eventual consistency testing:** For services employing eventual consistency, tests should ensure that delays in data synchronization do not introduce inconsistencies. In a test environment, simulate conditions such as network latency or temporary unavailability of the Warehouse service and verify that SalesOrder still functions as expected. Test scenarios should include both typical synchronization periods and high-load situations to ensure data consistency is maintained under varying conditions.

- **Contract testing for interservice communication:** Contract testing ensures that communication between services, such as SalesOrder and Warehouse, remains reliable. These tests validate that each service can correctly handle and interpret data or events from the other. For example, if SalesOrder receives an AvailabilityUpdated event from Warehouse, contract tests should confirm that SalesOrder processes it correctly and updates its local inventory cache.

- **Performance and load testing for database scalability:** Load testing is critical in understanding how the database will perform under high concurrency. By simulating heavy read and write loads, load tests reveal bottlenecks in schema design, indexing, and caching strategies. These tests can simulate high-traffic scenarios where SalesOrder frequently checks stock levels, helping to tune the database for optimal performance.

Deployment strategies for modular databases

Deploying a database in a modular architecture requires a strategy that minimizes downtime, preserves data integrity, and allows smooth updates across services. Since each module now operates independently, deployment processes must ensure that schema changes, migrations, and updates occur without disrupting interdependent services. The following are some strategies to consider:

- **Blue-green deployments for zero downtime:** Use a blue-green deployment strategy for database changes, where two environments (blue and green) run concurrently. Changes are applied to the blue environment while green continues to serve production traffic. Once testing confirms the new schema, traffic is switched to the updated environment, ensuring zero downtime and a quick rollback if issues arise.

- **Schema migration patterns (expand/contract)**: The expand/contract pattern (explained in detail in the *Principles of database refactoring and identifying domain boundaries* section) helps manage schema changes in a modular database. When refactoring shared data between SalesOrder and Warehouse, expand the schema to support both the old and new structures, maintaining compatibility during the transition. Only after all services are compatible with the new schema should the old schema be removed:

    - **Expand**: Add new fields or tables for the refactored data
    - **Contract**: Update services to use the new schema, then deprecate the old fields/ tables

- **Versioned migrations for incremental updates**: Database version control tools such as *Flyway* or *Liquibase* can manage schema changes as versioned migrations. Each migration is tested individually, applied incrementally, and rolled back if issues arise. This approach allows for phased updates where schema changes are compatible across versions until full deployment.

- **Data duplication for a seamless transition**: During refactoring, use data duplication to ensure data availability across services. For example, duplicate stock data in SalesOrder and Warehouse to prevent dependencies from causing downtime. Event-based data duplication patterns ensure data consistency without requiring immediate updates in each service.

- **Feature flags for gradual rollout**: For complex deployments, use feature flags to control new features that depend on schema changes. By enabling or disabling features per service or environment, you can test schema updates gradually and ensure stable operation across services. This strategy is especially helpful when deploying new data models or migrating to a distributed data source.

Feature flags

A **feature flag**, or **feature toggle**, is a powerful software development concept that allows you to enable or disable specific features without deploying new code. Feature flags serve different purposes, and it is essential, as a software architect, to consider these categories when creating and maintaining toggles. While they add flexibility, they also increase complexity, which is why it is wise to limit the number of toggles in your system to keep things manageable. You can use feature flags for the following:

- **Accelerated releases**: Safely deploy new features to production and manage risk by hiding unfinished features until they are ready
- **A/B testing**: Test new features with a subset of users to gather feedback and assess performance before a full rollout
- **Rollbacks made easy**: Quickly disable problematic features without needing to roll back the entire deployment

Generally speaking, feature flags help you develop and deliver features faster, safer, and with more flexibility. By using them, you can focus on building, refactoring, testing, and refining.

- **Deployment pipeline with continuous integration and testing**: Automated pipelines ensure that every schema change or deployment passes through CI/CD stages with automated testing. Incorporating database tests, schema migrations, and performance tests in the CI/CD pipeline allows for faster feedback, reducing the risk of deployment errors.

Let's apply the preceding strategies to deploy changes to the SalesOrder and Warehouse services in a way that ensures continuous availability and smooth transitions:

1. **Blue-green deployment**: Set up a blue environment to apply and test schema changes (e.g., duplicating availability data across SalesOrder and Warehouse). Traffic remains routed to the green environment, which operates with the stable version (once the blue environment is stable for production it becomes the new green).

2. **Expand/contract**: Expand the schema by adding new tables to store inventory in the local database of SalesOrder. Update SalesOrder to access this new schema gradually. Once validated, apply the contract step by step, deprecating old fields in Warehouse and re-routing stock-level queries to SalesOrder.

3. **Event-driven data synchronization**: Use event-based updates to keep SalesOrder and Warehouse inventory data consistent. An Availability event triggers SalesOrder to update its local stock cache, achieving eventual consistency without high-latency synchronous queries.

4. **Continuous deployment with feature flags**: Enable feature flags on SalesOrder to selectively access the new inventory data from its local schema. Feature flags control access to both old and new schemas during testing, allowing a gradual transition.

Testing and deploying a distributed database in a modular architecture requires a thoughtful blend of testing strategies, schema migration patterns, and deployment practices. By ensuring that schema updates are incremental, tested, and reversible, we can achieve a stable deployment pipeline that supports modular service independence without sacrificing data integrity or performance. These practices allow the architecture to evolve flexibly, providing a foundation for future scalability and resilience as services continue to decouple and scale.

Summary

In this chapter, you learned how to refactor your database, exploring fundamental patterns to help achieve this goal. Database refactoring is never an easy task, nor is it one that an architect can tackle alone—it requires collaboration with a database administrator. The primary challenge often lies not in the technical approach, but in overcoming resistance from stakeholders and DBAs who may be reluctant to split the database. However, if your goal is to move toward a microservices architecture, database separation becomes essential.

First, you need to identify which tables in the original database are relevant to each service's responsibilities. Previous chapters introduced patterns such as bounded contexts and aggregates to help guide this process. Once you've defined these responsibilities, you can apply one of the patterns explored throughout our journey in the database world.

Lastly, many legacy systems rely heavily on stored procedures. While efficient, this approach creates tight coupling between applications and the database, making it challenging to test and maintain. As with tables, you can't simply migrate stored procedures to the code base in one step; instead, you must proceed gradually, testing at each stage.

At the end of this chapter, you have now gained the skills to do the following:

- Split tables from the original database to the new, service-specific databases
- Migrate stored procedures into your code base
- Use incremental, carefully tested steps to ensure data integrity and maintain system behavior

With these skills, you're now equipped to transition from a monolithic solution to a microservices architecture, where each bounded context or microservice is responsible for its own database.

However, database splitting introduces additional complexity, particularly in managing long and intricate processes. When moving tables and services from a monolithic system to microservices, you may need to implement logic to coordinate processes across distributed systems. *Chapter 12, Orchestrating Complexity*, will introduce the saga pattern, a solution for handling these challenges in a microservices environment.

Before that, in the next chapter, we will cover DDD patterns for CI/CD and learn how to harness the power of automation, modularity, and iterative design to deliver high-quality software that serves your domain effectively.

9

DDD Patterns for Continuous Integration and Continuous Refactoring

After looking at how to refactor the database, it is now time to unlock the synergy between DDD and **Continuous Integration/Continuous Deployment (CI/CD)**. Whether you're refactoring legacy code or building new applications, you'll learn how to harness the power of automation, modularity, and iterative design to deliver high-quality software that serves your domain effectively.

In this chapter, you will learn how to do the following:

1. Bridge DDD and CI/CD practice to align business needs with technical delivery through frequent, reliable feedback loops

2. Refactor bounded contexts using proven patterns such as splitting and merging to improve modularity and adapt to changing requirements

3. Use automation and tooling to maintain code quality, reduce errors, and streamline your CI/CD pipelines

By the end of this chapter, you'll have learned practical strategies to ensure your domain models and CI/CD workflows reinforce each other for long-term success.

Integrating DDD with CI/CD

CI/CD and refactoring are not practices strictly tied to DDD—at least not exclusively! In the early days of software development, practices often borrowed concepts from manufacturing, with methods such as the Waterfall model shaping both large-scale processes and smaller tasks such as integration. In the 1990s, engineers on the C3 project, led by Kent Beck, introduced **eXtreme Programming (XP)**, which emphasized automation and frequent feedback as essential drivers of productivity in software engineering. By the 2000s, these principles extended into the realm of operations, giving rise to DevOps and automating many previously manual tasks. Automation enables teams to move faster and more confidently by providing reliable feedback to prevent unexpected issues. As a result, feedback loops and automation have become cornerstones of modern software development practices.

Like in the Whirlpool Process (we referred to this in *Figure 2.7* in the *Problem and solution space* section in *Chapter 2, Understanding Complexity: Problem and Solution Space*), DDD emphasizes a continuous cycling of learning, modeling, and refining the domain as new insights emerge. Such an iterative approach goes hand in hand with CI, where frequent integration with short feedback cycles is encouraged. While the Whirlpool Process focuses on adapting the domain model to evolving business needs, CI/CD ensures that these refinements are rapidly tested, validated, and deployed.

So, CI/CD is more than a technical practice; it is a discipline that enables teams to deliver software in smaller, safer, and more predictable increments. Through the continuous merging and testing of code changes, integration risks are reduced; confidence increases, and collaboration is fostered. It is, however, heavily dependent on the structure and clarity of the code base. That is why DDD complements CI/CD: aligning software structure with business intent means that changes can remain focused, isolated, and testable. In this way, DDD and CI/CD can reinforce each other in reducing the accelerating development while preserving long-term maintainability.

One of the critical pieces of such synergy comes from DDD's notion of bounded contexts. Each bounded context defines a clear boundary of responsibility, making it easier to isolate and test individual parts of the system. This modular design simplifies testing, supports incremental deployment, and minimizes the risk of changes affecting unrelated parts of the application. By ensuring that bounded contexts evolve independently while maintaining consistency with the overall domain model, DDD reinforces CI/CD's goal of a stable, continuously deployable code base.

Why CI/CD benefits from DDD

Modern software systems are complex, often comprising interconnected domains with competing priorities and evolving requirements. Without a clear strategy to manage this complexity, CI/CD can easily become a bottleneck. Large, tangled code bases make changes prone to errors, tests fragile, and deployments unpredictable.

DDD introduces principles and patterns that combat these challenges directly:

1. **Clear boundaries through bounded contexts**: By partitioning the system into bounded contexts, each with a certain business focus, DDD ensures changes in one area of the system are less likely to affect another. This isolation is vital for CI/CD pipelines because it enables smaller pieces that can be independently integrated and tested.

2. **Explicit communication via domain events**: DDD provides a clear call to domain events, which handle semantic business events; these improve communications in the domain model and act as natural integration points between contexts. In CI, these events provide simpler testing and debugging because system behavior becomes more predictable.

3. **Evolving models by refactoring continuously**: The iterative nature of DDD marries well with the incremental approach of CI. Regular refinement of the models keeps the code base representative of the current understanding of the domain, reducing technical debt and preventing stagnation.

Bridging business and technology

In a nutshell, the integration between DDD and CI/CD is fundamentally about bridging the gap that exists between business needs and technical delivery. The iterative processes of CI/CD demand a code base that is not only technically sound but also reflects the increasing understanding of the domain. DDD facilitates this in the following ways:

1. **Ubiquitous language**: Developers, domain experts, and stakeholders have a common language, meaning changes in code truly will represent business needs. This sets up the basis for trusted and meaningful CI/CD pipelines.

2. **Supporting incremental delivery**: DDD allows system design around autonomous contexts such that teams can deliver value incrementally without compromising on the integrity of the overall system.

Setting up a feedback loop

One of the primary goals of CI/CD is to create a rapid **feedback loop**. When integrated with DDD, this loop becomes not just about technical correctness but also about domain alignment. Automated tests validate not only that the code works but also that it serves its intended purpose in the domain. Domain events, for instance, provide immediate feedback about business processes, helping teams quickly identify and address misalignments.

Figure 9.1 shows how this loop works in practice:

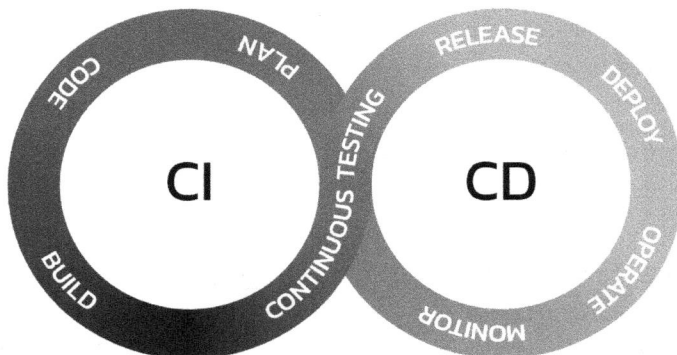

Figure 9.1 – CI/CD loop

This feedback loop becomes a powerful tool for continuously refining both the technical architecture and the domain model. As teams adopt patterns for splitting and merging bounded contexts, described later in this chapter, they can be assured that each context evolves independently according to business priorities.

This concept is also reinforced when refactoring bounded contexts by applying patterns such as splitting or merging, as you will see in the next section.

Patterns and techniques for effective DDD refactoring

Refactoring is not just about cleaning up code. In a DDD context, it's a way to ensure the system evolves alongside the business domain. Splitting bounded contexts is one of the most impactful techniques for aligning technical boundaries with shifting business needs. Effective refactoring in a DDD environment requires structured approaches to managing bounded contexts and refining domain models.

By exploring the patterns and techniques that support this process, you will see that they are the same as already discussed in the earlier chapters of this book. That's because the fundamentals of DDD also apply beautifully to this aspect of refactoring.

As you know, bounded context is a fundamental DDD concept that encapsulates a consistent domain language and model. Over time, as business needs evolve, these contexts may require splitting, merging, or redefinition. In this subsection, we will cover two techniques for managing such transitions: **splitting bounded contexts** and **merging bounded contexts**.

Splitting bounded contexts

When a bounded context grows too large or begins serving conflicting purposes, splitting it into smaller, more focused contexts can improve clarity and maintainability. For this reason, we can leverage domain decomposition or context mapping

Domain decomposition

Domain decomposition involves breaking down the responsibilities of a bounded context into smaller, distinct parts that align with specific subdomains or business capabilities. This approach helps identify natural seams in the domain model, enabling the creation of new, smaller contexts that better reflect business requirements.

Firstly, you need to understand the current context. As you already know by now, the only effective way is to work with the domain experts to map the existing responsibilities, workflows, and data flows within the bounded context. Do note that you can use tools such as EventStorming (see the *EventStorming* subsection in *Chapter 2, Understanding Complexity: Problem and Solution Space*, for a quick explanation) or domain storytelling to visualize how the current model operates.

Then, you can move on to identify subdomains by separating core subdomains from supporting and generic subdomains.

Look for areas with distinct business logic or teams that already work semi-independently. Find natural seams by examining where invariants (rules that must be enforced) are localized. These areas are prime candidates for new contexts. After that, assess boundaries defined by team ownership, user roles, or external dependencies and plan dependencies. You must decide how the split contexts will interact. For example, some may exchange domain events, while others may rely on APIs or asynchronous messaging.

For example, a *shipping* context in an e-commerce system might handle both route optimization and delivery tracking. Over time, these responsibilities could diverge significantly:

- **Route optimization** could become its own context, focused on advanced algorithms and integrations with mapping services
- **Delivery tracking** could be a separate context, concerned with customer-facing updates and integration with external logistics systems

To recap, the refactoring steps could be summarized as follows:

1. Isolate related aggregates into smaller clusters.
2. Introduce domain events to define clear communication between the new contexts.
3. Gradually refactor dependent code to respect the new boundaries.

Context mapping

Context mapping visualizes the relationships between bounded contexts, offering insights into their interactions, dependencies, and potential conflicts. It is an essential tool for planning and executing a split.

The steps are straightforward. You start by identifying the contexts already interacting with the one being split and then map the existing relationships, such as **shared kernel**, **partnership**, or **upstream/downstream**. As you analyze the new split contexts, represent each new context on the map, highlighting its relationship to the existing system. For example, after splitting, one context might depend on domain events produced by another.

After that, you must redefine the interaction patterns by adjusting patterns to match the new architecture. For example, you might change tight coupling such as **shared kernel** to a looser integration such as **published language** and transform a dependency-heavy relationship such as **conformist** into a partnership that allows for more autonomy.

Lastly, you must always validate with the domain experts. Collaborate with them to be able to confirm that the new boundaries align with business needs and workflows.

For example, in a *Customer Support* context of a telecommunications system, the split might result in two new contexts:

- **Ticket Management**: Focused on tracking customer support tickets and their lifecycle.
- **Knowledge Base**: Responsible for managing and updating help articles.

The context map would show the following:

- `Ticket Management` produces domain events (e.g., `Ticket Closed`) consumed by `Knowledge Base` to trigger content updates
- The two contexts share a customer ID but otherwise operate independently

Finally, remember to use anti-corruption layers to manage communication between the old and new contexts during the transition period (look at the *ACL* subsection in *Chapter 3*, *Strategic Patterns*, for a refresher) and verify that the split contexts communicate effectively through well-defined domain events or APIs with well-written integration tests (refer to the *Understanding tests and their role in refactoring* section in *Chapter 5*, *Introducing Refactoring Principles*, for an explanation of tests and their different types).

Splitting bounded contexts is a complex yet rewarding process that enhances system modularity and business agility. By leveraging domain decomposition and context mapping, teams can make informed decisions, ensuring a smooth evolution toward a more maintainable and scalable architecture.

Merging bounded contexts

Conversely, merging contexts may be necessary if boundaries are no longer meaningful or cause excessive friction. To merge contexts, you must first identify redundancies such as overlapping models, duplicate logic, or tight coupling between two contexts. Only then can you establish a new shared language and ensure the merged context adopts a unified ubiquitous language to eliminate inconsistencies. In short, the refactoring steps that you can then follow consist of consolidating aggregates into a shared model, deprecating redundant domain events and replacing them with shared ones, and lastly revisiting context maps to reflect the new, simplified structure.

A merge becomes necessary in scenarios such as when the domain models of two contexts have significant overlap, making their separation redundant. This often happens when different teams or phases of a project initially create boundaries that, over time, no longer reflect the current business landscape. Similarly, if two contexts frequently interact to the point that the integration overhead outweighs the benefits of separation, it is worth considering a merge. Changes in business strategy, such as consolidating operations or redefining team responsibilities, can also reveal opportunities for merging contexts that once served distinct purposes.

The process of merging begins with a thorough understanding of the existing contexts. The teams involved should analyze the responsibilities, domain models, and workflows of each context to identify overlaps and redundancies. Collaboration with domain experts is essential to uncover shared concepts and ensure the unified context aligns with the business' needs. This step often involves documenting the interactions and dependencies between the contexts to understand how the merge will affect the system as a whole.

Once a clear picture of the current state emerges, you can define the unified context. This involves creating a single domain model that consolidates shared entities and concepts while eliminating duplications. Careful thought must be given to the new boundaries of the merged context, ensuring it encapsulates all relevant responsibilities without becoming a monolith. The merged context should maintain cohesion, focusing on a consistent set of business capabilities.

For example, consider a situation where the Warehouse context handles stock management and shipments, while the Sales context manages orders and payments. Initially, these contexts were distinct to allow focused development. Over time, however, the Warehouse context's stock availability began to influence the Sales context's ability to accept orders, creating a dependency. The frequent need for synchronization between these contexts led to bottlenecks and integration challenges. In such a scenario, merging Warehouse and Sales into a single context might simplify operations by providing a unified model for managing orders and stock. This new context could include a consistent invariant, such as ensuring a beer cannot be sold if it is out of stock.

The transition from separate to unified contexts should be gradual to reduce risks. During the initial stages, shared domain events can act as a bridge between the contexts, maintaining existing functionality while the unified domain model is developed. For example, the Sales context could continue to rely on domain events such as AvailabilityUpdated from the Warehouse context until a unified stock management system is ready. As the integration progresses, entities and business rules can be migrated incrementally into the new context, ensuring that each step aligns with the unified model.

Another important aspect of merging is redefining the relationships between the new unified context and other parts of the system. Upstream and downstream dependencies must be adjusted to reflect the new architecture. In the case of the Warehouse and Sales merge, external systems such as *Customer Service* would need to interact with the unified context to retrieve stock and order information. These changes require careful planning to avoid disruptions.

Validating the success of a merge involves extensive testing and collaboration with domain experts. The unified context must meet both technical and business expectations. Domain experts play a critical role in confirming that the new model aligns with the company's workflows and goals. Testing ensures that the system's performance and reliability remain unaffected during and after the transition.

For example, in the case of the merged Warehouse and Sales context, the team must validate that the unified model supports both backend operations, such as stock tracking, and customer-facing processes, such as order confirmations. Performance bottlenecks introduced by the merge, such as slower order processing due to combined responsibilities, must be identified and addressed.

Merging bounded contexts is a strategic decision that requires careful planning and execution. When done correctly, it reduces the complexity of managing separate systems, streamlines communication, and ensures the architecture remains aligned with the domain's realities. By focusing on creating a cohesive, well-defined context, teams can enhance both technical efficiency and business agility.

While the patterns and techniques discussed in this section provide a strong foundation for effective DDD refactoring, maintaining a well-aligned domain model requires an ongoing commitment to continuous refactoring.

Continuous refactoring within a DDD context

The nature of DDD makes **continuous refactoring** particularly important because domains are dynamic. Business needs change, markets shift, and organizational strategies evolve. In a static code base, these changes can lead to misalignment between the system's implementation and the real-world processes it aims to model. Left unchecked, this drift introduces inefficiencies, impairs communication, and hampers agility. Continuous refactoring addresses this by embracing change as a natural part of software development.

At its heart, continuous refactoring in a DDD context is about weaving domain refinement into the fabric of day-to-day development. This means refactoring is not reserved for isolated *cleanup* phases; it happens every time a new feature is introduced, a bug is fixed, or a domain concept is clarified. For example, when a domain expert provides a new insight into how a business rule operates, the development team should immediately reflect this understanding in the domain model, ensuring that the system continues to accurately represent the business.

To enable continuous refactoring, robust practices must be in place. One key aspect is maintaining a clear and well-articulated ubiquitous language. As teams engage with domain experts and refine their understanding of the domain, this shared language evolves. Continuous refactoring ensures that the code base evolves in tandem, incorporating changes to entities, aggregates, and domain events to reflect the updated language. This process prevents inconsistencies and ensures that the code remains a reliable reference for the domain.

Another critical enabler is the use of automation to support frequent and safe iterations. Automated tests, particularly those focused on business logic, are indispensable in a DDD context. These tests act as a safety net, allowing developers to refactor with confidence. By capturing the intent and constraints of the domain, automated tests help ensure that refactoring efforts do not inadvertently disrupt functionality. Additionally, tools such as linters, static analyzers, and dependency scanners can proactively identify code smells or architectural drift, prompting timely intervention.

Continuous refactoring also thrives on collaboration. In a DDD environment, it is not solely a technical activity, it is inherently tied to domain exploration. Developers must work closely with domain experts to identify areas of the model that need refinement. These discussions often uncover opportunities to simplify complex workflows, consolidate overlapping concepts, or eliminate redundancies. For instance, a domain expert might reveal that two similar-sounding domain events—such as `OrderPlaced` and `OrderInitiated`—are effectively describing the same business action. Continuous refactoring would merge these events into one, reducing ambiguity and enhancing clarity.

In practice, continuous refactoring requires teams to be mindful of the boundaries of their bounded contexts. Misaligned or poorly understood boundaries often introduce friction, leading to unnecessary coupling or inefficiencies. By regularly revisiting these boundaries, teams can make minor adjustments to keep them relevant. This might involve redefining the scope of a context to better fit current business capabilities or restructuring interactions between contexts to reflect updated workflows.

An essential outcome of continuous refactoring is that it prevents architectural decay. Over time, even well-designed systems can accumulate technical and conceptual debt as new features are added or shortcuts are taken to meet deadlines. By treating refactoring as an integral part of feature development, teams ensure that the system does not degrade under the weight of these changes. For example, when implementing a new feature, developers can seize the opportunity to clarify ambiguous domain concepts, simplify convoluted code paths, or replace outdated patterns with more effective alternatives.

One significant challenge in continuous refactoring is balancing improvement efforts with delivery timelines. Teams must prioritize changes that provide the most value, ensuring that refactoring efforts align with business priorities. Small, incremental adjustments are often the most effective approach, as they minimize disruption while delivering steady progress. This incrementalism aligns well with agile practices, where frequent iterations allow for rapid feedback and course correction.

Continuous refactoring within a DDD context is not just about maintaining code quality but is about preserving the connection between the system and the business it serves. By embedding this practice into daily workflows, teams can ensure that the software remains a faithful and effective representation of the domain, capable of adapting to whatever challenges and opportunities the future holds. This commitment to ongoing refinement transforms refactoring from a reactive activity into a proactive strategy for long-term success.

To support continuous refactoring in a DDD context, leveraging the right automation and tooling is essential for maintaining efficiency and consistency. We will discuss this next.

Automation and tooling

Automation and tooling are the backbone of modern software development practices, and their importance grows exponentially when applying DDD within a CI/CD pipeline. While DDD provides strategic and tactical patterns for designing robust systems, automation ensures these patterns are implemented efficiently and consistently across the development lifecycle. From code generation and automated testing to infrastructure as code and deployment pipelines, the right tools not only enhance productivity but also reduce human error, enabling teams to focus on solving domain problems. In this section, we are going to explore the tools and automation practices that bring DDD and CI/CD to life, ensuring smooth integration, testing, and deployment at scale.

At the heart of this synergy lies the *source code repository*, which acts as much more than a simple storage medium for code. It serves as the foundation for collaboration, traceability, and automated workflows, enabling the seamless orchestration of every step in the CI/CD pipeline.

Platforms such as *GitHub*, *GitLab*, *Bitbucket*, and *Azure DevOps*, to name a few, have become full-blown tools to support and automate the CI/CD pipeline. All of them offer a location for online code storage and capabilities for issue tracking and CI/CD.

The first platform to provide developers with an integrated CI/CD system, beyond just source control, was GitLab. GitLab introduced its CI/CD system in 2015, offering a fully integrated solution that allowed developers to manage both source code and the entire development lifecycle, from automated testing to deployment. This was innovative compared to platforms such as GitHub and Bitbucket at the time, which required external tools (such as *Jenkins*, *Travis CI*, or *CircleCI*) to handle CI/CD workflows.

GitLab's CI/CD integration was particularly advantageous for the following reasons:

- It enabled the configuration of build, test, and deploy pipelines directly through a YAML file in the repository
- It provided a seamless, centralized experience without the need for external tools
- It was open source and available in a self-hosted version as well

Later, other platforms, such as *GitHub* (with *GitHub Actions*), *Bitbucket* (with *Bitbucket Pipelines*), *Azure DevOps* (with *Azure Pipelines*), and *AWS* (with *AWS CodePipeline*), introduced their own integrated CI/CD systems to offer similar capabilities.

All these platforms exemplify this critical role by providing tools for managing source code while also acting as a hub for automation, integration, and much more (i.e.: Kanban boards, tickets, etc.). Through features such as branching, pull requests, and code reviews, they facilitate a CI/CD workflow where teams can collaborate efficiently and maintain high-quality code standards.

So, the repository becomes not just a tool but an enabler of streamlined development practices, where every aspect of software delivery, from ideation to production, is tightly integrated and continuously optimized.

Along with unit tests, integration tests, and so on, an important tool for code quality is **SonarQube** (`https://www.sonarsource.com`). It is a powerful open source tool for maintaining and improving code quality by examining source code and delivering detailed insights and reports on various quality metrics for your project. By integrating both static and dynamic analysis techniques, SonarQube allows teams to track and enhance code quality consistently throughout the development lifecycle.

Static code analysis is meant to detect bugs, vulnerabilities, code smells, and duplications across various programming languages. The key features that SonarQube offers are as follows:

- **Code quality gates**: Enforces standards to ensure that code meets quality requirements before deployment
- **Multi-language support**: Supports over 25 programming languages, such as Java, Python, JavaScript, and C#

- **Integration**: Works seamlessly with CI/CD pipelines, DevOps tools (e.g., Jenkins, GitLab, GitHub, Azure DevOps), and IDEs
- **Security**: Detects security vulnerabilities such as SQL injection and **cross-site scripting (XSS)**
- **Custom rules**: Enables custom rules for specific project requirements

As a result of all these features, consequently, you end up with the following benefits:

- **Improved code quality**: Continuous monitoring helps developers produce cleaner, more maintainable code
- **Reduced technical debt**: Identifies areas that need refactoring to reduce long-term maintenance costs
- **Enhanced security**: Early detection of vulnerabilities reduces risks in production
- **Team collaboration**: Promotes shared standards and accountability across teams

SonarQube can be introduced as part of the development pipeline, ensuring every piece of code aligns with the organization's quality and security standards.

SonarQube and GitLab example

The following code is an example of a complete workflow for GitLab that also takes advantage of SonarQube features:

```
stages:
  - cleanup
  - build
  - test
  - sonarqube
  - deploy

cleanup:
  stage: cleanup
  script:
    - docker system prune --all --force
  tags:
    - shell
build:
  stage: build
  image: mcr.microsoft.com/dotnet/sdk:9.0
```

```yaml
    script:
      - dotnet build
    tags:
      - docker
test:
  stage: test
  script:
    - dotnet test --collect:"XPlat Code Coverage;Format=opencover"
--results-directory TestResults
  artifacts:
    paths:
      - TestResults/
      - TestResults/**/*.trx
      - TestResults/**/coverage.opencover.xml
  tags:
    - docker


sonarqube-check:
  stage: sonarqube
  image: mcr.microsoft.com/dotnet/sdk:9.0
  variables:
    SONAR_USER_HOME: "${CI_PROJECT_DIR}/.sonar"  # Defines the location of
the analysis task cache
    GIT_DEPTH: "0"  # Tells git to fetch all the branches of the project,
required by the analysis task
  cache:
    key: "${CI_JOB_NAME}"
    paths:
      - .sonar/cache
  script:
    - "apt-get update"
    - "apt-get install --yes default-jdk"
    - "dotnet tool install --global dotnet-sonarscanner"
    - "export PATH=\"$PATH:$HOME/.dotnet/tools\""
    - "dotnet sonarscanner begin /k:\"iris-poc-api\" /d:sonar.
login=\"$SONAR_TOKEN\" /d:sonar.host.url=\"$SONAR_HOST_URL\" /d:sonar.
cs.opencover.reportsPaths=\"TestResults/**/coverage.opencover.xml\""
    - "dotnet build"
```

```
        - "dotnet sonarscanner end /d:sonar.login=\"$SONAR_TOKEN\""
    allow_failure: true
    tags:
      - docker

deploy:
  stage: deploy
  script:
    - deploy commands (any container registry, ftp, etc.)...
  tags:
    - deploy
```

In the preceding code, the first stage is `cleanup`, which in this case consists of cleaning the Docker environment. This is done with `docker system prune --all -force`, which forces the deletion of all the unused images, containers, and networks.

The second stage, `build`, proceeds to build the solution, and then the following stage, `test`, runs the tests. You read about the importance of testing in the *Understanding tests and their role in refactoring* section in *Chapter 5*, and it is important to understand that if any of the tests fail the deployment process will fail and, as a result, nothing must be deployed in production till all tests are passed.

If the tests pass, the script moves on to the sonarqube stage, which evaluates the quality of your software. SonarQube allows you to set specific test coverage thresholds to ensure that your code base meets quality standards. It analyzes your project's test results and measures how much of the code is exercised by your test cases, typically displayed as a percentage. You can configure coverage goals in your quality gate, such as requiring at least 80% coverage. If the coverage falls below the set threshold, SonarQube will flag it as a failure, prompting developers to improve test coverage before merging or deploying the code. This helps maintain robust testing practices and ensures higher code reliability.

Finally, the last stage, `deploy`, kicks in and our application is deployed in staging or production depending on the rules engaged.

GitHub Actions example

The following is another example but with GitHub Actions:

```yaml
name: 🚀 BrewUp.Rest deploy pipeline

on:
  workflow_dispatch:
  push:
    paths:
      - './**'
    branches:
      - develop
    tags:
      - '*'

env:
  SOLUTION_PATH: ./BrewUp.Rest.sln
  DOCKERFILE_PATH: ./BrewUp.Rest/Dockerfile
  STAGING_MY_CLOUD_PROVIDER_APP: BrewUp-staging
  PRODUCTION_MY_CLOUD_PROVIDER_APP: BrewUp-staging
  IMAGE_NAME: ${{ github.repository }}-BrewUp
  DOCKER_CONTEXT_PATH: ./

jobs:
  build_and_test:
    name: 🔧 Build and Test
    runs-on: ubuntu-latest
    steps:
      - name: 💻 Get latest code
        uses: actions/checkout@v4
      - name: 🔧 Setup .NET Core
        uses: actions/setup-dotnet@v4
      - name: 🔧 Restore dependencies
        run: dotnet restore ${{ env.SOLUTION_PATH }}
      - name: 🔨 Build
        run: dotnet build ${{ env.SOLUTION_PATH }}
      - name: 🧪 Run tests
```

```
            run: dotnet test ${{ env.SOLUTION_PATH }}


  build_and_push_staging_image_amd64:
    name: 🏗️ Build and push develop amd64 Docker image to GitHub Container
Registry
    runs-on: ubuntu-latest
    needs: build_and_test
    if: startsWith(github.ref, 'refs/heads/develop')
    steps:
      - name: 🖥️ Get latest code
        uses: actions/checkout@v4
      - name: 🔑 Login to GitHub Container Registry
        uses: docker/login-action@v3
        with:
          registry: ghcr.io
          username: ${{ github.actor }}
          password: ${{ secrets.REGISTRY_HUB_SECRET }}
      - name: 🔨 Build and push image
        uses: docker/build-push-action@v6
        with:
          context: ${{ env.DOCKER_CONTEXT_PATH }}
          file: ${{ env.DOCKERFILE_PATH }}
          platforms: linux/amd64
          push: true
          tags: ghcr.io/${{ env.IMAGE_NAME }}:develop


  build_and_push_production_image:
    name: 🏗️ Build and push tag Docker image to GitHub Container Registry
    # Like staging. Here is the configuration for the production
environment


  deploy_staging:
    name: 🚀 Deploy to Staging
    runs-on: ubuntu-latest
    needs: build_and_push_staging_image_amd64
    if: startsWith(github.ref, 'refs/heads/develop')
    steps:
      - name: 🌐 Deploy to my cloud provider
```

```yaml
        uses: my_cloud_provider/app_action@v1.0.0
        with:
          app_name: ${{ env.STAGING_MY_CLOUD_PROVIDER_APP }}
          token: ${{ secrets.MY_CLOUD_PROVIDER_TOKEN }}


  deploy_production:
    name: 🚀 Deploy to Production
    # Like staging. Here is the configuration for the production
environment


  notify_on_failure:
    name: 🔔⚠️ Notify Microsoft Teams of deployment failure
    runs-on: ubuntu-latest
    needs: [build_and_test, build_and_push_staging_image_amd64, build_and_
push_production_image, deploy_staging, deploy_production]
    if: |
      always() &&
      (
        needs.build_and_test.result == 'failure' ||
        needs.build_and_push_staging_image_amd64.result == 'failure' ||
        needs.build_and_push_production_image.result == 'failure' ||
        needs.deploy_staging.result == 'failure' ||
        needs.deploy_production.result == 'failure'
      )
    steps:
      - name: 📮 Send Microsoft Teams Notification
        uses: jdcargile/ms-teams-notification@v1.4
        with:
          github-token: ${{ github.token }}
          ms-teams-webhook-uri: ${{ secrets.MS_TEAMS_WEBHOOK_URL }}
          notification-summary: ${{ github.workflow }} failed by deploying
${{ github.ref_name }}, check the workflow run for more information.
          notification-color: dc3545
          timezone: Europe/Rome
          verbose-logging: true
```

The preceding code comprises a more complex example, but we will not delve into explaining all the steps because it is out of this book's scope. However, this example basically follows the same stages explained in the GitLab example we covered before this one and, as a plus, includes an example of integration with Microsoft Teams for failures.

Summary

In this chapter, you discovered how integrating DDD with CI/CD can transform the way you build and maintain software. You explored how these methodologies complement each other, helping you deliver systems that are modular, aligned with business goals, and easy to evolve. By combining DDD's strategic insights with CI/CD's technical rigor, you've gained tools to tackle complexity while fostering agility and maintainability.

Here's what you learned:

- How DDD enhances CI/CD workflows, enabling frequent, safe updates through modularity and alignment with domain models
- Techniques for refactoring bounded contexts
- The importance of automation and tools, such as SonarQube and CI/CD pipelines, in ensuring code quality and seamless delivery

With these insights, you're now equipped to create resilient systems that keep pace with both technical and business demands.

Remember that effective DDD refactoring is not just about improving code; it's about evolving systems in harmony with the domain. By mastering these patterns and techniques, you can ensure your system remains both technically robust and aligned with business needs.

The next chapter is about microservices architecture and when it makes sense to move your perfectly working monolith to a more complex system such as one made of microservices.

Get this book's PDF version and more

Scan the QR code (or go to packtpub.com/unlock). Search for this book by name, confirm the edition, and then follow the steps on the page.

UNLOCK NOW

Note: Keep your invoice handy. Purchases made directly from Packt don't require an invoice.

Part 3

Moving from Monolith to Microservices

In this final part of the book, you'll explore how to move from a modular monolith to microservices. You'll learn when and why it's time to transition to microservices, and how to effectively manage the evolution of events within this new structure. You'll also dive into advanced approaches for orchestrating complex business processes, equipping you with the tools to navigate the challenges of distributed systems while maintaining agility and scalability. By the end of this section, you'll be ready to embrace the flexibility and power of microservices in your own projects.

This part of the book includes the following chapters:

- *Chapter 10, When and Why You Should Transition to a Microservices Architecture*
- *Chapter 11, Dealing with Events and Their Evolution*
- *Chapter 12, Orchestrating Complexity: Advanced Approaches to Business Processes*

10

When and Why You Should Transition to a Microservices Architecture

In recent years, microservices architecture has gained significant attention as a solution to the limitations often associated with monolithic systems. But what does it actually mean, and why has this architecture become such a popular choice? Fundamentally, a microservices architecture divides an application into a set of small deployable services. Each service is built to perform a single specific role and to interact with the rest using well-defined APIs.

This is quite different from the architecture of monolithic systems, in which all functionalities are tightly coupled and work as an integral unit. While monoliths are easier to develop and deploy at the beginning, their tightly coupled nature may result in challenges regarding scalability, maintainability, and development speed as the application grows. Microservices promote modularity and flexibility, thus being an attractive choice for organizations that look for agility and scalability.

Understanding the difference between monolithic and microservices architectures is crucial to determining whether a move to microservices aligns with an organization's goals. This chapter lays out the foundational knowledge and practical insights needed to determine when and why microservices may be the right choice for your organization, focusing on the migration from a modular monolith—a step many organizations take as they explore this architectural approach.

We specifically explore how to migrate from monolithic solutions to microservices architectures, focusing on aligning technical decisions with business needs. By delving into foundational concepts and practical approaches, you'll gain the tools to navigate this transition effectively.

This chapter will cover the following:

- The role of modular monoliths as a foundation for transitioning to microservices
- Insights into the trade-offs and complexities inherent in distributed systems
- Practical steps for evolving your architecture incrementally, minimizing risk, and maximizing value

The complete code for this chapter can be found in the `02-monolith_with_cqrs` (https:// github.com/PacktPublishing/Domain-driven-Refactoring/tree/02-monolith_with_cqrs), `03-monolith_with_cqrs_and_event_sourcing` (https://github.com/PacktPublishing/ Domain-driven-Refactoring/tree/03-monolith_with_cqrs_and_event_sourcing), and `04-microservices` (https://github.com/PacktPublishing/Domain-driven-Refactoring/ tree/04-microservices) branches in the book's GitHub repository.

Exploring microservices architecture

At its heart, **microservices** emphasize building distributed systems composed of small, independently deployable components, each responsible for a specific functionality. While this architectural style has reshaped how we think about scalability, agility, and maintainability, its alignment with the core principles of DDD is where its true potential lies.

One of the key advantages of microservices is their alignment with business capabilities. By structuring services around specific domains, teams can work more independently, reducing bottlenecks and enabling faster iteration. This approach dovetails naturally with DDD principles, which emphasize organizing software around the core domains and subdomains of a business.

Microservices can offer the following:

- **Improved scalability**: Every single service can scale independently as per its demand
- **Enhanced resilience**: When one service fails, it will not necessarily bring down the whole application
- **Faster development cycles**: Self-sufficient teams can develop, deploy, and iterate on services independently, reducing time to market for new features

While these benefits are impressive, they are not without a trade-off: microservices architectures are inherently more complex than monolithic systems. This added complexity raises questions about when the transition makes sense and how to execute it effectively.

Moving from a modular monolith to microservices

In general, the leap to microservices is framed as a natural evolution rather than a complete overhaul for organizations transitioning from a modular monolith. After all, modular monoliths already incorporate some of the principles foundational to microservices, such as clear module boundaries and separation of concerns. This similarity makes them a common starting point for organizations contemplating the switch.

However, the decision to adopt microservices should never be based solely on trends or perceived industry best practices. It must be grounded in a deep understanding of the organization's current needs, future goals, and the constraints of its existing systems. Factors such as team structure, operational readiness, and the complexity of the domain should play a pivotal role in shaping this decision.

Figure 10.1 shows the transformation from a modular monolith to the microservices equivalent in simple terms. As you can see, the components in every layer of the monolith are moved to a standalone service.

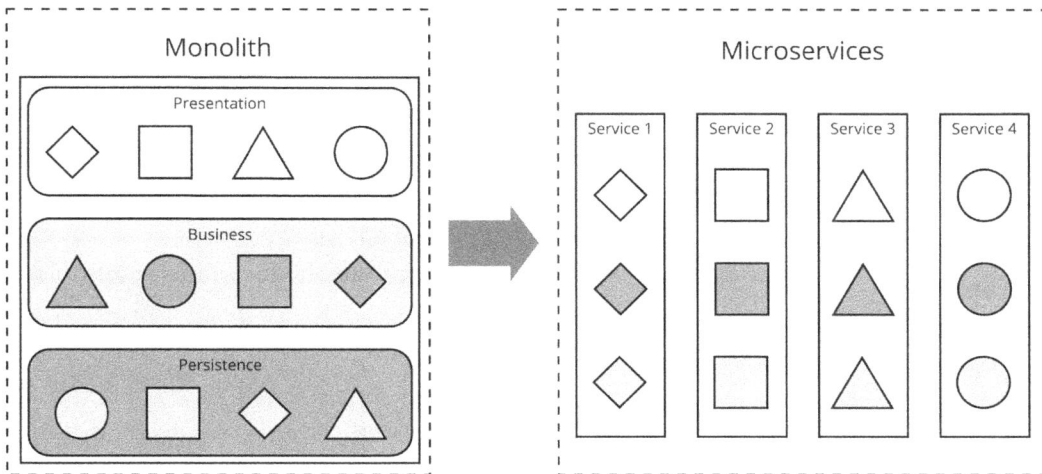

Figure 10.1 – Moving from a modular monolith to microservices

Monolith versus microservices

To understand when and why moving to microservices might be beneficial, it is crucial to first explore the key differences between monolithic and microservices architectures across several dimensions:

- **Development**: Monolithic systems are developed as a single, unified code base. This approach clearly simplifies initial development since all components are part of the same system. However, as the code base grows, coordinating changes among teams becomes increasingly challenging. Microservices, in contrast, allow different teams to work on separate services with minimal interdependencies. So, each team can focus on its domain, leading to shorter development cycles and fewer bottlenecks. However, it is important to note that starting a greenfield project with microservices is significantly more complex and costly than with a well-structured modular monolith, as it requires setting up infrastructure, service communication, and deployment automation from the outset.

- **Deployment**: A monolith is deployed as a single unit, simplifying deployment pipelines but making updates riskier. A small change in one component requires the entire application to be redeployed. Instead, with microservices, each service is independently deployable and enables faster and more frequent updates while minimizing the impact of changes on unrelated services.

- **Scalability**: Scaling a monolith usually involves adding more resources (known as vertical scaling), which has physical and cost limitations. On the other hand, microservices enable horizontal scaling, allowing specific services to be scaled independently based on their needs. For example, a high-demand service such as a recommendation engine can be scaled without affecting the rest of the system.

- **Resilience**: A failure in a monolithic application can bring down the entire system since all components are tightly coupled. In a microservices architecture, failures are isolated to individual services, improving the overall resilience of the system. It is worth noting that this advantage heavily depends on robust service communication and error-handling mechanisms.

- **Complexity**: Monolithic architectures are less complex to design and manage initially. The fact that all components reside in the same code base reduces the need for sophisticated infrastructure and operational practices. Microservices introduce significant complexity, requiring advanced DevOps practices, distributed system design, and monitoring to manage multiple services and their interactions.

- **Team autonomy**: Monolithic systems force all teams to use the same technology stack, which can limit innovation and create dependencies between teams. Microservices grant teams the freedom to choose the best technology for their specific service, enabling experimentation and optimization. This autonomy also aligns better with DDD principles.

- **Maintenance and performance**: Over time, monoliths become harder to maintain as the code base grows larger and more intertwined. Microservices, with their smaller and more focused code bases, are easier to maintain but introduce performance challenges due to network overhead in service-to-service communication.

- **Startup costs**: Monoliths have lower initial development and infrastructure costs, making them suitable for start-ups or small applications. Microservices require investment in tooling, automation, and infrastructure, which can be a barrier for smaller organizations.

Table 10.1 summarizes these key points for a quick reference:

Aspect	Monolithic Architecture	Microservices Architecture
Development	Simplified development with a single code base	Teams can develop independently, enabling faster iterations
Deployment	A single deployment unit makes deployment straightforward	Independent deployment of services allows flexibility
Scalability	Vertical scaling (increasing hardware capacity)	Horizontal scaling (scaling individual services)
Resilience	A failure in one component can crash the whole system	Failures are isolated to individual services
Complexity	Less initial operational complexity	High operational complexity due to the distributed nature
Team Autonomy	Teams must coordinate tightly, leading to bottlenecks	Teams can work autonomously on different services
Technology Flexibility	Single technology stack across the application	Freedom to use different technologies per service
Performance	No network overhead; everything runs in one process	Network latency between services impacts performance

Aspect	Monolithic Architecture	Microservices Architecture
Maintenance	Challenging as the code base grows larger and more intertwined	Easier to maintain; smaller, focused code bases
Startup Cost	Lower initial cost for setup and infrastructure	Higher upfront investment in tools and infrastructure

Table 10.1 – Monolith vs. microservices

The microservices movement has not only influenced system design but has also prompted a rediscovery and renewed appreciation of DDD concepts such as bounded contexts. Many organizations, while grappling with the challenges of implementing microservices, have stumbled upon a revelation: to design microservices effectively, understanding and applying DDD is not just helpful, it's essential.

DDD and microservices share a symbiotic relationship. Microservices provide an operational lens, a way to structure and deploy software systems in a distributed fashion. DDD, on the other hand, offers a conceptual and strategic foundation, particularly through its emphasis on modeling the problem space and aligning software design with business domains. The most significant bridge between these two paradigms is the bounded context, a concept in DDD that maps cleanly to the boundaries and responsibilities of microservices.

However, we need to handle this relationship with care. A bounded context defines a semantic boundary, meaning that within it, every element of the software model has a well-defined meaning and role, shaped by the domain's language and logic. It is structured around the purpose and conceptual integrity of the model.

A microservice, on the other hand, defines a physical boundary—it is a deployable unit of an application, encapsulated within infrastructure elements such as containers or virtual machines. You can think of this boundary as containing a Docker image or runtime environment.

While, in some scenarios, the driving forces behind defining a bounded context and a microservice may overlap, they serve different purposes: one ensures *conceptual clarity*, and the other enforces *deployment and operational independence*.

You can have a microservice with more than one bounded context, but you cannot have a bounded context split through many microservices! Keep your boundaries logically clean and enforce physical separation when it is worth the cost.

The rationale behind microservices

There isn't a clear definition for **microservices architecture**, except in a famous blog by Martin Fowler and James Lewis entitled *Microservices* (https://www.martinfowler.com/articles/microservices.html), published in March 2014, which explains the characteristics of microservices architecture. Scrolling through the characteristics in the article, you can find many of them really align with bounded context principles. If you are asking yourself why you should move your project to a microservices architecture style, you need to analyze these characteristics and check how they relate to DDD. Four of them must capture your attention:

- **Organized around business capabilities**: Usually, when breaking down a large application into smaller parts, management often organizes teams based on technological layers. This is a direct consequence of *Conway's Law* (Melvin Conway, 1968, https://martinfowler.com/bliki/ConwaysLaw.html). This approach can create significant bottlenecks due to the need for additional approvals even for minor changes. The microservices approach, on the other hand, advocates for splitting up the application into services organized around specific business capabilities and encourages cross-functional teams to focus on addressing these specific business problems. This is very much in line with the Ubiquitous Language pattern, which is a vertical language for a specific business problem.

- **Decentralized governance**: Companies with centralized governance have the tendency to standardize on single technology platforms, but, as you know, not every problem is a nail, and not every solution is a hammer. When splitting your monolith into microservices, you must choose the right technology for a specific problem. This approach aligns with the idea of having a model that fits the business purpose in DDD.

- **Decentralized data management**: This is one of the most critical aspects of microservices architecture. Unlike traditional architectures that rely on a single centralized database for persistence, microservices adopt a different approach. Because of the principles of DDD, which emphasize the importance of private persistence for maintaining language consistency within a bounded context, each microservice must have its own dedicated database.

- **Evolutionary design**: One of the main purposes of microservices practitioners is evolutionary design. They view service decomposition as an additional tool that empowers application developers to manage changes in their systems without hindering the pace of development. Here, the match with DDD starts with the Whirlpool approach to the problem. The system grows with your knowledge about the domain itself.

In their blog, Martin Fowler and James Lewis provide a more comprehensive exploration of other characteristics of microservices architecture. Some of these are orthogonal to DDD, while others coexist without issues or conflicts. The real question, after reading and analyzing the whole blog, is *Why do you have to move from monolith to microservices architecture?*

Remember the second law of software architecture: *The why is more important than the how.*

After outlining the benefits and challenges of microservices, you could dive deeper into the connection between bounded contexts and how they mitigate some of the challenges while enhancing the advantages.

The bounded context seems to be a natural microservices boundary. By aligning each microservice with a bounded context, you can minimize the risk of shared dependencies or unclear responsibilities that often plague poorly implemented microservices. This alignment helps maintain the cohesion and autonomy of each service while allowing the system to evolve naturally alongside the domain.

As an architect, you must analyze the trade-off of the cost of autonomy versus duplication of data models and the increased complexity in orchestration. DDD provides patterns such as anti-corruption layers, domain events, and shared kernels that can help manage these complexities. For example, an anti-corruption layer ensures that communication between services respects their individual boundaries without introducing coupling or leaking domain details.

If you are asking yourself why to transition to microservices, the decision often needs to be taken when the limitations of a monolithic architecture become apparent. These may include slower development cycles to include new features, bottlenecks in scaling specific parts of the application, or challenges in onboarding new teams. Microservices offer a solution by creating modular, independently deployable units of functionality. But the question remains: *Do the benefits outweigh the operational and development costs in your specific context?*

The transition from a monolith to microservices is not a one-size-fits-all process. It is critical to identify the most problematic or independent bounded context first. These are often the areas where the business domain is well understood, and the potential for scalability or independent development is most significant. Start small, evaluate the result, and iterate incrementally. Remember, the goal is not to create microservices for their own sake but to solve real-world challenges more effectively.

Figure 10.2 shows the process to adopt when moving from monolith to microservices. Keep your boundaries logically clean and enforce physical separation when it's worth the cost.

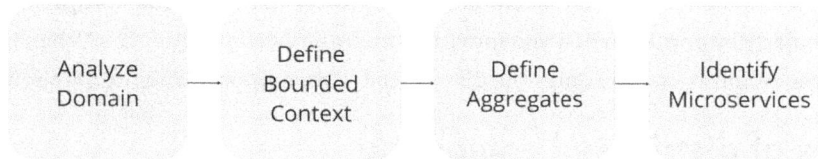

Figure 10.2 – Domain analysis first

As shown in the preceding figure, the process begins with the most critical step: analyzing the domain. This foundational activity is essential for understanding the problem space and identifying the appropriate bounded contexts. These contexts help to encapsulate distinct areas of your domain and provide clarity for defining aggregates, which represent the core business models and rules within each context.

Once these conceptual steps are complete, you can move on to the design phase, determining the physical boundaries within your system. At this stage, you can decide whether to implement a microservices architecture immediately or adopt a modular monolithic approach, deferring the physical separation until it becomes necessary.

Challenges and considerations

Microservices represent a distributed architecture, meaning each service runs in its own process. However, we must beware of the fallacies of distributed systems! We will cover these in detail in the upcoming subsection. Transitioning from a monolith to a microservices architecture involves analyzing numerous factors. So far, we have focused on the architectural aspects of the system and explored how to gradually refactor your code to prepare your monolith for decomposition.

Introducing the events in your monolith seems to be an over-engineering approach, and it is if you don't need to split the monolith. However, because you are looking for a safe appropriate approach, it isn't! With events, you can easily debug the whole system, even if the communication is asynchronous, by setting the appropriate breakpoints in your code and inspecting the process. At the end of this step, you can be confident that the system still works after moving to a microservices architecture—at least for the functional requirements.

On the other hand, it is time to take a look at the non-functional requirements. As Fred Brooks said in his famous paper *No Silver Bullets – Essence and Accident in Software Engineering* in 1986, there are two kinds of complexity: **accidental complexity** and **essential complexity**. The first one is particularly important when you move to a microservices architecture. When moving to a microservices architecture, you enter the distributed systems world, and the game rules change.

Fallacies of distributed computing

Back in 1994, L. Peter Deutsch, one of the original Sun fellows, created a list of seven fallacies, starting from a list of four created by Bill Joy and Dave Lyon. In 1997, James Gosling, the inventor of Java, added the eighth fallacy.

The fallacies of distributed computing are a set of assertions describing false assumptions that programmers, new to distributed applications, invariably make.

Table 10.2 shows the **eight fallacies of distributed computing**.

Fallacy	Description
The network is reliable	Assumes that the network will always work perfectly, with no failures or interruptions
Latency is zero	Assumes that messages sent over the network will arrive instantly, ignoring delays
Bandwidth is infinite	Assumes that there is unlimited network capacity, disregarding limitations such as congestion or speed
The network is secure	Assumes that the network is inherently secure, ignoring vulnerabilities and threats
Topology doesn't change	Assumes that the network structure is static, ignoring changes such as nodes joining or leaving
There is one administrator	Assumes that a single authority manages the network, ignoring decentralized ownership
Transport cost is zero	Assumes that data transfer has no cost, ignoring expenses related to bandwidth and latency
The network is homogeneous	Assumes that all systems in the network are identical, ignoring differences in hardware, software, or configurations

Table 10.2 – The eight fallacies of distributed computing

Later, Udi Dahan, a well-known expert in distributed systems and software architecture, expanded on the original list by adding two more fallacies. These additional fallacies address modern challenges in distributed systems, as shown in *Table 10.3*

Fallacy	Description
The system is consistent	Assumes that the system will always maintain consistency across all nodes, ignoring the challenges of eventual consistency in distributed systems
The system is predictable	Assumes that the system will behave in a predictable manner under all conditions, ignoring the impact of varying loads, failures, and delays

Table 10.3 – Udi Dahan's two fallacies

These two additional fallacies reflect the complexity of modern distributed systems and emphasize the need for architects and developers to account for inconsistency and unpredictability in their design.

In distributed systems, achieving strong consistency (where all nodes see the same data at the same time) is extremely difficult due to network delays and partitions. Many systems rely on eventual consistency, where consistency is achieved over time, not instantly. Because of network latency, distributed systems often face unpredictable behavior. Assuming that the system will behave predictably under all conditions is unrealistic.

Over the years, other authors have added more fallacies to the original list. While not officially part of the original set, these are often discussed in the context of modern distributed systems. *Table 10.4* highlights these additional fallacies.

Fallacy	Description
The system has infinite resources	Assumes that computing resources (e.g., CPU, memory, and storage) are unlimited, ignoring real-world constraints
The system is free of state	Assumes that stateless systems are easier to scale and maintain, ignoring the challenges of managing distributed state
Scaling is easy	Assumes that scaling a system (horizontally or vertically) can be done seamlessly, ignoring bottlenecks and architectural limitations

Fallacy	Description
Failures are rare	Assumes that failures (hardware, software, or network) are infrequent, ignoring the inevitability of failure in large-scale systems
Time is consistent	Assumes that clocks across distributed systems are synchronized, ignoring clock drift and issues with event ordering

Table 10.4 – Additional fallacies relevant to modern distributed systems

Let's discuss the fallacies from the preceding table in more detail. The first is the assumption that systems have infinite resources, such as CPU, memory, or storage, particularly in cloud environments where resources appear abundant but remain limited and costly. Secondly, there is a belief that systems are free of state, assuming that stateless designs are inherently scalable while ignoring the challenges of managing distributed states, such as coordinating sessions or ensuring consistency across databases. The third fallacy is that scaling is easy, as developers often underestimate the complexity of partitioning data, managing load balancing, and avoiding bottlenecks as systems grow.

Fourthly, there's the false assumption that failures are rare, when, in reality, hardware, software, and network failures are inevitable, and systems must be designed to handle them gracefully. Finally, distributed systems often rely on time synchronization, leading to the fallacy that time is consistent across all nodes. In practice, **clock drift** and synchronization issues can cause inconsistencies, making event ordering and coordination a significant challenge. These additional fallacies highlight the importance of recognizing the practical limitations of distributed systems and designing for resilience, scalability, and consistency. These fallacies also reflect the evolving challenges in distributed systems as they grow in scale, complexity, and reliance on cloud infrastructure. While not part of the *original* list, they are widely recognized in modern system design discussions.

As you can see, transitioning to a microservices architecture means embracing the challenges of distributed systems. In a monolithic solution, most of the problems you face are *essential*, as the infrastructure's complexity is minimal—your entire application runs on a single machine. However, in distributed systems, you must also contend with *accidental* problems. These arise because your application is no longer confined to one machine but spans multiple machines or nodes, each with its own memory and processing capabilities. These nodes work together as a single system, communicating over a network, which introduces latency, potential failures, and other complexities.

Benefits and trade-offs in moving to microservices

So, why move to a distributed system? The answer lies in the benefits: distributed systems are designed to handle increased workloads by distributing tasks across multiple nodes. This architecture improves performance, fault tolerance, and scalability compared to centralized systems. For example, adding a new feature in an independent microservice is often simpler and less risky than modifying a large, tightly coupled monolithic system.

Does this mean there are only advantages to moving from a monolith to microservices? Absolutely not. While microservices offer significant benefits, they also come with trade-offs. You must carefully evaluate the characteristics of each architectural style, understand the specific needs of your stakeholders, and choose the approach that best aligns with your goals and constraints. Moving to microservices is not a one-size-fits-all solution; it's a strategic decision that requires balancing the risks and rewards.

Table 10.5 shows a translation of domain concerns to architecture characteristics, like the one that Mark Richards and Neil Ford summarized in their book, *Fundamentals of Software Architecture*. This table was created with the aim of supporting architects in identifying the right architectural style in the face of stakeholder demands.

Domain Concern	Architecture Characteristics
Mergers and acquisitions	Interoperability, scalability, adaptability, and extensibility
Time to market	Agility, testability, and deployability
User satisfaction	Performance, availability, fault tolerance, testability, deployability, agility, and security
Competitive advantage	Agility, testability, deployability, scalability, availability, and fault tolerance
Time and budget	Simplicity and feasibility

Table 10.5 – Domain concerns vs. architecture characteristics

Once you have this table, the next step is to create a rating for each characteristic in each architectural style, as the authors did in their book. For our purpose, we have summarized this epic battle in *Table 10.6*

Architecture Characteristic	Modular Architecture	Microservices Architecture
Partition type	*Technical*	*Domain*
Number of quanta	*One*	*One to many*
Deployability	☆ ☆ ☆	☆ ☆ ☆ ☆
Elasticity	☆	☆ ☆ ☆ ☆ ☆
Evolutionary	☆ ☆ ☆	☆ ☆ ☆ ☆ ☆
Fault tolerance	☆	☆ ☆ ☆ ☆
Modularity	☆ ☆ ☆	☆ ☆ ☆ ☆ ☆
Overall cost	☆ ☆ ☆ ☆ ☆	☆
Performance	☆ ☆ ☆	☆ ☆
Reliability	☆ ☆ ☆	☆ ☆ ☆ ☆
Scalability	☆	☆ ☆ ☆ ☆ ☆
Simplicity	☆ ☆ ☆ ☆	☆
Testability	☆ ☆ ☆	☆ ☆ ☆ ☆

Table 10.6 – Modular architecture vs. microservices architecture

This table is not intended to be the definitive answer, but a guide. Think of it as one more tool in your toolbox for evaluating all aspects of your decision.

Assessing readiness for microservices

The decision to adopt a microservices architecture is as much about organizational and technical readiness as it is about aspiration. While the allure of microservices is strong—offering scalability, resilience, and team autonomy—the transition involves considerable complexity. Moving prematurely or without the necessary groundwork can lead to significant setbacks, technical debt, or even failure.

Signals of readiness for microservices

Before moving to microservices, evaluate your current architecture, team capabilities, and organizational needs. The following are strong indicators that the move can be made with minimum risk:

- **Clear domain boundaries**: You have well-defined domains and subdomains based on DDD principles. This ensures that the boundaries of each microservice align naturally with business capabilities, reducing the risk of overlapping responsibilities or fragmented logic.

- **Scaling pressures on specific areas**: Certain parts of your system require scaling due to high demand, while others do not. This imbalance is a strong indicator that horizontal scaling through microservices could be advantageous, so it enables targeted scaling of high-demand components.

- **Independent development needs**: Your teams are frequently blocked by interdependencies in a monolithic code base. Moving to microservices can enable teams to work autonomously, deploying updates without coordinating with unrelated parts of the application.

- **Operational maturity**: Your organization has invested in DevOps practices, including CI/CD, robust monitoring, and automated testing. These capabilities are essential to manage the complexity of a microservices architecture effectively.

- **Technical expertise**: Your development teams are proficient in distributed system design, including handling challenges such as eventual consistency, network latency, and service failures.

- **Business justification**: The decision to move is driven by measurable business needs, such as reducing time to market, improving system reliability, or enabling rapid scaling, rather than by trends or external pressures.

The role of a modular monolith as a foundation

Before transitioning to microservices, it's often best to develop a modular monolith. A modular monolith applies to many of the same principles as microservices—such as clear boundaries and separation of concerns—within the context of a single deployable unit. This approach provides a strong foundation for eventual decomposition into microservices. Here's why:

- **Eases transition**: A modular monolith enforces clean boundaries between modules, making it easier to identify which modules can be extracted as independent services. Without this preparation, disentangling a tightly coupled monolith can be a daunting task.

- **Simplifies testing and deployment**: Modules within a monolith can be tested and deployed together, simplifying operational overhead. This allows your teams to refine their understanding of domain boundaries without the complexity of managing distributed systems from the outset.

- **Supports incremental decomposition**: Once the modular monolith is stable, you can gradually extract services one at a time. This reduces risk and provides flexibility to adapt as your understanding of system requirements evolves.

Why the mediator pattern falls short for decoupling

Many modular monoliths rely on a **mediator pattern** for communication between modules. While this approach centralizes control and simplifies interactions within a monolith, it inherently keeps modules tightly coupled. The mediator acts as a hub, making all modules dependent on it for communication. This tight coupling can create challenges when breaking down modules into independent microservices:

- **Centralized dependencies**: The mediator becomes a critical dependency, limiting the autonomy of individual modules
- **Difficult to extract services**: Because modules rely on the mediator, you may need to rewrite significant portions of code to enable independent communication between services

Transitioning to event-driven communication

A more effective approach to decoupling modules is adopting event-driven communication within the modular monolith. This method replaces synchronous interactions through the mediator with asynchronous event-based messaging. Events are published by one module and consumed by others, enabling the following:

- **Loose coupling**: Modules no longer depend directly on one another, making them easier to extract as independent services
- **Scalability**: Event-driven systems can handle higher throughput as modules communicate asynchronously
- **Simplified service extraction**: Since modules are already communicating through events, the same messaging infrastructure can be used when transitioning to microservices

Preparing for microservices

Before embarking on a transition to microservices, consider these preparatory steps:

1. **Refactor toward modularity**: Establish clear boundaries between modules, ensuring they align with DDD principles. Replace the mediator pattern with event-driven communication to decouple modules.

2. **Invest in operational readiness**: Build the necessary infrastructure for CI/CD, monitoring, and automated testing.

3. **Start with pilot services**: Identify one or two modules that are self-contained and have a high impact. Extract these as microservices to validate your approach and refine your processes.

By carefully assessing your readiness and laying a solid foundation with a modular monolith, you can transition to microservices more effectively, avoiding many common pitfalls. This approach ensures that your organization is positioned to fully realize the benefits of microservices while minimizing risks and disruptions.

Strategies for transitioning to microservices

It is time to dive into the code of our ERP system to bring all the patterns discussed in this chapter together. The first step in transitioning from a monolith to microservices is identifying the contexts and establishing clear boundaries around them. This ensures proper subdomain isolation, which is critical for successful migration.

Figure 10.3 shows the solution as found in the `02-monolith_with_cqrs` branch of the book's GitHub repository:

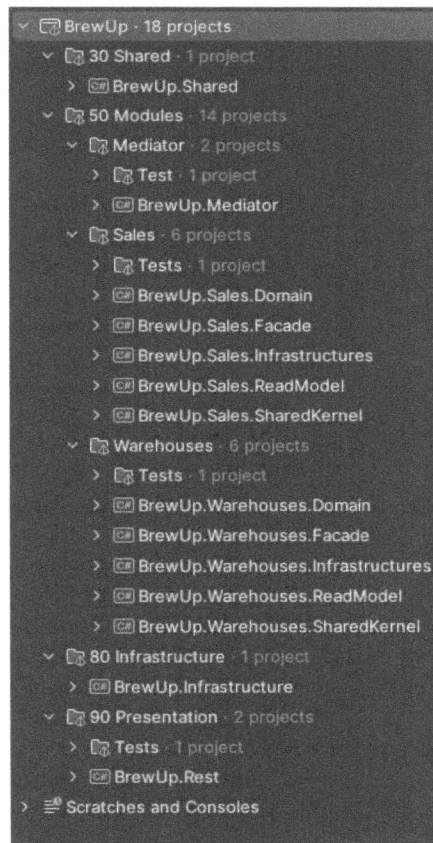

Figure 10.3 – Modular architecture with mediator

It's crucial to progress in small, manageable steps. Once you've split the solution into clearly defined bounded contexts, it's essential to ensure that each bounded context remains independent, with no dependencies on one another. At this stage, you can leverage fitness functions (see the *Testing and stabilizing* section in *Chapter 6, Transitioning from Chaos*) to validate your design.

As discussed earlier, while the mediator pattern isn't ideal for preparing a monolith to transition into microservices, it serves as an effective intermediate solution. Jumping directly to an event-driven architecture introduces unnecessary complexity at this stage, which you should avoid. The mediator pattern provides a simpler way to manage communication between bounded contexts during this phase of refactoring.

The following code snippet demonstrates how the mediator facilitates communication between the `Sales` and `Warehouse` bounded contexts, ensuring that they do not directly interact with each other:

```
public class BrewUpMediator(ISalesFacade salesFacade, IWarehousesFacade
warehouseFacade) : IBrewUpMediator
{
    public async Task<string> CreateOrderAsync(SalesOrderJson body,
CancellationToken cancellationToken)
    {
        List<BeerAvailabilityJson> availabilities = new();

        foreach (var row in body.Rows)
        {
            var availability = await warehouseFacade.
GetAvailabilityAsync(row.BeerId, cancellationToken);
            if (availability.TotalRecords > 0)
                availabilities.Add(availability.Results.First());
        }

        // Prepare the list of rows that are available for sale
        List<SalesOrderRowJson> rowsForSale = (from row in body.Rows
            let beerAvailability = availabilities.Find(a => a.BeerId == row.
BeerId.ToString())
```

```
        where beerAvailability != null && beerAvailability.Availability.
  Available >= row.Quantity.Value
        select row).ToList();

    if (rowsForSale.Count == 0)
    {
        return "No beer available for sale";
    }

    body = body with { Rows = rowsForSale };
    return await salesFacade.CreateOrderAsync(body, cancellationToken);
  }
}
```

As shown in the preceding code, BrewUpMediator receives the façades for both Sales and Warehouse. This allows it to facilitate communication between these bounded contexts and manage the process of order creation without establishing direct dependencies between them.

After completing this step and verifying that everything functions as expected, you can proceed to replace the mediator pattern with an event-driven communication pattern. At first, introducing events into a monolithic project might appear to be unnecessary overhead—and it would be if you intended to maintain the project in its monolithic state. However, our goal is to prepare the solution for eventual decomposition into multiple microservices. Therefore, replacing the mediator with events becomes a crucial step. Making this change within the monolithic project allows for simpler testing and reduced risk. As always, prioritize simplicity and avoid adding unnecessary complexity during this transition.

Figure 10.4 shows the new structure of our ERP solution. You can find the whole solution in the 03-monolith_with_cqrs_and_event_sourcing branch in the book's GitHub repository:

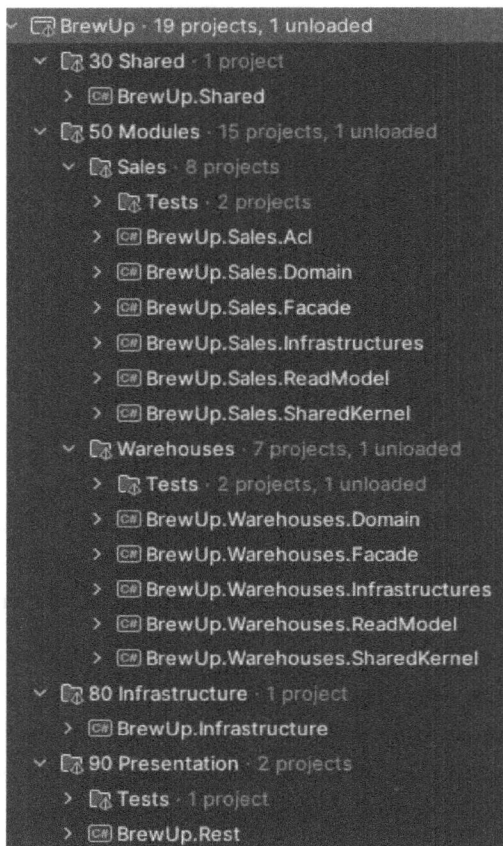

Figure 10.4 – Modular architecture with events

At this stage, as you can see, the mediator has been removed, and communication between Sales and Warehouse is now managed through events. This eliminates the need for a mediator to orchestrate interactions between bounded contexts.

In this setup, the Sales bounded context maintains a copy of the availability data, while Warehouse owns the Availability aggregate. Naturally, the copy in Sales follows an eventual consistency model, so it's essential to ensure that this approach aligns with your business requirements.

The following code snippet demonstrates how the Warehouse bounded context raises an integration event whenever its availability is updated:

```
public class AvailabilityUpdatedDueToProduction
OrderForIntegrationEventHandler(ILoggerFactory loggerFactory,
    IEventBus eventBus) : DomainEventHandlerBase<AvailabilityUpdated
DueToProductionOrder>(loggerFactory)
```

```
{
    public override async Task
HandleAsync(AvailabilityUpdatedDueToProductionOrder @event,
        CancellationToken cancellationToken = new())
    {
        cancellationToken.ThrowIfCancellationRequested();

        var correlationId =
            new Guid(@event.UserProperties.FirstOrDefault(u => u.Key.
Equals("CorrelationId")).Value.ToString()!);

        AvailabilityUpdatedForNotification
availabilityUpdatedForNotification = new(@event.BeerId, correlationId, @
event.BeerName, @event.Quantity);
        await eventBus.PublishAsync(availabilityUpdatedForNotification,
cancellationToken);
    }
}
```

The following code snippet receives and manages the integration event within the Sales bounded context anti-corruption layer:

```
public sealed class
AvailabilityUpdatedForNotificationEventHandler(ILoggerFactory
loggerFactory, IServiceBus serviceBus) : IntegrationEventHandlerAsync
<AvailabilityUpdatedForNotification>(loggerFactory)
{
    public override async Task
HandleAsync(AvailabilityUpdatedForNotification @event,
        CancellationToken cancellationToken = new())
    {
        cancellationToken.ThrowIfCancellationRequested();

        var correlationId =
            new Guid(@event.UserProperties.FirstOrDefault(u => u.Key.
Equals("CorrelationId")).Value.ToString()!);

        UpdateAvailabilityDueToWarehousesNotification command = new(@event.
BeerId, correlationId, @event.BeerName, @event.Quantity);
```

```
        await serviceBus.SendAsync(command, cancellationToken);
    }
}
```

Another approach to managing a process like this is to use a long-running process or saga. You'll learn more about this pattern in *Chapter 12, Orchestrating Complexity – Advanced Approaches to Business Processes.*

Transitioning from the modular event-driven architecture we developed throughout this book to a microservices architecture can be considered a straightforward process. We have demonstrated this in the 04-microservices branch of the book's GitHub repository. The key steps involved isolating the Sales and Warehouses modules into their own solutions. This was achieved by moving all related projects (including BrewUp.Shared) and exposing their respective endpoints. The result is two fully independent services, each capable of evolving at their own pace. *Figure 10.5* illustrates the structure of these newly created solutions.

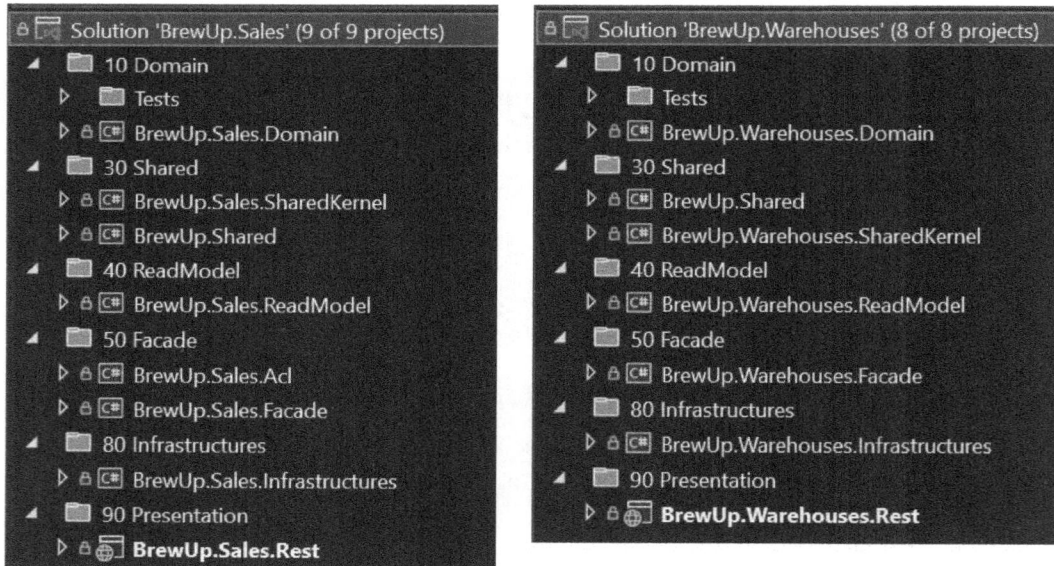

Figure 10.5 – The new solutions for Sales and Warehouses

To conclude, it's best to avoid introducing unnecessary complexity at the outset of your refactoring process. Instead, as demonstrated, you can achieve your goals through incremental steps that not only enable you to gain deeper insights into your domain but also empower you to make well-informed decisions at the right time.

Summary

In this chapter, you explored the critical considerations and strategies for transitioning from a monolithic solution to a microservices architecture. You learned that architectural decisions require careful alignment between technical and business needs, balancing domain concerns with technical constraints to evolve systems effectively and without unnecessary complexity.

The transition begins with identifying appropriate bounded contexts and ensuring clear boundaries. Initial communication between these contexts can be handled with simpler patterns such as the mediator, which can later be replaced with event-driven communication. This prepares the monolith for eventual decomposition into independent microservices aligned with specific bounded contexts.

In this chapter, you should have learned the following:

- How to recognize and utilize bounded contexts as a foundational element for microservices architecture
- How to adopt a step-by-step approach to transition from a monolithic to a microservices architecture, reducing risks and maintaining system stability
- What the roles of mediator and event-driven patterns are in decoupling and facilitating communication during the transition
- What accidental complexities are and strategies to address them, including handling the fallacies of distributed computing
- How to evaluate key organizational and technical signals to assess preparedness for adopting microservices

By following these principles, you can ensure a structured and deliberate evolution of your system, prioritizing simplicity, business alignment, and long-term scalability.

In the next chapter, we will explore advanced topics, focusing on event versioning—a critical aspect of managing and maintaining consistency in event-sourced systems.

11

Dealing with Events and Their Evolution

As software systems grow and adapt to new requirements, managing the evolution of data structures becomes critical. In this chapter, we will explore strategies to handle event versioning in event-sourced systems. By the end of this chapter, you will know how to do the following:

- Implement basic event versioning techniques
- Apply strategies such as upcasting and weak schemas for managing evolving events
- Leverage advanced approaches such as content negotiation and copy-replace for more complex scenarios

While we aim to introduce you to practical solutions, it's important to acknowledge that event versioning is a vast and nuanced topic. Due to space constraints and the focused scope of this book, we cannot go too deep into all aspects of this subject. However, the strategies and examples provided here will equip you with a solid foundation to start managing event evolution effectively. For those who wish to explore this topic further, we recommend additional resources such as Gregory Young's comprehensive work on versioning, *Versioning in an Event Sourced System*.

Let's dive into how to navigate the challenges of event versioning and ensure your systems remain robust and adaptable over time.

The complete code for this chapter can be found in the `03-monolith_with_cqrs_and_event_sourcing` branch in the book's GitHub repository here: https://github.com/PacktPublishing/Domain-driven-Refactoring/tree/03-monolith_with_cqrs_and_event_sourcing.

CQRS, event sourcing, and the event streaming misconception

Modern software systems often face challenges such as scalability, flexibility, and traceability, especially in domains with complex business logic. As you learned in the previous chapters, two architectural patterns, **Command Query Responsibility Segregation and Event Sourcing (CQRS+ES)**, have emerged as powerful tools to address these challenges.

CQRS is an architectural pattern that separates the responsibilities of commands (which represent write operations) and queries (which represent read operations). This separation allows the system to handle these operations independently, optimizing each one for its specific purpose. Unlike traditional CRUD systems, where reading and writing often share the same data model, CQRS employs distinct models for each function. Thus, commands in CQRS act as transporters of data for the aggregate, which ensures data consistency and enforces business logic during state changes. The query model, on the other hand, is tailored for efficient data retrieval and presentation. This division not only improves scalability by allowing each model to evolve and scale independently but also enhances maintainability by clearly defining the responsibilities of each operation. Additionally, CQRS enables better alignment with DDD principles, as it allows for more expressive models that reflect the unique requirements of reading and writing in a given domain.

The key concepts of CQRS include the following:

- **Commands**: Represent actions that change the system's state, such as CreateSalesOrder in our ERP example
- **Queries**: Represent requests for retrieving data without modifying it, such as GetSalesOrders
- **Write model**: Handles commands and enforces business rules
- **Read model**: Optimizes for querying and returning data efficiently

The primary reason for choosing CQRS is scalability. Since the read and write models are separate, they can be scaled independently to meet specific demands. For example, in a system with significantly more read operations than write operations, the read model can be scaled horizontally without affecting the write model. This separation also simplifies the code base by isolating the logic for reading and writing, making the system easier to maintain and understand. Additionally, the read model can be optimized and tailored to specific query patterns, improving performance and user experience by delivering precisely the needed data in the most efficient way.

While CQRS focuses on separating the responsibilities of commands and queries to improve scalability and maintainability, the second pattern, ES, complements it by storing the state of an application as a sequence of events. Together, they create a powerful synergy: CQRS defines how the system interacts with data, and ES defines how the data is stored and evolves over time.

ES is a pattern that captures state changes as a sequence of immutable events. Unlike traditional approaches that store the current state of an entity in a database, ES maintains a complete history of all events that have led to the current state. This means that the system doesn't just know what the current state is, it also knows how it got there. This approach provides a richer and more detailed understanding of the system's behavior over time.

An **event** is an immutable record raised by an aggregate when it processes a command and persists in a specialized database called an **event store**. The event store serves as the single source of truth, containing all the events that have occurred in the system. When the state of an aggregate is needed, the system replays these stored events to rebuild the aggregate's current state. This approach ensures consistency and allows the system to process new commands based on the reconstructed state.

One of the key benefits of ES is its ability to provide full traceability of business processes. By maintaining a complete history of all changes, it supports auditing, debugging, and compliance requirements. For example, if an issue arises, developers or auditors can trace back through the event history to understand exactly what happened and why. This level of transparency is invaluable in systems where accountability and accuracy are critical.

A common mistake is to conflate ES with event streaming, but these are distinct patterns with different purposes. Understanding their key features and the differences between the two is crucial.

Key features of event streaming are as follows:

- You subscribe to a stream of events, but you cannot directly read all the events as you would in an event store
- Event streaming does not inherently provide guarantees for optimistic concurrency checks or strong consistency
- The primary focus of event streaming is to move data from one part of the system to another, enabling real-time communication between components
- While event streaming systems offer durable storage for fault tolerance and resilience, they are not designed to act as a source of truth for your application

Key features of ES are as follows:

- In ES, events represent the immutable history of changes that define the current state of the aggregate

- When a new command is processed in an event-sourcing system, the workflow typically looks like this:

  - The repository reads all events for the aggregate from the event store.

  - These events are applied sequentially to rebuild the aggregate's current state.

  - The aggregate evaluates the command, executes the business logic, and raises a new event.

  - The repository appends this new event to the event store.

- An event store supports strong consistency and optimistic concurrency, and often guarantees global ordering of events, making it suitable as the source of truth for your application

The purpose of an event store is to provide a consistent and reliable mechanism for storing and replaying events to rebuild the application state. In contrast, the purpose of event streaming is to facilitate the movement of data across systems, enabling real-time processing but without the guarantees required to act as the authoritative source of truth.

As with any software application, systems built with CQRS and ES evolve over time. New business requirements often necessitate changes to the structure and meaning of events. Managing these changes effectively is a critical part of system design. This process, often referred to as negotiation, involves ensuring that updates to events maintain backward compatibility and minimize disruptions for existing consumers. As you'll learn in this chapter, there are several strategies for managing event evolution, all of which begin with **event versioning**. By versioning events, the system can support both old and new formats, allowing for a smooth transition during updates and ensuring continued functionality across all components.

The lifespan of events: why evolution matters

Event-sourced systems, being an append-only model, are subject to versioning issues, and you must handle them effectively to ensure the system's long-term viability. Events, once written to the event store, are immutable and represent a historical record of what has occurred in the system. This immutability is a core strength of event sourcing, providing a complete audit trail and the ability to reconstruct the state from past events. However, the immutability of events also introduces challenges when the structure or meaning of events needs to evolve, as older events must coexist with newer ones in the same system. Since aggregates rely on replaying historical events to reconstruct the state, they must remain compatible with all previous event versions.

In traditional systems, managing changes to a database schema is often straightforward. You apply a schema update script, and as long as you add columns or make non-breaking changes, the system continues to operate smoothly. Modern systems, however, rarely follow this monolithic update approach. Instead, changes are deployed incrementally, often with multiple versions of the same software running concurrently in production. If you modify the structure of an event, not all event handlers across the system are updated at the same time. Moreover, projections and event handlers must always be able to process events written years ago, even if the logic or structure has changed.

These factors make event evolution critical. Without careful planning and strategies such as versioning, upcasting, and schema compatibility, systems risk inconsistencies and failures. Properly managing the lifespan of events ensures that your system remains flexible, scalable, and capable of supporting both historical and future requirements without breaking existing functionality.

In the context of event-sourced systems, modifying an existing event can lead to two distinct scenarios: versioning or creating a new event. When you add or remove a property from an existing event while preserving its core meaning and purpose, you are creating a new version of the same event. This approach maintains continuity with the original event, allowing older and newer versions to coexist while ensuring backward compatibility. However, if you rewrite the event entirely, changing its meaning, structure, or purpose, you are effectively creating a new event. This new event represents a fundamentally different concept or domain activity and is treated as distinct from the original event, with no implicit compatibility between the two. Properly distinguishing between these cases is crucial to maintaining the integrity and evolution of an event-sourced system.

Adopting CQRS+ES: overcoming technical and cultural challenges

While CQRS+ES is a powerful architectural pattern, it's important to recognize that it's not a silver bullet or a universal solution. Much like owning a hammer doesn't turn every problem into a nail, CQRS+ES is most effective when applied to the right scenarios. As with any tool, its adoption should be thoughtful and context-driven.

In practice, it is perfectly valid, and often advisable, to apply CQRS+ES selectively within a system. For example, it is particularly effective in core business modules where capturing the complete history of changes, ensuring strong consistency, and enabling complex business logic are critical. ES shines in these areas by allowing the system to rehydrate the current state of an aggregate from a sequence of events, providing a detailed audit trail and enabling powerful features such as temporal queries and event replay.

However, not all parts of a system require this level of complexity. For supportive modules, where the primary goal is to manage data rather than enforce intricate business rules, a traditional CRUD approach is often more appropriate. In such cases, modules can be treated as "data bags," simple repositories for storing and retrieving information, which support the core domain. This works because we are not concerned with the history of changes or the exact sequence of events leading to the current state. Instead, we prioritize simplicity, efficiency, and ease of implementation.

As discussed in the *Architectural quanta* callout in *Chapter 6, Transitioning from Chaos*, introducing modules helps create pragmatic, maintainable systems by aligning code structure with bounded contexts and business responsibilities. By applying CQRS+ES where it provides the most value and using CRUD elsewhere, you can strike a balance between the benefits of event-driven architectures and the simplicity of traditional data management. Ultimately, the goal is to tailor the architecture to the needs of your system rather than forcing every part of it into a single paradigm. Remember what you learned in the *Problem and solution space* section in *Chapter 2, Handling Complexity, the Problem, and Solution Space*: you do not have to start from the solution, but you must listen to the problem, and then propose the solution. Possibly a solution that can grow with the features of your system.

While these technical considerations are crucial when searching for a solution, they are not the only factors to address. Socio-technical challenges often prove to be even more significant. Broadly speaking, we can categorize these challenges into three main scenarios:

- A winning team doesn't change. This principle holds true not only in sports but also in our environment.
- The team could improve their game with better training or players but believes their current strategy is enough to win.
- The team believes they need a new playbook to win but they lack the skills and experience to execute it effectively.

The first scenario is straightforward: if you have a strong team that consistently wins, there's no need to fix what is not broken. Similarly, if your traditional layered architecture is performing well for both your team and your customers, adopting new approaches purely for the sake of innovation isn't practical or necessary.

In the second scenario, the team recognizes issues with their current setup but lacks the motivation to propose an alternative solution. In our experience, this reluctance often stems not from the team itself but from the company culture. *This is how we've always done it, why change the strategy?* is the mindset typically driving management in such cases. Also, this mindset becomes self-reinforcing. When a company prioritizes maintaining the status quo, its employees often adopt the same outlook. It is important to remember that our goal is to deliver effective business solutions, not to indulge in learning new frameworks for personal satisfaction. As you have learned, an architect must make critical decisions at the start of a project when the least information is available. While introducing accidental complexity may not seem significant initially, your role goes beyond technical choices, you must also act as a motivator, fostering a culture of learning and growth within the team and the company.

The third scenario is more challenging. The team acknowledges the need for change and is willing to explore new approaches but lacks the experience or confidence to execute them effectively. This can lead to hesitation, missteps, or an overreliance on external tools without fully understanding their implications. In such cases, the architect's role extends beyond proposing the right solution; you must also guide the team in acquiring the necessary skills and provide a clear, incremental path forward. Mentorship, prototyping, and safe spaces to experiment become critical enablers for long-term success.

Regardless of which scenario your team is in, the guiding principle we have followed in this book is *start simple – grow big*. This approach is especially important during a refactor phase, where it is crucial to begin with supporting and generic domain components. If you make mistakes here, the consequences are minimal; you won't face significant setbacks or financial loss. The functionalities you deal with during this phase are often straightforward, giving you the opportunity to learn more about the domain you are working in. The approach also allows your team time to explore and experiment with new frameworks and patterns. A pragmatic approach ensures that new concepts are introduced gradually, allowing the team and company to adapt before they are integrated into the system.

That said, if you choose to implement CQRS+ES, be prepared to handle event versioning; it's not optional but inevitable, as change is a constant, and events are immutable by design.

Event versioning strategies

Now that you understand how events can evolve over time, let's explore how to manage this evolution effectively. There are several strategies to handle event versioning, each with its own advantages and drawbacks. Before diving into specific solutions, let's review some fundamental principles that are crucial when working with events:

- **Immutability**: Events are immutable records of occurrences in the past. Once an event is published, it cannot be altered or removed without compromising the integrity of your system's history. Instead of modifying an event, you should publish a compensating or corrective event to address any required changes.

- **Event handlers**: After an event is in production, any changes to its structure or meaning must be managed with caution. If you modify an event or its corresponding handlers, you must consider the impact on historical data. During an event replay, old events will retain their original structure, potentially causing compatibility issues with updated handlers.

So, where to start? First, it's important to note that commands are not subject to versioning. This is because commands represent actions that trigger changes immediately and are not typically stored in the event store for rebuilding the aggregate state. Instead, our focus must be on versioning events, since they form the persistent history that defines how the state is reconstructed.

Let's begin with the most straightforward technique.

Simple event versioning

As an example, let's consider the `SalesOrderCreated` event:

```
public sealed class SalesOrderCreated(SalesOrderId aggregateId, Guid
commitId, SalesOrderNumber salesOrderNumber,
    OrderDate orderDate, CustomerId customerId, CustomerName customerName,
    IEnumerable<SalesOrderRowDto> rows) : DomainEvent(aggregateId,
commitId)
{
    public readonly SalesOrderId SalesOrderId = aggregateId;
    public readonly SalesOrderNumber SalesOrderNumber = salesOrderNumber;
    public readonly OrderDate OrderDate = orderDate;

    public readonly CustomerId CustomerId = customerId;
    public readonly CustomerName CustomerName = customerName;
```

```
    public readonly IEnumerable<SalesOrderRowDto> Rows = rows;
}
```

Let's say that the preceding code is the first version you put into production. After some time, new requirements emerge, and you need to add a Boolean property called IsReseller, indicating whether the order was made by a regular customer or a reseller. The simplest way to address this, without encountering the problems discussed earlier, is to create a new version of the event called SalesOrderCreated_V2:

```
public sealed class SalesOrderCreated_V2(SalesOrderId aggregateId, Guid
commitId, SalesOrderNumber salesOrderNumber,
    OrderDate orderDate, CustomerId customerId, CustomerName customerName,
    IEnumerable<SalesOrderRowDto> rows, bool isReseller) :
DomainEvent(aggregateId, commitId)
{
    public readonly SalesOrderId SalesOrderId = aggregateId;
    public readonly SalesOrderNumber SalesOrderNumber = salesOrderNumber;
    public readonly OrderDate OrderDate = orderDate;

    public readonly CustomerId CustomerId = customerId;
    public readonly CustomerName CustomerName = customerName;

    public readonly IEnumerable<SalesOrderRowDto> Rows = rows;
    public readonly bool IsReseller = isReseller;
}
```

Regardless, this requires a bit of work on your end. For the reasons explained in the *The lifespan of events: why evolution matters* section earlier in the chapter, our aggregate must always be able to load older versions of an event. So, we must retain the older Apply methods and create a new one. Therefore, the code in our aggregate must change by implementing a new Apply method for the new version and the old one should handle default values (if needed).

Let's look at the relevant code in the SalesOrder aggregate:

```
    private SalesOrder(SalesOrderId salesOrderId, Guid correlationId,
  SalesOrderNumber salesOrderNumber, OrderDate orderDate,
        CustomerId customerId, CustomerName customerName,
  IEnumerable<SalesOrderRowDto> rows)
    {
```

```
        RaiseEvent(new SalesOrderCreated(salesOrderId, correlationId,
    salesOrderNumber, orderDate, customerId, customerName, rows));
    }

    private void Apply(SalesOrderCreated @event)
    {
        Id = @event.SalesOrderId;
        _salesOrderNumber = @event.SalesOrderNumber;
        _orderDate = @event.OrderDate;
        _customerId = @event.CustomerId;
        _customerName = @event.CustomerName;
        _rows = @event.Rows.MapToDomainRows();
    }
```

With the new event, you add a new `Apply` method and change the `RaiseEvent` call using the new event version:

```
    private SalesOrder(SalesOrderId salesOrderId, Guid correlationId,
    SalesOrderNumber salesOrderNumber, OrderDate orderDate,
        CustomerId customerId, CustomerName customerName,
    IEnumerable<SalesOrderRowDto> rows, bool isReseller)
    {
        RaiseEvent(new SalesOrderCreated_V2(salesOrderId, correlationId,
    salesOrderNumber, orderDate, customerId, customerName, rows, isReseller));
    }

    private void Apply(SalesOrderCreated @event)
    {
        Id = @event.SalesOrderId;
        _salesOrderNumber = @event.SalesOrderNumber;
        _orderDate = @event.OrderDate;
        _customerId = @event.CustomerId;
        _customerName = @event.CustomerName;
        _rows = @event.Rows.MapToDomainRows();
        _isReseller = false; // Default value that we choose
    }

    private void Apply(SalesOrderCreated_V2 @event)
    {
```

```
        Id = @event.SalesOrderId;
        _salesOrderNumber = @event.SalesOrderNumber;
        _orderDate = @event.OrderDate;
        _customerId = @event.CustomerId;
        _customerName = @event.CustomerName;
        _rows = @event.Rows.MapToDomainRows();
        _isReseller = @event.IsReseller;
    }
```

The same goes for the event handlers in your read model. You should retain the old handler with default values for new properties and implement a new handler for the new event, like what was done in the aggregate.

This approach is straightforward to implement, but it comes with significant drawbacks that shouldn't be overlooked. The main issue lies in the growing number of event versions. Imagine reaching version 19, or even having multiple events, each with several versions. This can quickly lead to a proliferation of Apply methods in your aggregate. Over time, the code becomes increasingly bloated, making it harder to maintain, understand, and reason about. The readability of your aggregate suffers, and managing changes across these numerous methods becomes a daunting task, ultimately jeopardizing the scalability and maintainability of the solution. As a rule of thumb, remember what Greg Young wrote on versioning in his book, *Versioning in an Event Sourced System* (https://leanpub.com/esversioning/read):

> *"A new version of an event must be convertible from the old version of the event. If not, it is not a new version of the event but rather a new event."*

This implies that new events should be convertible to the older versions, and vice versa.

If you are struggling with how to convert your old event to its new version, maybe it is an entirely new event. That said, what other solutions do we have?

How to manage event evolution outside the aggregate

We can approach the problem by handling event evolution over time while keeping aggregates manageable and avoiding unnecessary complexity. This means managing changes to event structures and versions in a way that keeps the code base clean and maintainable. To achieve this, we can move the problem outside the event by using upcasting, weak schema, content negotiation, or copy-replace.

Upcasting

Upcasting is a technique for handling event versioning in a way that avoids proliferating multiple versions of event handlers. Instead of maintaining multiple versions of an event, you can create a converter (or "upcaster") that transforms older versions of an event into the most recent version. This transformation typically occurs as the event is read from the event stream, applying any necessary default values or adjustments to match the latest schema.

A possible implementation, again using SalesOrderCreated with the added IsReseller property, could be as follows:

```
public class EventUpcaster
{
    public DomainEvent Upcast(DomainEvent oldEvent)
    {
        return oldEvent switch
        {
            SalesOrderCreated v1 => new SalesOrderCreated_V2
            {
                Id = v1.Id,
                SalesOrderNumber = v1.SalesOrderNumber,
                OrderDate = v1.OrderDate,
                CustomerId = v1.CustomerId,
                CustomerName = v1.CustomerName,
                Rows = v1.Rows,
                IsReseller = false // Default value for new field
            },
            _ => throw new NotSupportedException($"Unknown event type:
{oldEvent.EventType}, version: {oldEvent.Version}")
        };
    }
}


public class EventProcessor
{
    private readonly EventUpcaster _upcaster = new();

    public void ProcessEvent(IEvent evt)
    {
```

```
            // Upcast the event to the Latest version if necessary
            var upcastedEvent = evt.Version < 2 ? _upcaster.Upcast(evt) : evt;
            // Handle the Latest version of the event
            Handle((SalesOrderCreated_V2)upcastedEvent);
        }

        private void Handle(SalesOrderCreated_V2 evt)
        {
            Console.WriteLine($"Processing SalesOrderCreated_V2: {evt.Id}");
            //process the event...
        }
    }

    // Example usage
    class Program
    {
        static void Main()
        {
            var oldEvent = new SalesOrderCreated
            {
                Id = Guid.NewGuid(),
                SalesOrderNumber = "2025.12",
                OrderDate = DateTime.UtcNow,
                CustomerId = Guid.NewGuid(),
                CustomerName = "Jane Doe",
                Rows = new List<string> { "Item1", "Item2" }
            };

            var processor = new EventProcessor();
            processor.ProcessEvent(oldEvent);
        }
    }
```

Upcasters must correctly transform old events to maintain the integrity of the data. It is crucial to rigorously test them as they form a critical part of the event-handling pipeline.

With this approach, you only need one event handler for the latest version of the event, simplifying your event processing logic. However, upcasting introduces some challenges, particularly in distributed or multi-node systems.

If two versions of the application or two separate services are running concurrently, one may not yet be updated to handle the latest event version.

A workaround is to implement a **double publish** mechanism where all versions of the event are saved in the event store. Each node reads only the versions it can handle. However, this approach introduces potential complexities such as additional storage and maintenance overhead for multiple event versions.

For example, if the latest version of the event has not been written to the event store at the time of reading, the consuming node must wait or reprocess events later. This means that if the latest version of the event is not yet written in the event store while the service tries to read it, it can look ahead in the stream and read the events again. As you can imagine this process can become complex very fast.

Weak schema

In an event-sourced application, **weak schema** refers to a flexible, loosely defined structure for the event payloads. Instead of enforcing a rigid, strongly typed schema (as is typical in relational databases), a weak schema approach allows for variability in the structure and fields of events over time. In practice, this often means storing data in formats such as JSON, where the exact structure of fields is not fully predefined or tightly validated. Weak schemas are particularly useful because, as events evolve, older versions of events can still be read and processed, even as new fields are introduced or removed. This approach also allows for the easy introduction of new event versions without breaking existing consumers.

Let's look at this event in JSON format:

```
{
    "id" = 10,
    "salesOrderNumber" = "2025.12",
    "orderDate" = "2025-01-09",
    "customerId" = 12345,
    "customerName" = "John Doe",
    "rows" = [{row-1}, {row-2}, ..., {row-n}]
    "isReseller" = false;
}
```

The preceding code easily maps to both `SalesOrderCreated` and `SalesOrderCreated_V2` events. The `isReseller` property is simply ignored during deserialization for version 1 of the event and this does not disrupt existing consumers. This approach would also simplify the code in our aggregate because we do not need more than one `Apply` method for each event.

As a best practice tip, you should always include a version identifier in the event metadata to distinguish between different schemas. Doing so allows consumers to better handle missing fields gracefully and ignore unexpected ones.

But what are the cons of this kind of implementation? The first and most obvious one is that weak schema delays validation until runtime, increasing the risk of invalid or malformed events being saved in the event store. Secondly, consumers must handle multiple event versions, deal with missing or unknown fields, and implement fallbacks for default values or error-handling mechanisms. Thirdly, without a strongly enforced schema, the structure of events in the system becomes harder to understand leading to confusion, double efforts, and errors when a developer misinterprets the event or adds duplicate fields.

Content negotiation

Content negotiation is a strategy where, instead of managing versioning within the event store, version control is handled at the producer-consumer communication layer. Producers and consumers negotiate both the format and version of events, similar to how HTTP content negotiation works using headers such as `Accept` and `Content-Type`. This approach enables dynamic, flexible schema evolution.

The flow of this approach goes through the following sequence:

1. **Version metadata**: Each event includes metadata that specifies its version (e.g., `SalesOrderCreated:v1` or `SalesOrderCreated:v2`).

2. **Consumer declaration**: Consumers declare which event versions they can process, either at subscription time or during the event processing phase.

3. **Producer negotiation**: Producers adapt the events they emit to match the versions supported by each consumer.

4. **Middleware transformation**: Middleware or an adaptation layer dynamically converts events to a format and version acceptable to the consumer if the exact match isn't available.

This sequence, in practice, allows older consumers to continue processing events in a version they understand, while newer consumers can take advantage of updated schemas. By requesting explicitly the versions they support, the risk of misinterpretation or failure due to unsupported schemas is reduced.

Producers can evolve event schemas without requiring immediate updates from all consumers. Middleware can handle version transformations on the fly. Middleware can act as a bridge, converting older event versions into newer ones (or vice versa) as needed.

One way to implement this kind of version-aware communication is by using a transport mechanism that supports extensibility and version tagging. **Atom feeds** offer this capability: they were originally designed for syndicating structured data with built-in support for version metadata, schema links, and content type negotiation. By leveraging these features, Atom feeds can serve as a practical foundation for content negotiation in event-driven architectures.

By adapting the versioning and extensibility features of Atom feeds to an event-sourced architecture, you can support schema evolution more effectively. One added advantage is that, since the list of events is immutable, it can be safely cached across multiple nodes to reduce read latency and improve scalability.

Here is an example Atom feed that illustrates how multiple versions of an event can be published and negotiated using content-type metadata:

```
<feed xmlns="http://www.w3.org/2005/Atom">
  <title>SalesOrder events</title>
  <updated>2025-01-09T12:00:00Z</updated>
  <entry>
    <id>urn:uuid:1234-5678-91011</id>
    <title>SalesOrderCreated</title>
    <updated>2025-01-09T12:01:00Z</updated>
    <content type="application/vnd.brewup.event.
salesorder+json;version=1">
        {
            "id" = 10,
            "salesOrderNumber" = "2025.12",
            "orderDate" = "2025-01-09",
            "customerId" = 12345,
            "customerName" = "John Doe",
            "rows" = [{row-1}, {row-2}, ..., {row-n}]
```

```
            }
        </content>
        <link rel="schema" href="https://schemas.brewup.com/salesorder/
    v1.json"/>
      </entry>
      <entry>
        <id>urn:uuid:1234-5678-91012</id>
        <title>SalesOrderCreated</title>
        <updated>2025-01-09T12:05:00Z</updated>
        <content type="application/vnd.brewup.event.
    salesorder+json;version=2">
            {
                "id" = 10,
                "salesOrderNumber" = "2025.12",
                "orderDate" = "2025-01-09",
                "customerId" = 12345,
                "customerName" = "John Doe",
                "rows" = [{row-1}, {row-2}, ..., {row-n}]
                "isReseller" = false;
            }
        </content>
        <link rel="schema" href="https://schemas.brewup.com/salesorder/
    v2.json"/>
      </entry>
    </feed>
```

To optimize further, consider that, usually, an event does not evolve into a new version frequently. So, asking for a specific version of the event every time could be a waste of calls. The consumer could instead register the content types they support beforehand, and the publisher consequently can directly expose the correct versions and formats for that specific consumer, reducing the requests per message.

Copy-replace

Copy-replace is a versioning strategy where you create a new event stream by selectively copying events from an existing one, often transforming, merging, or omitting events in the process. This approach was defined by Greg Young as *the nuclear option of versioning*, which, for all intents and purposes, it is, and is typically used when other strategies fall short.

For example, look at *Figure 11.1*.

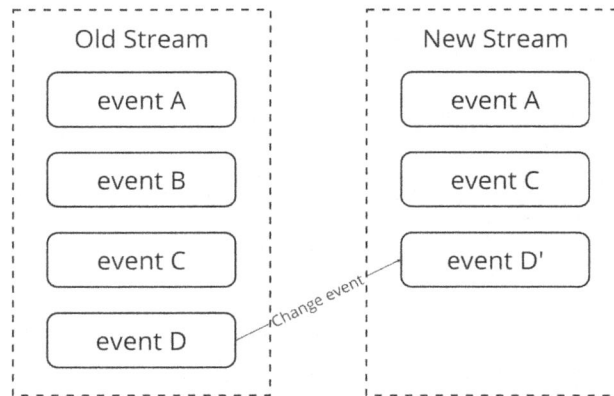

```
┌ ─ ─ ─ ─ ─ ─ ─ ─ ─ ─ ─ ┐     ┌ ─ ─ ─ ─ ─ ─ ─ ─ ─ ─ ─ ┐
│      Old Stream       │     │      New Stream       │
│   ┌───────────────┐   │     │   ┌───────────────┐   │
│   │    event A    │   │     │   │    event A    │   │
│   └───────────────┘   │     │   └───────────────┘   │
│   ┌───────────────┐   │     │   ┌───────────────┐   │
│   │    event B    │   │     │   │    event C    │   │
│   └───────────────┘   │     │   └───────────────┘   │
│   ┌───────────────┐   │     │   ┌───────────────┐   │
│   │    event C    │   │     │   │    event D'   │   │
│   └───────────────┘   │     │   └───────────────┘   │
│   ┌───────────────┐   │     │                       │
│   │    event D    │   │     │                       │
│   └───────────────┘   │     │                       │
└ ─ ─ ─ ─ ─ ─ ─ ─ ─ ─ ─ ┘     └ ─ ─ ─ ─ ─ ─ ─ ─ ─ ─ ─ ┘
```

Figure 11.1 – An event is omitted, and one has changed

But is copy-replace really the definitive solution? Of course not; there are many aspects, as per the other solutions described, that you must keep in mind if you want to go down this road.

Problems especially arise when you use this solution with a live system. If you need, at some point, to do a full replay and both the events and the streams have new IDs, what will happen to our consumers? A simple solution could be to save the old ID together with the new one. But what if you created a brand-new event? Also, what if the data in the copied events has changed and is not the same anymore?

The answers to these questions could be to simply take down the entire system, perform a copy-replace, and then bring the system back up again. But what if you have 90 gigabytes of events? Are you sure you can take the system offline for 8 or more hours?

A less invasive alternative, if your event store supports it (EventStoreDB does), is that you can use the `truncate before` property. This function allows you to delete all the events before a specific one in the stream. This approach could be useful if your use case allows it because you do not need to copy events in a new stream but simply move the pointer to the new first event of the stream and the event store will automatically delete the older events.

For example, you can consider a stream of events where you just keep the account balance of a customer, and you do not care about the past years. At the end of the current year, you can create an event that represents a snapshot of the customer's balance and mark it with the `truncate before` property.

In conclusion, whichever solution fits your scenario, always ask: *What happens if we need to replay the entire event stream from scratch?* Assume that, sooner or later, you'll need to. And when that time comes, you don't want to find out your assumptions were wrong because, by then, it's too late.

As noted at the start of this chapter, event versioning is a vast and nuanced topic. What we've covered here only scratches the surface, but it should give you a solid foundation for tackling the most common versioning challenges.

Summary

In this chapter, we explored the challenges and strategies for managing the evolution of events in event-sourced systems. Event versioning is an unavoidable aspect of maintaining the integrity and adaptability of modern software architecture. By addressing the immutability of events and the coexistence of old and new formats, you've learned how to ensure your system remains flexible and functional over time.

The skills you've gained in this chapter include the following:

- Understanding event immutability and its implications on system design and versioning strategies
- Implementing simple event versioning techniques, such as creating versioned event classes
- Utilizing advanced strategies such as upcasting, weak schemas, and content negotiation for event schema evolution
- Exploring copy-replace approaches for managing large-scale event transformations
- Planning for replays and long-term maintainability when designing versioning strategies

While we have covered several foundational techniques, event versioning remains a complex and expansive topic. Remember, the principles discussed here are just the beginning, and deeper exploration may be required depending on your system's needs.

In the next chapter, we will turn our focus to another critical aspect of distributed systems: managing workflows that span multiple bounded contexts or services. We will explore sagas and process managers, two patterns for orchestrating and coordinating workflows in systems where a single transaction cannot encompass all the necessary steps. By understanding these patterns, you'll be equipped to handle complex workflows with consistency, resilience, and efficiency.

Get this book's PDF version and more

Scan the QR code (or go to packtpub.com/unlock). Search for this book by name, confirm the edition, and then follow the steps on the page.

UNLOCK NOW

Note: Keep your invoice handy. Purchases made directly from Packt don't require an invoice.

12

Orchestrating Complexity: Advanced Approaches to Business Processes

In modern distributed systems, managing business processes across multiple services is a complex challenge. Traditional transaction management strategies, such as two-phase commit, provide strong consistency guarantees but struggle to meet the demands of scalable and resilient architectures. As a result, alternative approaches such as sagas have emerged as a more flexible way to handle long-running transactions while maintaining system availability.

This chapter explores advanced techniques for orchestrating business processes in distributed environments. It will introduce you to the trade-offs between different coordination patterns—choreography and orchestration—and how they impact fault tolerance, consistency, and system scalability. Lastly, we will discuss the role of compensating transactions, durable execution, and event-sourced sagas as key strategies for ensuring reliability in modern applications.

By the end of this chapter, you will be able to do the following:

- Understand the limitations of two-phase commit and why alternative transaction management patterns are necessary for distributed systems
- Be able to differentiate between orchestration and choreography in the context of business process coordination and recognize when to use each approach
- Know how to implement compensating transactions to handle failures gracefully and maintain consistency without strict atomicity

Through real-world examples and design considerations, this chapter will equip you with the knowledge to architect robust business processes that balance consistency, performance, and resilience.

Complexity has always been a thing

In distributed computing, ensuring consistency across multiple systems is a challenging task, especially when transactions involve multiple services.

When the services involved in your business logic were in a single piece of code, the easy way to solve this kind of problem was to use an **atomic transaction**. This left the hard part to the database, which was to guarantee data consistency at the end of the process.

With the introduction of the **Simple Object Access Protocol (SOAP)**, distributed services, and databases, this pattern wasn't valid, and another pattern became the standard, the **two-phase commit (2PC)**.

2PC

This pattern is a widely used distributed algorithm designed to achieve atomicity in transactions that span multiple nodes. When multiple nodes participate in a transaction, there is always a risk that one node may fail, leading to an inconsistent state. The 2PC protocol ensures that all nodes commit a transaction successfully or abort it entirely, preventing partial updates that could lead to data corruption. The pattern consists of two main phases:

- **Phase 1—Voting (or prepare) phase:**

  1. A coordinator node sends a `prepare` request to all participants' nodes involved in the process.

  2. Each participant validates whether they can commit the transaction.

  3. Participants reply with either `YES`, if they can commit the transaction, or `NO`, if they cannot commit.

- **Phase 2—Decision (or commit) phase:**

  - If all participants respond `YES`, the coordinator sends a `commit` message, and all participants commit the transaction

  - If any participant responds `NO`, the coordinator sends an `abort` message, and all participants roll back any changes

This process ensures that all participants agree on the final transaction state, either they all commit or none commit.

Figure 12.1 shows the phases of the 2PC protocol applied to our ERP. For each service or participant, the coordinator sends a prepare message, asking them whether they are ready to commit the transaction. Each service acquires a lock on the resource and replies with either a YES or NO message, indicating whether they can commit (the voting phase).

The coordinator decides to commit the transaction if all services or participants have responded with a YES message, otherwise, it aborts the transaction (the decision phase).

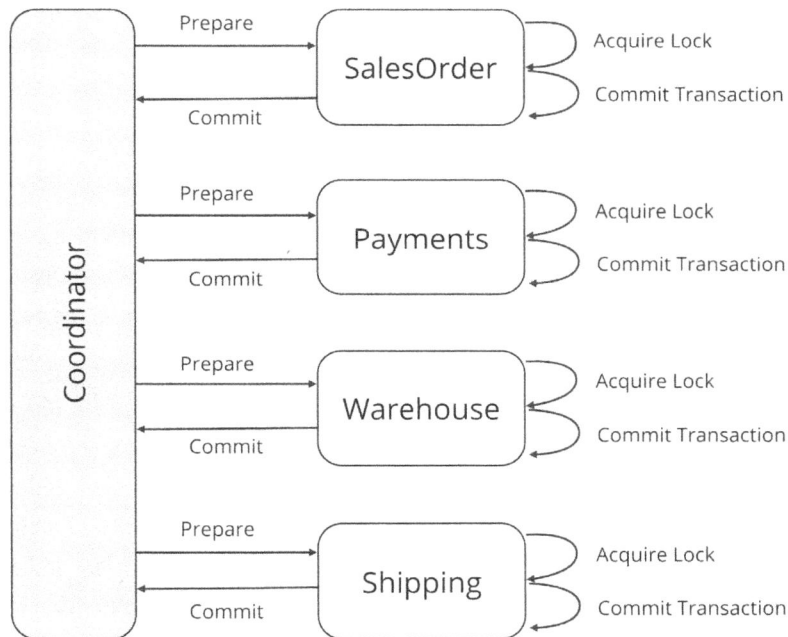

Figure 12.1 – 2PC

While 2PC is effective in ensuring consistency, it has five key drawbacks that make it challenging for modern distributed architectures:

- **Blocking nature**: Participants must wait for the coordinator's decision, potentially locking resources for an extended period. If the coordinator fails before sending the final decision, participants remain stuck in a locked state, unable to proceed.

- **Single point of failure**: The coordinator becomes a critical point in the system—if it crashes, recovery mechanisms must be in place to prevent indefinite blocking.

- **Lack of fault tolerance**: This fragility can be problematic in large-scale distributed environments where reliability is crucial.

- **Performance overhead**: Multiple communication rounds between the coordinator and participants introduce network latency and slow down transaction processing, making 2PC inefficient in high-throughput systems.

- **Scalability issues**: As the number of participants grows, the likelihood of failure increases. This not only reduces efficiency but also risks inconsistent states—such as when a participant crashes after responding "prepared" but before receiving the commit. Complex recovery techniques, such as log-based recovery, are required to handle these failures.

Due to these limitations, modern distributed systems increasingly adopt alternative approaches, such as **sagas**, that offer better fault tolerance, higher availability, and improved performance.

Sagas

Sagas are an alternative approach to handling distributed transactions in environments where the strong consistency guarantees from 2PC may not be feasible due to performance and availability concerns. Instead of enforcing a global commit or rollback, a saga breaks a transaction into a sequence of smaller, independent steps, each capable of executing compensating actions to undo changes if a failure occurs. This makes the Saga pattern particularly suitable for long-running business processes that require resilience and flexibility in handling failures.

The Saga pattern enhances fault tolerance and scalability by eliminating resource locking, as each step completes independently without waiting for a global commit. However, this pattern also comes with a trade-off: eventual consistency rather than strict atomicity. This means that intermediate states may be temporarily visible before a transaction fully completes or compensates for failures. Sagas are well suited for applications where a degree of flexibility is acceptable, and system availability is a priority.

There are two main approaches to implementing sagas: choreography and orchestration. In **choreography**, services react to events independently, enabling a decentralized flow without a central coordinator. **Orchestration**, on the other hand, relies on a central **saga orchestrator** to control the execution flow and handle compensations. Each approach has its trade-offs, which we'll explore in detail in the next section.

However, choosing between choreography and orchestration is just one aspect of designing a saga. As Neil Ford and Mark Richards discuss in their book, *Software Architecture: The Hard Parts*, three key forces influence architectural decisions: coordination, consistency, and communication. Here is how:

- **Coordination** refers to how services interact—either through a decentralized event-driven approach (choreography) or a central orchestrator controlling the flow
- **Consistency** determines whether the system guarantees strong consistency, ensuring immediate correctness at the cost of performance, or eventual consistency, prioritizing responsiveness while allowing temporary inconsistencies
- **Communication** can be synchronous, providing immediate responses but introducing latency, or asynchronous, allowing greater scalability but requiring more complex error handling

There is no one-size-fits-all solution, the right approach depends on the business rules and operational needs of the system. Ford and Richards propose a decision matrix that maps out different combinations of these factors and the types of sagas they can support, offering valuable guidance in selecting the most suitable design.

Table 12.1 summarizes all possible combinations of the three forces—communication, consistency, and coordination—and provides an evaluation of their resulting coupling:

Pattern name	Communication	Consistency	Coordination	Coupling
Epic Saga	Synchronous	Atomic	Orchestrated	Very high
Phone Tag Saga	Synchronous	Atomic	Choreographed	High
Fairy Tale Saga	Synchronous	Eventual	Orchestrated	High
Time Travel Saga	Synchronous	Eventual	Choreographed	Medium
Fantasy Fiction Saga	Asynchronous	Atomic	Orchestrated	High
Horror Story Saga	Asynchronous	Atomic	Choreographed	Medium
Parallel Saga	Asynchronous	Eventual	Orchestrated	Low
Anthology Saga	Asynchronous	Eventual	Choreographed	Very low

Table 12.1 – The matrix with all combinations

For a deeper understanding of all these saga variations, we highly recommend reading the book *Software Architecture: The Hard Parts*; it's a masterpiece. However, for our purpose, we'll focus on one key aspect: coordination, which comes down to a choice between orchestration and choreography.

Choreography versus orchestration

When designing distributed systems, especially those leveraging the Saga pattern, one of the most critical decisions is how to coordinate service interactions. As discussed in the previous section, there are two primary approaches: orchestration and choreography.

Before diving into their details, let's take a step back and examine their fundamental differences.

Both approaches facilitate workflows across multiple services but they differ in how control and responsibilities are distributed. These distinctions are crucial when implementing sagas, as they influence communication patterns, responsibility allocation, and transaction management. The choice between them directly impacts scalability, maintainability, fault tolerance, and overall system complexity.

Choreography

Choreography relies on event-driven interactions, where services react to changes in the system state. Each service listens to the events it is interested in and decides how to proceed based on its own logic—without a central authority coordinating the process. Instead, services collaborate through events to accomplish a business goal.

This approach is particularly beneficial when services are designed to be independent and loosely coupled, minimizing dependencies.

Figure 12.2 illustrates how a SalesOrder workflow could unfold in a choreographed system.

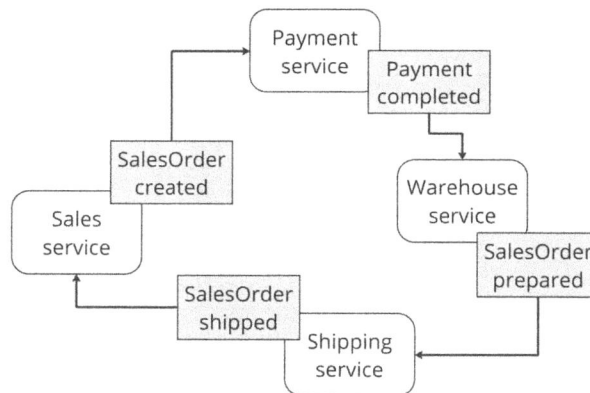

Figure 12.2 – Choreographed workflow of SalesOrder

As you can see, the process starts when the sales service emits a SalesOrderCreated event. From there, other services react to the events they are subscribed to, emitting their own events in turn. The flow continues until no further events are generated.

So, choreography enhances scalability and flexibility, as new services can be added or modified with minimal disruption. The approach works well for event-driven domains where different components must react asynchronously to changes.

But what if you need to keep the customer updated at every step of the order process shown in *Figure 12.1*? You guessed right! The Order service should subscribe to every event to be able to do that.

And what if an error occurs during the flow? Suppose the Warehouse service emits a QuantityNotFound event because the available stock is insufficient—perhaps due to an inventory miscalculation.

The flow would change to something like in *Figure 12.3*.

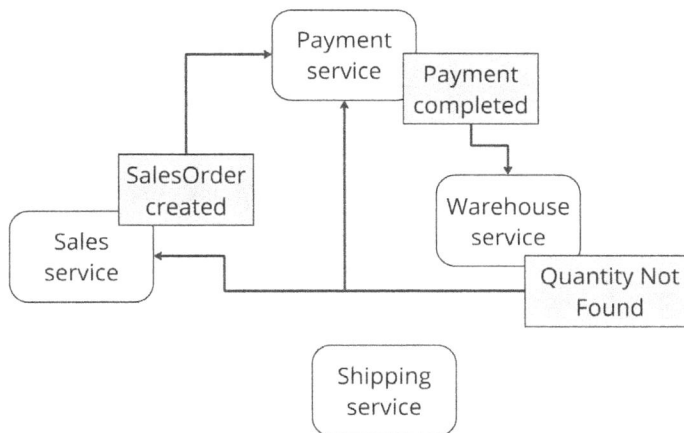

Figure 12.3 – Workflow for beers not available

In this case, both the Order and Payment services must handle the failure. They should subscribe to the QuantityNotFound event and react accordingly.

The Payment service processes a refund, while the Order service updates the order status to Canceled. This decentralized approach enhances resilience by isolating failures since each service manages its own reactions to events and also prevents a single point of failure from disrupting the entire system.

But what if the number of services increases or the failure conditions and their rollback operations grow over time? You should already know where this is going.

Despite its advantages, choreography comes with challenges. As the number of services (and failure conditions) grows, so do the complexity and operational overheads.

Since there is no central controller, tracking the overall progress of a process can be difficult and debugging and monitoring becomes complex because tracing the flow across multiple services and events requires significant effort. Additionally, if an event is not properly handled or a service fails to process it, unintended consequences may ripple through the system, leading to cascading failures. The cost of handling transaction rollbacks can grow unexpectedly, especially in systems with increasing service interactions.

To conclude, while choreography enables flexibility and scalability, the trade-offs must be carefully considered when designing event-driven workflows.

Orchestration

Orchestration, on the other hand, introduces a dedicated component—the orchestrator—that explicitly manages the workflow. The orchestrator is responsible for invoking services, handling responses, and deciding the next steps based on business logic. This approach is particularly useful for complex business processes that require explicit control over service execution order. With orchestration, monitoring and observability are significantly improved since the orchestrator maintains a global view of the process, simplifying tracking, debugging, and logging. Additionally, error handling and compensation mechanisms are more efficient because the orchestrator can implement compensating transactions and rollback strategies in a structured manner. The orchestrator also ensures that business rules requiring strict sequencing or dependencies are consistently enforced.

Going back to our example, *Figure 12.4* shows how the order process changes using the orchestrator approach.

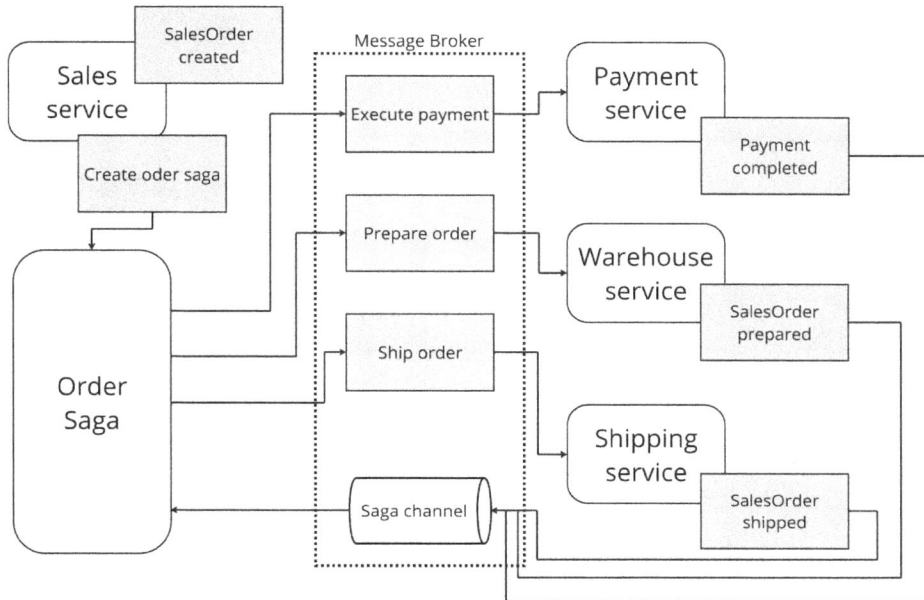

Figure 12.4 – Orchestrator workflow

The Order saga is the component responsible for orchestrating the flow and does so by emitting commands in response to receiving events. The process begins with an initiating command, after which the orchestrator emits the corresponding commands for each step in the workflow. In the preceding example, after receiving the CreateOrderSaga command, the orchestrator emits an ExecutePayment command to which the Payment service is subscribed. The service charges the customer's credit card and then emits a PaymentCompleted event. This event is subscribed by the Order saga, which moves to the next step of the process and emits the PrepareOrder command. And so on until the completion of the process.

The only goal of the orchestrator is to tell other services what to do by sending commands and waiting for responses in the form of events.

This approach could resemble the one of a state machine because every step is a command, and the flow is well-defined and, consequently, easily testable.

But as for the choreographer, what happens if the beers are not available?

The orchestrator will emit a command for a compensating action, as in *Figure 12.5*

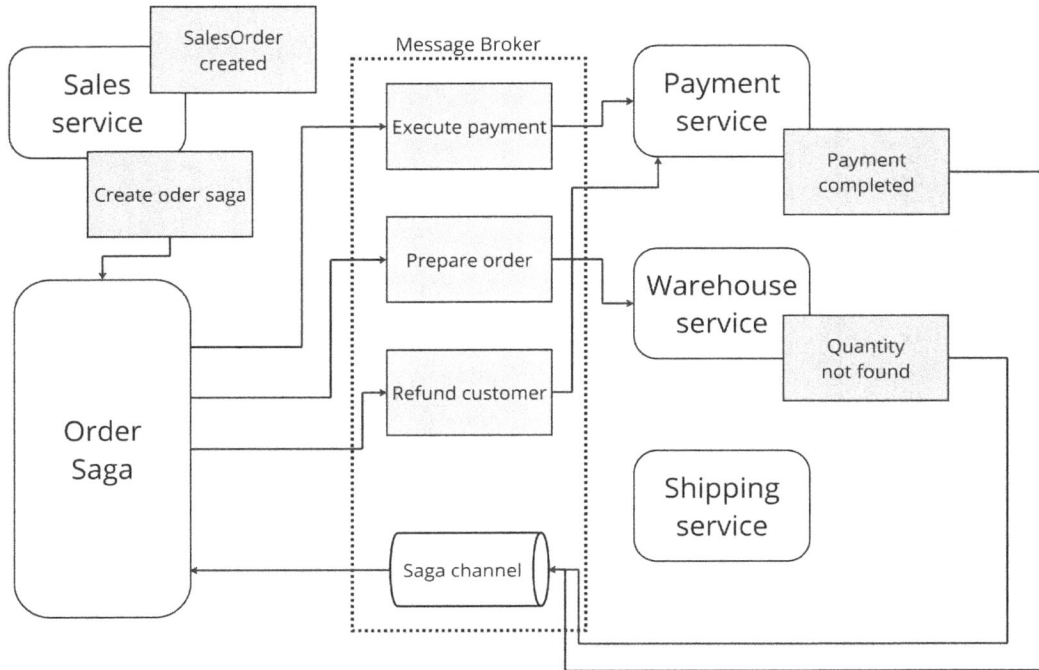

Figure 12.5 – Compensating action for beers not available

With orchestration, rollbacks are easier to manage compared to choreography, as only the orchestrator needs to subscribe to all events and handle compensation steps. This centralized control simplifies testing, monitoring, and debugging.

Another key advantage is the ability to handle complex compensating actions more effectively. For example, if a wire transfer fails to complete, the bank may deduct a processing fee before refunding the remaining amount to the customer's account. Managing such scenarios within an orchestrated workflow is more straightforward, as all rollback logic is centralized.

However, orchestration also comes with trade-offs. It introduces tighter coupling, as the orchestrator must be aware of all service interactions—meaning changes to individual services may require modifications to the orchestrator itself. Additionally, it creates a single point of failure; if the orchestrator goes down, the entire process can be disrupted. Scalability is another concern, as the orchestrator must manage an increasing number of processes, potentially becoming a bottleneck if not properly designed. Lastly, the orchestrator requires its own persistent storage, adding to the system's infrastructure complexity.

Consideration on versioning

Imagine a mortgage application: a customer subscribes to a 30-year mortgage today, but after a few years, the bank updates its business rules. What happens to existing mortgages? Typically, once a process has started, it remains unchanged—new rules apply only to new applications. In such cases, instead of modifying the existing orchestrator, a new version must be created to handle the new process while the old one continues managing active workflows.

Choosing between choreography and orchestration depends on the complexity of the workflow, the need for central control, and the system's resilience requirements.

Choosing between choreography and orchestration

When services should be loosely coupled and independent, choreography is a more suitable choice. On the other hand, when a workflow requires explicit control over execution order, orchestration provides a structured approach. If the system needs to scale dynamically with minimal dependencies, choreography is preferable, whereas if observability and monitoring are critical, orchestration offers better visibility. In cases where business processes involve compensating transactions, orchestration is the preferred method.

Table 12.2 lists some scenarios where using either choreography or orchestration is recommended.

Scenario	Choreography	Orchestration
Services should be loosely coupled and independent	✔	✘
The workflow requires explicit control over execution order	✘	✔
The system needs to scale dynamically with minimal dependencies	✔	✘
Observability and monitoring are critical	✘	✔
The business process involves compensating transactions	✘	✔

Table 12.2 – When to use choreography or orchestration

In many real-world applications, a hybrid approach is often the best choice. For example, an e-commerce order processing system might use choreography for payment validation and inventory reservation, where services operate independently, but rely on orchestration for complex returns and refund processes. By understanding the trade-offs between choreography and orchestration, developers can make informed decisions when implementing sagas, ensuring that business processes are robust, scalable, and maintainable.

Understanding the difference between process managers and sagas

Saga and **process managers** are often mistaken to be the same, but they serve distinct purposes. While both handle business processes in distributed systems, they operate differently.

Both Saga and Process Manager are patterns designed to handle long-running, distributed transactions, ensuring consistency across multiple services. However, they differ significantly in how they coordinate the workflow and manage state transitions. The process manager topic is an extensive one and falls beyond the scope of this book. We will focus only on the Saga pattern and how it differs from Process Manager. As an example, *Figure 12.6* shows how Process Manager would work applied to our ERP process.

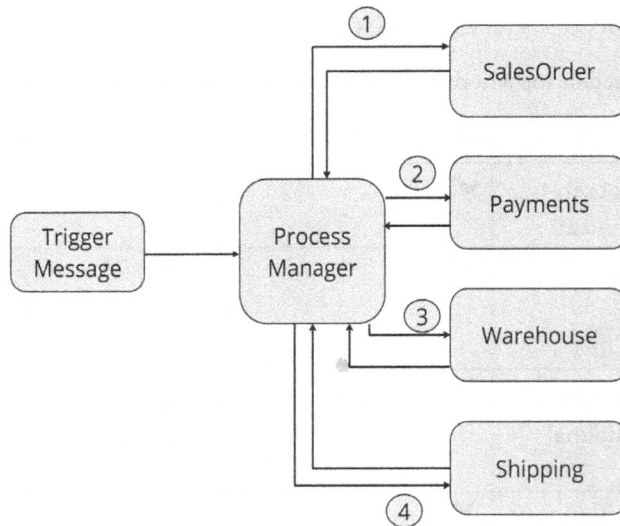

Figure 12.6 – Process Manager for our ERP

An incoming message, usually called a trigger message, initializes the process. Based on the rules inside the process manager, it sends a message to the first service, or processing step—in this case, the SalesOrder service. After SalesOrder completes its task, it sends a reply message back to the process manager. Next, the process manager determines that the next step to be executed is Payment responsibility, then sends a message to Payments and waits for the reply message. The process manager will do the same for all the services by the end of the process itself.

The centrality of the process manager is simultaneously its greatest strength and biggest weakness. By consolidating business logic, state management, error handling, and decision-making into a single entity, it ensures a structured and controlled workflow. However, this centralization also makes the process manager a single point of failure and introduces tight coupling, making the system less flexible and harder to modify.

On the other hand, a saga is a decentralized approach where each service is responsible for handling its part of a long-running transaction. A saga is a sequence of local transactions where each service performs its operation and initiates the next step through events or messages, maintaining data consistency.

Why Saga and Process Manager are not interchangeable

While both Saga and Process Manager provide control over distributed transactions, they are not interchangeable.

Saga is an event-driven approach where each participating service executes its step independently and triggers an event to notify the next service in sequence. If you choose to choreograph a saga, there is no central authority dictating the flow. Instead, services react to events and either execute compensating actions in case of failure or proceed to the next step if the previous one succeeded. This decentralized nature fosters loose coupling and scalability, making it well-suited for event-driven microservices. Because each service independently determines when to proceed, tracking execution flow and handling failures across multiple services can become complicated.

In contrast, the Process Manager pattern introduces a centralized coordinator that explicitly manages the transaction flow and dictates the sequence of steps. Unlike the decentralized, event-driven nature of Saga, Process Manager maintains an explicit state of the transaction, keeping track of which steps have been completed, what needs to happen next, and how to handle failures. Process Manager directly calls services in a predefined order, ensuring more structured control over execution. This approach makes it easier to handle complex workflows, enforce business rules, and maintain visibility over the transaction's process. The downside is that the process manager becomes a single point of failure and can introduce tight coupling between services, making modifications more complex.

You can argue that an orchestrated saga can indeed maintain state, much like a process manager, and it often simplifies error handling compared to a choreographed saga. The distinction between the two is more about the role of the coordinator and how it manages the transaction rather than whether it stores state.

With an orchestrated saga, the saga orchestrator explicitly tracks the process of the transaction and ensures that each step is executed in the correct order. This means the orchestrator can maintain stateful information about which steps have been completed, and which service invokes after receiving back a message; it doesn't matter whether this is a successful message or an error message. Since the orchestrator has a centralized view of the workflow, it simplifies error handling and rollback mechanisms, making failure recovery more predictable. Additionally, this structured approach allows for clear monitoring, logging, and debugging, as all actions pass through a single coordinating entity.

However, an orchestrated saga is not exactly the same as a process manager. While both manage state and control execution, a process manager is typically used for more complex workflows that may involve branching logic, whereas an orchestrated saga primarily focuses on transactional consistency through a linear sequence of compensable operations. A saga does not have direct knowledge of the logic behind a compensation action. Instead, it simply invokes the appropriate service based on the event it receives, triggering the next step without distinguishing whether it is a compensation action or a regular operation.

How 2PC relates to Saga and Process Manager

At this point, it is useful to clarify the relationship between 2PC, Saga, and Process Manager. While 2PC, as previously discussed, is a strict distributed transaction protocol ensuring atomicity, both Saga and Process Manager provide alternative approaches that embrace eventual consistency.

Unlike 2PC, which enforces global atomicity through a blocking mechanism, Saga ensures consistency by executing a sequence of local transactions, each with its own compensating action in case of failure. Process Manager, on the other hand, does not enforce strict transactionality but coordinates workflows centrally, keeping track of state and execution flow. While 2PC prioritizes strong consistency at the cost of scalability, Saga and Process Manager favor availability and resilience, making them better suited for distributed systems where strict atomicity is impractical.

Both Saga and Process Manager aim to handle distributed transactions but take fundamentally different approaches. Saga, whether choreographed or orchestrated, provides a decentralized, event-driven model that enhances scalability and loose coupling, making it ideal for microservices architectures. However, it can introduce complexity in tracking execution flow and handling failures.

On the other hand, Process Manager offers centralized orchestration, making workflows more structured and predictable, with clear error handling and monitoring. However, this comes at the cost of tighter coupling and a single point of failure, which can impact system resilience and flexibility.

Ultimately, the choice between Saga and Process Manager depends on the specific needs of the system. If scalability and autonomy are key, a Saga-based approach is more suitable. If explicit control, complex workflows, and strict sequencing are required, Process Manager may be the better fit. If neither approach provides the required level of consistency, 2PC may still be necessary, though it is often impractical in highly distributed environments.

Error handling and transaction recovery in sagas

One of the fundamental motivations for using a saga in a distributed system is its ability to manage errors and ensure system resilience. As seen earlier, the process manager centralizes the control flow and handles errors in a more procedural manner while the saga embraces the nature of distributed transactions by defining compensating actions and allowing decentralized recovery strategies. Understanding how the saga handles failures and ensures transactional integrity is key to designing robust business processes.

Failures in a saga can occur at various stages of execution, and each type of failure requires a different strategy for resolution. The two main failure categories are as follows:

- **Step failures**: A single step in the saga may fail due to network issues, service unavailability, or validation errors. The system can attempt retries with exponential backoff or invoke a compensating transaction to undo the operation.

- **Saga-wide failures**: If a failure affects the entire business process, the system must ensure that previous successful operations are compensated correctly. Unlike a process manager, which would centrally manage the rollback, a saga delegates compensation to individual services, ensuring greater flexibility and decentralization.

As illustrated in *Figures 12.2*, *12.3*, *12.4*, and *12.5*, the failure recovery mechanisms in both choreographed and orchestrated sagas follow the same core principles. As explained in the *Choreography versus orchestration* section, in a choreographed saga, each service independently listens to events and reacts accordingly, executing compensating actions when needed. In an orchestrated saga, a central orchestrator directs the sequence of steps and invokes compensating transactions explicitly.

However, in both cases, the handling of failures depends on the same core principles: detecting failures, retrying when possible, and executing compensations when necessary. The choice between choreography and orchestration affects system design and coupling but does not change the underlying failure recovery strategies.

Compensating transactions and recovery strategies

When a step in a saga fails and cannot be retried, immediate compensation is triggered to undo the effects of the failed operation. For example, if the payment transaction fails after an order is placed, the system must cancel the order to maintain consistency. In some cases, sagas allow compensation to be deferred until a final decision is reached, which is useful when failures are temporary and recovery may still be possible within a predefined window. To prevent unintended side effects, all compensating transactions must be idempotent, ensuring that if a compensation step is retried multiple times due to intermittent failures, it does not introduce further inconsistencies.

Sagas embrace both forward and backward recovery strategies:

- **Forward recovery**: Instead of rolling back changes, the system attempts an alternative solution. For example, if a primary shipping provider fails, an alternative provider may be used without requiring compensation for previous steps.

- **Backward recovery**: When a failure is irrecoverable, the saga must execute compensating transactions to undo the operations that have already been performed.

Also consider that some business processes allow partial completion, where certain steps succeed while others fail gracefully. For example, in a multi-step booking system, if a hotel reservation fails but a flight booking succeeds, the user might be given the option to proceed with only the flight.

Durable execution: ensuring reliability in sagas

Durable execution is a critical requirement for sagas because, firstly, it ensures that sagas can continue processing even in the presence of failures, crashes, or system restarts. To achieve this, the saga's state must be persisted reliably so that it can be resumed without inconsistencies. This persistence is often managed using event logs, message queues, or dedicated databases that store each step's progress. If a failure occurs, the system can reload the saga's last known state and resume execution from the point of interruption.

Secondly, durable execution also requires that all operations within a saga be **idempotent**. Since failures may cause steps to be retried multiple times, idempotency ensures that repeated execution does not produce unintended side effects. Each step must be designed in such a way that executing it twice produces the same result. This is particularly crucial for compensating transactions, as a failure during compensation must not leave the system in an inconsistent state.

Thirdly, durable execution ensures timeout handling. Some steps in a saga may take longer than expected due to system load or external dependencies. To prevent indefinite waiting, sagas should define explicit timeouts for each step. If a step is not completed within the allocated time, the system should either trigger a compensation action or escalate the issue to a fallback mechanism.

Finally, durable execution is closely linked to dead letter handling. When a step in a saga repeatedly fails despite retries, the message (also known as a poison message) associated with the failed operation should not be lost. Instead, it should be placed in a dead letter queue for further inspection. This allows system administrators to analyze persistent failures, apply manual interventions if necessary, and improve system resilience over time.

Event-sourced sagas

An alternative approach to durable execution is **event-sourced sagas,** as suggested by Jonathan Oliver (`https://blog.jonathanoliver.com/cqrs-sagas-with-event-sourcing-part-i-of-ii/`). In this model, each step of the saga is recorded as an event in an event store. The saga state is derived from the sequence of past events rather than being stored as a mutable record. This approach provides a robust way to reconstruct and resume sagas after failures, ensuring consistency even in complex distributed environments. Event sourcing allows the saga to be replayed from its last successful step, enabling a precise recovery mechanism without relying on explicit state management. Furthermore, it integrates seamlessly with CQRS, allowing efficient queries on saga progress and compensation.

In conclusion, by implementing these principles, sagas provide a robust and scalable mechanism for handling errors in distributed systems. Ensuring durable execution minimizes the impact of transient failures, allowing long-running business processes to complete reliably even under adverse conditions.

Summary

In this chapter, we explored two primary approaches to implementing sagas: choreography and orchestration. Choreography enables decentralized, event-driven workflows that enhance flexibility and scalability but can lead to complex failure handling and debugging. Orchestration, on the other hand, centralizes process control through an orchestrator, making monitoring and compensation easier but introducing tighter coupling. We also examined the Process Manager pattern, which provides structured workflow control but can become a single point of failure if not properly managed.

Additionally, we discussed key strategies for error handling and transaction recovery, including compensating transactions, durable execution, and event-sourced sagas. These techniques ensure that distributed transactions remain reliable even in the face of system failures.

The skills you have learned by completing this chapter include the ability to do the following:

- Evaluate different coordination patterns and choose the right approach based on business and technical requirements

- Implement compensating transactions to recover from failures while maintaining system consistency

- Design resilient workflows using durable execution strategies, ensuring long-running processes can withstand crashes and recover gracefully

- Leverage event-sourced sagas to enhance observability, simplify rollback mechanisms, and enable efficient process tracking

With these skills, you can confidently design robust distributed systems that handle business process complexity while optimizing performance and fault tolerance.

Throughout the 12 chapters in this book, we have navigated the complexities of refactoring with DDD—starting from chaos, recognizing emerging patterns, and shaping a more flexible and modular system. Each chapter has been a step toward a deeper understanding of how to transform legacy code into an architecture that fosters evolution and resilience. Now, the challenge is yours: apply these principles in your own context, experiment, and keep improving. Code will change, but the thinking behind it is what truly makes a difference.

‹packt›

packtpub.com

Subscribe to our online digital library for full access to over 7,000 books and videos, as well as industry leading tools to help you plan your personal development and advance your career. For more information, please visit our website.

Why subscribe?

- Spend less time learning and more time coding with practical eBooks and Videos from over 4,000 industry professionals
- Improve your learning with Skill Plans built especially for you
- Get a free eBook or video every month
- Fully searchable for easy access to vital information
- Copy and paste, print, and bookmark content

At www.packt.com, you can also read a collection of free technical articles, sign up for a range of free newsletters, and receive exclusive discounts and offers on Packt books and eBooks.

Other Books You May Enjoy

If you enjoyed this book, you may be interested in these other books by Packt:

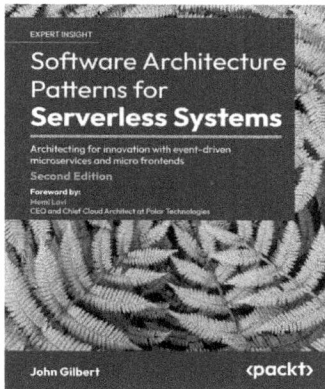

Software Architecture Patterns for Serverless Systems

None Gilbert

ISBN: 978-1-80323-544-8

- Explore architectural patterns to create anti-fragile systems
- Focus on DevSecOps practices that empower self-sufficient, full-stack teams
- Apply microservices principles to the frontend
- Discover how SOLID principles apply to software and database architecture
- Gain practical skills in deploying, securing, and optimizing serverless architectures
- Deploy a multi-regional system and explore the strangler pattern for migrating legacy systems
- Master techniques for collecting and utilizing metrics, including RUM, Synthetics, and Anomaly detection

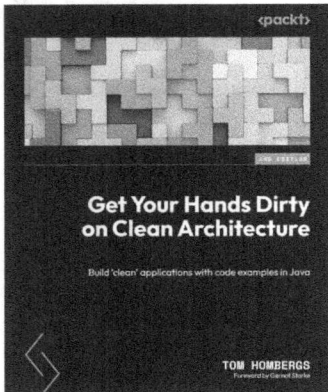

Get Your Hands Dirty on Clean Architecture

Tom Hombergs

ISBN: 978-1-80512-837-3

- Identify potential shortcomings of using a layered architecture
- Apply varied methods to enforce architectural boundaries
- Discover how potential shortcuts can affect the software architecture
- Produce arguments for using different styles of architecture
- Structure your code according to the architecture
- Run various tests to check each element of the architecture

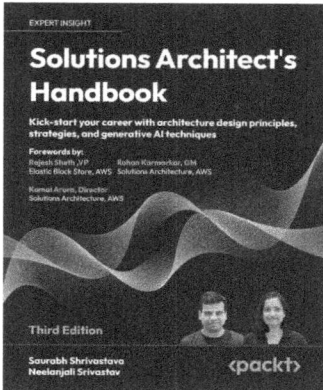

Solutions Architect's Handbook

Saurabh Shrivastava, Neelanjali Srivastav

ISBN: 978-1-83508-423-6

- Explore various roles of a solutions architect in the enterprise
- Apply design principles for high-performance, cost-effective solutions
- Choose the best strategies to secure your architectures and boost availability
- Develop a DevOps and CloudOps mindset for collaboration, operational efficiency, and streamlined production
- Apply machine learning, data engineering, LLMs, and generative AI for improved security and performance
- Modernize legacy systems into cloud-native architectures with proven real-world strategies
- Master key solutions architect soft skills

Packt is searching for authors like you

If you're interested in becoming an author for Packt, please visit authors.packtpub.com and apply today. We have worked with thousands of developers and tech professionals, just like you, to help them share their insight with the global tech community. You can make a general application, apply for a specific hot topic that we are recruiting an author for, or submit your own idea.

Share your thoughts

Now you've finished *Domain-Driven Refactoring*, we'd love to hear your thoughts! If you purchased the book from Amazon, please click here to go straight to the Amazon review page for this book and share your feedback or leave a review on the site that you purchased it from.

Your review is important to us and the tech community and will help us make sure we're delivering excellent quality content.

Index

Download a free PDF copy of this book

Thanks for purchasing this book!

Do you like to read on the go but are unable to carry your print books everywhere?

Is your eBook purchase not compatible with the device of your choice?

Don't worry, now with every Packt book you get a DRM-free PDF version of that book at no cost.

Read anywhere, any place, on any device. Search, copy, and paste code from your favorite technical books directly into your application.

The perks don't stop there, you can get exclusive access to discounts, newsletters, and great free content in your inbox daily

Follow these simple steps to get the benefits:

1. Scan the QR code or visit the link below

https://packt.link/free-ebook/9781835889107

2. Submit your proof of purchase
3. That's it! We'll send your free PDF and other benefits to your email directly

www.ingramcontent.com/pod-product-compliance
Lightning Source LLC
Chambersburg PA
CBHW061802210326
41599CB00034B/6846